Enjoy the Journey!

Eleanor

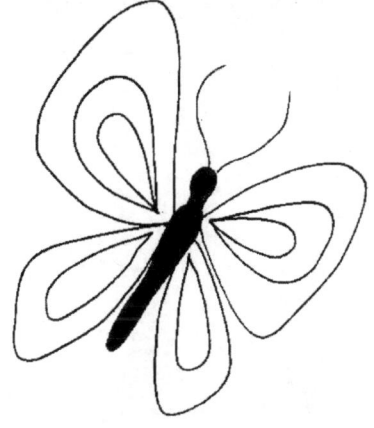

10 Days in May, 1966
... freely recieve... freely give

10 Days in June, $1000
... BONUS: 10 Seminars

10 Days in July, 2020
... lock down... open up

I am not what happened to me.
I am what I choose to become.
　　—Carl Jung

a memoir by
Eleanor Deckert
Book 6 & 7 & 8
BONUS: 10 Seminars

 **FriesenPress**

One Printers Way
Altona, MB R0G 0B0
Canada

www.friesenpress.com

Disclaimer: This content is not intended to be a substitute for professional advice, diagnosis, or treatment and is a reflection of the author's experiences only.

Copyright © 2022 by Eleanor Deckert
First Edition — 2022

Cover Art: Doris Scarff
Drawing for Title Pages: Eleanor Deckert
Page Breaks: Eleanor Deckert
Back Cover Photo Credit: Young Eleanor: Daddy
Back Cover Butterfly Dance Photo Credit: Kevin Deckert

 *Seven Predictable Patterns* ®

Photos, Reviews, Events, Ordering Info are found on Author's Web Page
www.eleanordeckert.com
To Protect Privacy, names of people and places in this memoir have been changed.

All rights reserved.

No part of this publication may be reproduced in any form, or by any means, electronic or mechanical, including photocopying, recording, or any information browsing, storage, or retrieval system, without permission in writing from FriesenPress.

ISBN
978-1-03-913333-4 (Hardcover)
978-1-03-913332-7 (Paperback)
978-1-03-913334-1 (eBook)

1. Biography & Autobiography, Personal Memories
2. Self-Help, Personal Growth, Self-Esteem
3. Self-Help, Personal Growth, Success

Distributed to the trade by The Ingram Book Company

DEDICATION

This book is dedicated to two little girls.

One of them is Little Me.

The other one is my newly born One-and-Only Granddaughter.

I hope my stories of The Innocence of Youth, Developing Self-Concept and Triumph Over Negative Messages will remind, encourage and inspire *me* to continue my own Path to Self Awareness, Creativity and the precious Sense of Satisfaction during each phase of my life.

Dear Darling Grand-Daughter, I hope my stories of Natural Born Talent, ever-expanding Creative Curiosity and Focused Transformation will inspire *you* as you begin your Journey from Infancy to Adulthood, finding your own Talents, reaching your own Potential, sharing your own Song.

May your Curiosity nourish the Seed of your Creativity as it takes root, blossoms and bears fruit. May you find deep satisfaction and bring blessings to others.

> I think, at a child's birth,
> if a mother could ask a fairy godmother
> to endow it with the most useful gift,
> that gift would be curiosity.
> —*Eleanor Roosevelt*

ACKNOWLEDGEMENTS

Blessings. Gratitude.
For my parents, teachers and pastors who show me ways to participate in the world.
For my husband who encourages me to experiment, explore and expand my creativity.
For my children during many Golden Moments.
For opportunities given by my employers.
For mentors helping me see my Self.
For my Publisher's work and the Printer's tour.
For TV, radio, magazine and newspaper interviews.
For bookstores, libraries, organizations and schools hosting my seminars and book signing events.
For Readers asking, "When is your next book coming out?"
Mostly I am blessed by and grateful for the ideas that pop into my head. Where do they come from? I'm glad they arrive.

Lord, I asked for all things that I may enjoy life.
You gave me life that I may enjoy all things.
—author unknown

A NOTE TO THE READER

Most of what I have done in my life cannot be seen.
But, it can be told. So, I saved it all with ink on paper.
Read on! I wrote this for You!
I am going to tell you e-v-e-r-y-t-h-i-n-g.

Table of Contents

10 Days in May, 1966
... freely recieve... freely give

10 Days in June, $1000
... BONUS: 10 Seminars

10 Days in July, 2020
... lock down... open up

Dedication	v
Acknowledgements	vi
A Note to the Reader	vi
10 Days in May, 1966 ... freely receive... freely give	ix
10 Days in June, $1000 ... BONUS: 10 Seminars	111
10 Days in July, 2020 ... lock down... open up	283
Endnotes	337
What Readers Are Saying	338
Review	339
About the Author	340
Seminars Available	341

10 Days in May, 1966
... freely receive... freely give

The most important days of your life are
the day you were born
and the day you find out why.
 —Mark Twain

a memoir by
Eleanor Deckert
BOOK 6

Table of Contents
10 Days in May, 1966
... freely receive... freely give

Introduction	xi
Chapter 1 There *is* a Plan Sunday, May 1, 1966	1
Chapter 2 Go Out West Monday, May 2, 1966	11
Chapter 3 3-Room Cabin Tuesday, May 3, 1966	23
Chapter 4 3-Room School Wednesday, May 4, 1966	33
Chapter 5 "Look What I Made!" Thursday, May 5, 1966	49
Chapter 6 Chore Chart Friday, May 6, 1966	63
Chapter 7 Born to Dance Saturday, May 7, 1966	73
Chapter 8 Mother's Day Sunday, May 8, 1966	85
Chapter 9 I love to Read Monday, May 9, 1966	93
Chapter 10 Of Course I Can Write Tuesday, May 10, 1966	101
Epilogue	110

INTRODUCTION

I don't remember, but I've heard stories...
   ... my life began on Christmas Eve.
I don't remember, but I can imagine...
   ... the frantic effort of swimming, the excitement, the prize, the comfortable months of provision, the hours of pressure, the shock of cold air.
I don't remember, but there are photographs...
   ... newly born Little Me, wrapped in a soft, barely pink blanket. My Daddy is 27, focusing the camera. My Mommy is 23, smiling.
I don't remember, but I always wonder...
   ... about the nine days while I was sick. My mother, my father, both grandmothers taking turns around the clock, pressing hot compresses, worried, not allowed to hold me.
   Doesn't a newborn need the security of mother's arms? Does the root of my self-doubt begin here? Anxious. Alone. Flat on a bed. Longing to be cuddled.
   More photographs. Laughing in a basket. Splashing in the water. Baptism. Christmas. Birthday.
I don't remember, but I've been told...
   ... I was 15 months old when twins arrived. Boys!
   ... I was not quite 3-and-a-half years old when my sister arrived. Parents, grandparents, uncle, admiring her. My heart is hard, cold, heavy. "Doesn't anyone love *me*?"
   Now I am 8. My baby sister is here, too.
   To keep my place of importance I have to be so so good and so so smart. I am the Big Sister. Obedient. Bossy.

Chapter 1
Sunday, May 1, 1966
There *is* a Plan

> And the Day Came
> When the Risk to Remain Tight In a Bud
> Was More Painful
> Than the Risk It Took to Blossom.
> —Anais Nin

Freely Receive

Daddy takes us to church every Sunday.

So noisy when we pile into the car, jostling for who gets to sit by the window.

So quiet as we sit in the pew.

So glad as we sing.

So still as we listen.

So eager to be excused for Sunday School.

I tromp up the stairs. We have a young lady teacher. It's springtime! Sunshine is pouring in through the window.

May Chapter 1   There *is* a Plan

"What are some symbols we see in our church? the stained glass windows? the flag? the embroidery? the chancel? What do these symbols mean?"

Look! It's an interesting paper craft!

The spectrum of colors pours into my eyes, warming me the way hands wrapped around a mug of cocoa warms the whole body, nourishing me the way savory soup spreads vitality through my veins, stimulating me the way music calls my heart to express gladness through dance.

With so many deep, rich, variations in color to choose from, I reach for only three. The gentle blue looks like the Colorado sky. The goldenrod yellow looks like a butterfly opening its wings. The deep brown looks like the supporting branch where the caterpillar crawled, the cocoon was formed, the butterfly emerged.

And when I reach, I touch. The paper has a layer of soft velveteen!

While the other children chatter around the Sunday School craft table, I bring scissors and glue and move to sit alone. I need to close off distractions. While the other children cut stars and crosses and doves and hearts, each of these shapes conveying meaning, I need to focus on the message of this particular symbol.

In the same way that I have learned to make a Valentine, I fold the golden paper in half, and cut first one, then a second rounded wing. Next, I cut long, thin, brown strips to be the twigs that the butterfly stands on before first flight. Now the full page of blue sky frames the newly awakened insect. O! Did I see a flutter of wings?

A strange sensation comes over me. Far from the classroom, lost in time, silence, stillness, wide open, deep, I experience a 'knowing.'

Without words, the symbol is teaching me:

Sunday, May 1, 1966

'All is well.'
'Trust the cycle.'
'There is a Plan.'
'Follow the Path.'
'Listen. I will show you.'
'Your small Self is a part of the Universal Whole.'

Time's up. Tidy up. Line up.

The other children scurry out the door, scramble down the stairs, scatter to find their parents. "See what I made?" "May I have a cookie?"

Hovering in my heart, I am not finished with this inner experience. Leaving last, I sit on the stairs, holding, looking, entering the meaning of the open-winged butterfly. So fragile, so small, yet, conveying this essential truth: First you are 'that.' Then you wrap up, 'alone.' When the time is right, you become 'this.' There is no going back. There is no resisting the future. You will become what you are meant to be.

During this Golden Moment, I receive a gift of clarity: If this miraculous transformation is true for so simple a creature, if something so drab and low and slow can become something so colorful and swift and high, surely the Creator had something equally marvelous in mind when He created me?

I join my family, nibble on my cookie. We wait for Mommy to get the Baby from the nursery. Daddy starts the car. Our family of seven heads for home. Baby Carol is wrapped in a blanket in a little bed on the floor behind the driver's seat. Little Julie, who often gets car sick, sits on Mommy's lap in front, near the open window. In the back, James and Andrew have the window seats. I am in the middle. It is a short drive, across the creek, left into highway traffic, right into our driveway.

Daddy pulls off the pavement onto the gravel. "Get the paper, Andrew. Open the gate, James." I slide across the bench seat. I am by the window now.

Andrew unrolls the newspaper. Look! Sunday Funnies!

James lifts the latch, stands on the lowest rung, rides the swinging metal gate inward. Daddy pulls through, opens his car door. James climbs onto Daddy's lap. Little hands grip the steering wheel.

"Do you remember which is the window wiper? the headlights? the turn signals? Ready?" Daddy is coaching so that James will do well. Now Daddy gently shifts into first gear, touches the gas, and up the hill we go.

Am I jealous? Am I scared? Am I disapproving of 'breaking the rules'? Am I watching Mommy's face? Is she stressed? or laughing? Am I worried about my baby sister's safety as the car lurches and swerves? Am I nervous about the ditches? All of these feelings swirl in my mind and heart. Just hush. Be quiet. Sit back. We're almost home.

But, wait!

The dog is barking. Rex has treed a bear!

It's springtime in the rocky mountains and bears often come in close to buildings seeking bird feeders, pet food, garbage cans, litter along the roadsides. Anything that smells will attract a bear.

"Daddy! Look up! Past the bear! I think there is a cub!" We are parked so close to the tree. My neck is arched way back to try to see clearly.

Black dog. Barking. Barking. Circling.

Black bears. Up so high. How long can they hold on?

Sunday, May 1, 1966

"Rex has them cornered," Daddy states confidently. "Let's all go out on the passenger side."

"One. Two. Three. Go!" Daddy slides out Mommy's door, reaches behind the seat for the Baby. The house is not locked. The dog stays on guard. Barking. Barking. We are all safe.

The sliding glass door yields a clear view. We stand and watch. Daddy calls and calls for Rex to come inside. Rex wants to keep barking.

"Daddy! No!" My eyes are wide. My heart pounding. He grabs Rex by the collar and drags him indoors.

Anxiously pacing. Nervously whining. Rex is shut in another room.

We watch for a long time until the mother bear signals to her young one that it is time to go.

"OK. They are going back to their home now." Mommy ends this episode as we watch them amble away. "Go change into your play clothes," she commands as she begins to get Sunday Dinner on the table.

Before we left for church this morning, Mommy set the timer on the electric oven so that the chicken would be perfect by the time we arrived home. She had also peeled the potatoes and left them in cold water. While we get changed, she brings the pot to a boil, pours frozen peas into a smaller pot on the stove. She sets the pitcher of milk and a plate of butter on the table and gets the Baby settled into her high chair.

"Eleanor, set the table. Julie, put a napkin at each place." We are ready to begin.

May Chapter 1   There *is* a Plan

Hold hands. Bow heads. Close eyes. Recite together. "O give thanks unto the Lord, for He is good and His mercy is forever, Amen."

"Daddy, will you read the Funnies to us?" After the table is cleared, the Baby is napping, the long afternoon has more special Sunday events.

Daddy opens the newspaper pages on the smooth, new, pine floorboards so we can all gather around. On hands and knees, I watch as he patiently points to each square of the comics. He keeps changing his voice to demonstrate the personality of each character, explaining the vocabulary. Some stories stand alone each week. Some stories are in a series.

Snoopy and Charlie Brown in *Peanuts* are pretty easy to follow: baseball, football, school, silly dog dancing! *Henry* and *Nancy* also share the dilemmas of childhood.

Dagwood and Blondie have been around since Daddy was a little boy.

Li'l Abner sounds so funny when Daddy mimics the hillybilly contractions and accents, a high falsetto voice for the girls, a growling voice for Granny, the deeper voice for the young man who is always on the run while the buxom gal chases him. Until Leap Year. On February 29th, Sadie Hawkins Day arrives and *she* can propose to *him*!

I am bewildered by *Pogo*, the political opossum and his alligator friends. I hear Daddy's southern drawl, but I don't understand the jokes, no matter how he tries to explain them.

Sunday, May 1, 1966

My brothers love *Prince Valiant*. The lofty Olde English speech flows off of Daddy's tongue with such grandeur. I like the costumes. Red velvet cape. Flowing blue gown. Handsome guards. Flags. Trumpets. Horses. Castles. Deeds-of-daring-do.

My Daddy is a university professor. There is so much he talks about that I cannot understand. But this! Sunday Funnies! I try to keep up with his wit. Puns. Political jibes. I like to hear his voice, his laughter, his eagerness to share what he enjoys.

Next, we romp outside, climbing hills, building forts, noticing springtime flowers. Mommy calls us inside for baths and PJs.
Lassie is on TV at 5:30. We don't want to miss a minute.
Mommy brings a tray with bowls, cereal, milk.
The Wonderful World of Disney starts at 6:00.
7:00 It's time to brush teeth. Goodnight kisses.

"Mommy, did you like the butterfly I made in Sunday school?" It is especially nice to have a tiny moment with my mother. She is always so busy. Her eyes send love into my eyes.

"Do you remember the pet butterfly I had last summer? One wing was kind of folded. I carried it on my finger and took it from flower to flower. I felt the tiny feet and saw the tiny tongue uncurl and reach into the flower for nectar. I knew it would die. But, I gave it a good last day, don't you think?"

Mommy smooths my hair. "It *is* amazing to think of each tiny creature, first in an egg, starting life as a caterpillar, making a cocoon, then awakening one day, able to fly!"

May Chapter 1   There *is* a Plan

"How does the Lord do it all?" I wonder. "Think things up. Make so much variety. Protect each living thing. And remember to take care of all of the millions of people. And even me and you? Even stars!"

"That's why God is God," she answers the unanswerable questions of a child.

Mommy tucks me in.

All is well.

Before I close my eyes, I look again, admiring the butterfly I made today. The best part of the week is Sunday. The best part of Sunday is going to church. The best part of going to church is Sunday School. The best part of Sunday School is making a project so you don't forget the lesson.

I hung up the butterfly right beside my picture of Jesus. He is knocking at the door. "Behold, I stand at the door and knock. If anyone hears my voice and opens the door, I will come in to Him and sup with Him and He with me." Revelation 3:20

The Lord comes to me. And I come to Him. He made me. He loves me. He calls me. He has a plan for me. I want to listen!

All *is* well.

Freely Give
1972

Six years and two moves later, now we live in Canada. In September, the pastor announced, "We need teachers for Sunday School. Please sign up for one month."

My heart was beating hard when I spoke to him. "I can do it!"

Sunday, May 1, 1966

I was just turning 15 years old. Clearly, the Lord has given me this talent, and so, I give it freely. I signed up for the rest of the school year.

Right away I could see the problem. The kids were bored. They had been using the same lesson formula since they were five years old! Read the lesson. Answer questions. Color a picture.

I asked for a small budget and tried something new. Crafts. Textures. Music. Acting.

By the month of May, 1973, we had painted a mural for Thanksgiving, crafted Nativity figures out of decorated toilet paper tubes, used pine-cones spread with peanut butter and seeds to make bird feeders, cut felt for bookmarks, painted plaster of Paris, and built the Tabernacle from a kit. I wrote a song filled with action so the children could act out The Good Samaritan. We made props and a skit portraying the parable of the Sower. We went outside on a grassy hill to read the Sermon on the Mount.

Later

1978

After our summertime wedding, my husband, Kevin, drove our VW van out west. That autumn we built our tiny log cabin. The next year, I volunteered in the nearby town at the two-room school to develop trust with the parents and children. After that, I taught Sunday School for many years.

I always based each lesson on this verse.

Matthew 22: 38 Jesus said, "You shall love the Lord your God with all your heart, and with all your soul and with all your mind."

Heart. Soul. Mind. Body. This is who we are. Each part is hungry, seeking, growing. How can I provide nourishment, challenges, and satisfaction?

Heart: Music, art, creativity.
Spirit: Reverence, symbols, meaningful traditions.
Mind: Facts, maps, new vocabulary.
Body: Acting, skills, participation.

It didn't take long for every single child in town to come to Sunday School at least once. However, I noticed that there were few, if any, Bibles in their homes.

1984

I consulted with my husband. "This Christmas, we could buy enough paperback copies of the *Good News* Bibles to give to every child at the Community Christmas Concert. The tiny line drawings help even children who cannot read find their place and remember the stories."

So, we did.

Nearly 50 years after my first experience, teaching Sunday School is still my favourite thing to do!

To read more about the Plan Eleanor has for her life...
... turn to 10 Days in June Chapter 1, page 117.

Chapter 2
Monday, May 2, 1966
Go Out West

> Keep away from people
> who try to belittle your ambitions.
> Small people always do that,
> but the really great
> make you feel that you, too,
> can become great.
> —Mark Twain

Freely Receive

Monday morning. Up and out. Wait for the school bus. Bell rings. Line up.

Our school has three rooms. Each room has a door to the outside. Each room is one grade with one teacher. I am in Grade 3. We have Mrs. Thompson. She's the best teacher I've ever had in my whole life. On Monday, in the morning, we always start a new Spelling list. On Monday, after lunch, we always have Social Studies.

Sometimes Mrs. Thompson pulls down the huge map of the whole world. Oceans. Deserts. Glaciers. Rivers. Countries. Cities. We have been reading about how different people from all around the world first started coming to America in ships almost 500 years ago. I can see where we live now and I can see where my grandparents came from: Germany.

Sometimes Mrs. Thompson pulls down the huge map of the United States of America. Lakes. Rivers. Mountains. Prairie. States. Cities. We have been reading about the different tribes of people who lived in each place before settlers arrived. They lived in different climates with different resources to build different kinds of houses. We have been reading about how the Ute people lived right here. Then the pioneers came to Colorado in covered wagons about 100 years ago. I can see where we live now and I can see where we came from: Pennsylvania.

"As we have learned, some of the tribes stayed in one place with permanent dwellings. They had a reliable and abundant food source, such as fishing, or grew crops, such as corn. Other tribes had to move often, with portable dwellings, like tepees, so they could follow herds of buffalo or caribou. The Ute people who lived here, traveled from the flat grasslands, up Ute Pass, into the high country every summer, then returned to the low lands in the wintertime," Mrs. Thompson explained. "The original people who lived in North America could travel by walking, or on the waterways. Some had domesticated dogs to pull sleds or carry loads. Later, when Europeans brought horses, the people could travel faster, further, and more easily."

"Today we will begin to write about Travel," Mrs. Thompson begins. "Think about the way your family travels. You may choose one of three ways to write a story."

This sounds interesting!

Monday, May 2, 1966

"The first way you can write about travel is to tell a story about your own life. Have you been on a trip recently? Have you visited a famous place? the ocean? the city? the Grand Canyon? Have you had a ride on an airplane? boat? train? Where did you go? What did you see?"

I'm getting ideas already!

"Your second choice to write about travel is to tell a story about your family. Who first came to America? When? Why? How did they get here? Where did they first live? When did your family come to Colorado?"

I know things about my family!

"The third way you might write about travel will stretch your imagination: You can be someone real or pretend who is traveling anywhere in the world. Where are you going? How do you travel? What do you see?"

This sounds like a fun project!

"This assignment will take you two weeks. It is almost the end of the school year. This is your final project. It is important to share both facts and descriptions. This is how to begin. First, list your ideas such as the method of transportation, geographical features, facts. Then, write the first draft. Later, you can add details. And, finally, check your spelling and punctuation."

What will I decide to do?

Maybe I will write about the first topic: Trips our family has taken.

I remember Beth Ayers, Pennsylvania:

My Mommy walked two blocks up the hill, pulling the little red wagon along the sidewalk to the library. Sitting tightly together, three children could fit. Since I was the eldest, I walked beside the wagon. How else could she take four children?

Four pairs of hard leather shoes to tie. Three children in cloth diapers. Twin boys. One Baby. We made our own parade. One of the twins held the bag of books. The other wrapped his arms tightly around Baby Julie. I carried Mommy's library card in my little red purse. We were a team.

To go on an outing, we all had to help.

My Daddy walked two blocks down the hill to catch the train. He was a teacher at the college in Philadelphia. One day, I got to go with him. I ate a banana as the buildings zoomed by. It was so different to ride on a train. No seat belt. You can stand up. You can change seats. No stop signs. Big windows. Click-a-tee-clack. Rocking. Zipping trees. A zillion windows. Lights flashing. Bell clanging. Horn warning. Traffic stopping. People waving. A man in a uniform punched my ticket. I held Daddy's hand through the crowded station. Trotting to keep up with his long stride. Too much to see. Too many steps to climb. Too quiet in his office.

To go on an outing, I had to keep up.

Grammie and Grampa did not drive a car, but they were always traveling. They took the train. They stayed with relatives. They rented rooms. In every city, they took the bus or trolley. They have lived in New York, Massachusetts, Minnesota, Texas, Colorado, Vermont and Pennsylvania.

Grampa would find a job to earn the money. Sometimes he was a teacher. Sometimes a newspaper editor. Sometimes a proofreader. Sometimes a translator. Wherever they lived, Grampa was in the church choir.

Grammie stayed at home to take care of the children. She was a volunteer. Wherever they lived, Grammie taught Sunday School.

To go on an outing, they had to plan ahead.

Opa drove a big, black delivery van. But, he died. Oma did not drive. But, she liked to travel. She took the Greyhound.

Monday, May 2, 1966

Once she went to Canada. She brought back postcards of the snow-capped mountains, the crystal clear lakes, the red-coated Mounties, the wild animals, the bright cities, the brand new Canada flag. I saw the Queen on the coins. I sat close beside Oma. Listening. Asking. Looking.

To go on an outing, she wore white gloves.

Other people in my family have been to faraway places.

Uncle Ronald went to Paris and Amsterdam. He brought me a pair of wooden shoes.

Uncle Peter was a pilot. He was flying for the Air Force.

Aunt Kirsten came from South Africa. She had a maid.

We had a visitor from India. She wore a soft, green silk sari.

Where are these places? How do you get there?

Traveling. Ever since I can remember, someone in our family is always traveling. When I am grown up, I will travel, too.

Maybe I will write about the second topic: How our family came to Colorado.

Everybody in my family likes to move around. Crossing oceans. Climbing mountains. Driving across the continent. Trains. Buses. Airplanes.

It would take a lot of paper to tell about my family and how we came to live in Colorado.

My father's family came to America almost 200 years ago. They came from England to Baltimore. Later, Boston. Some had a farm, delivering milk. Some studied to become professionals.

When Grammie and Grampa brought their three children to Colorado, my Daddy was a cute little boy. They lived in a three-room cabin. Grampa worked at home, slowly and steadily translating books from Latin to English, mailing away thick, manila envelopes with typed pages. The cabin was up in the mountains. To get to town, they asked neighbors for rides to get groceries, to go to church, to bring metal cans of water from the spring. Later, when the fourth child was expected, they moved down the valley into the city. Colorado Springs had a hospital.

My mother's parents came from Europe.

Opa came on a ship from Switzerland to America to work for his uncle in New Jersey.

Oma came on a ship from Germany to Ellis Island when she was only seventeen. The first plan was for Oma's older sister to come. But, the sister got sick. So, Oma took her sister's coat and suitcase and used her sister's ticket. When it was time to leave, the sister said, "When you get there, please mail my coat and suitcase back to me."

After Opa died, Oma learned to drive a car. She decided to move to Colorado to be near our family. She lives in a little pink cottage. I can see it when the school bus drives along the highway.

It would be easy to tell about how my parents brought our family to Colorado.

We had been living in Grammie and Grampa's house in Pennsylvania, not too far from Mommy's relatives. But, Daddy said we were moving to Colorado! He owned property there! I remember the picnic at Oma's house with all of the cousins, and how people were worried about the wild wild west. They gave us blankets. And warnings.

Two-and-a-half years ago Mommy packed everything up. Daddy hitched the rented U-Haul trailer to the light blue Ford station wagon.

I remember the long, hot, boring ride across the prairies. I remember the chilly morning when we arrived at our property and celebrated by walking up the driveway for the first time. I was so tired. Daddy explained that there was less air to

Monday, May 2, 1966

breathe at high altitude. We had been living at almost sea level. Now we were at 8,000 feet! It took a few days to get used to it. Now I'm not tired.

Colorado. Ever since I can remember, someone in our family has been living in Colorado.

I had a bad *dream* about traveling once. I do not want to write about *that*.

I do not even want to talk about this or tell anyone. Ever. I would rather stuff this scary dream down inside and never talk about it. If I do, someone might laugh. They would not understand how frightened I was. To someone else, it might seem small. Someone might say, "It would never happen that way."

In the dream: It was my turn to steer the car up the driveway, like we do every Sunday on the way home from church.

"OK, Eleanor, hop in! It's your turn to steer."

Eagerly, I climbed into the front, up on Daddy's lap, my legs under the steering wheel, my back straight, my head high so I could see out of the window.

"OK, Daddy. I'm ready."

In the dream: He eased slowly forward and we started up the gentle slope. Wide grassy space was to the left. Young trees were growing close to the road on the right. I wanted to learn. I wanted to do well. I wanted to hear, "Good for you!"

Suddenly the engine revved. Loudly. The tires spun the gravel. The car lurched forward!

"Woo-Hoo!" my brothers cheered. "Let's GO!"

I screamed. "Daddy! No! Stop!"

Sudden stop. Everyone jerked forward.

Silence.

"Aw... You wrecked the fun!" my brothers whined.

"Do you want to drive?" Daddy asked.

"Yes."

He moved his hands. He moved his feet. Again he started the car forward. Slowly. As we reached the bend in the road, I gripped the steering wheel. Carefully I judged the distance up ahead, the arc of the turn, the width of the road, avoiding the ditches on either side.

But! Wait! What was happening?

In the dream: I was trying to ease the steering wheel just enough, but it wouldn't do what I wanted it to do. My knuckles were white. It felt like the steering wheel was locked. It wouldn't budge! We were headed for the ditch!

"Daddy! Help!" I was so scared. It will be all my fault if we crash!

Just at the last minute, the steering wheel swerved away. For a second I could relax.

In the dream: I screamed. "O, No! Look out! Here comes the other ditch!"

"Yahoo!" one brother called. "Yee-haw!" the other cheered.

Not me. This was not fun anymore.

"Stop. Please, Daddy. Stop! Stop!"

The engine idled. The family was silent. I tried to be calm.

"Keep going, Daddy. This is fun!" one brother coaxed. "Can we do this when it is my turn?" the other begged. They were leaning over Daddy's shoulder, excited by the thrill.

In the dream: Daddy moved his feet. Now we were moving... backwards? No! This is an emergency! The slope was not steep, but the highway was behind us. I had no power to stop the car. No understanding of what to do next. I wish I had never tried to drive. Machines are too scary! O, when will this danger end?

Some kind of sound came out of me. Terrified.

Whew. We stopped.

Monday, May 2, 1966

"We were having fun..." someone mumbled from the back seat. "Girls always ruin the day..."

In my dream: The door opens. "Do you want to get out? You can walk home."

My heart is pounding. I wake up.

Shall I go downstairs and ask Mommy or Daddy to listen? to comfort me?

I am only eight years old! I can't figure it out.

The feelings from the dream seem so real. I am the oldest. It is my job to take care of the others. I don't understand why the car kept jerking? Fast. Stop. Swerve. Back. Did I do that? I must be very stupid. Heavy shame fills and floods. I cannot see. I cannot hear. I am immobilized.

One thing I know: I don't want another turn to drive up the driveway. Maybe I will never even try to drive a car. Or any other machine. Ever.

Maybe I'll just write about the third topic: a pretend trip.

One thing for sure: It won't be about me driving a car!

I could travel by train or boat, by camel or dog-sled, by horse or goat cart. I could hike or bike or drift downstream on a raft or paddle a canoe.

I could live in a lighthouse. I could be a servant in a castle. I could explore the mountains. I could find a little valley with a rushing creek, good soil, tall trees, wild animals, and a place for a garden to grow my own food. I would go there all by myself. I would take a camera and sell my photographs of beautiful scenery to make into calendars.

Yes, I will write about a place where I am alone so no one will tease me. I will write about a place where I can live that will have all the necessities, so I would not need to drive a car.

Fresh mountain air and crystal clear water, trees to build a cabin and to burn for warmth, a garden and chickens for food. And books, I would have to bring lots of books... or else write my own.

Later

1971

Daddy flew from Toronto, Ontario, to London, England for an international conference. Meanwhile, that summer Mommy drove the red VW van out to Colorado, taking the five of us kids (now 6-13 years old) on a camping trip.

Every day she gave us each a 10¢ allowance. While we stopped at a gas station, we could look over the candy, pop, chips, comic books and souvenirs. What to buy? When to spend?

Every day she drove about 350 miles. We stopped early. We agreed to a regular routine. First set up the tent. Then go swimming.

We made our own food. No restaurants for us. Mommy had a big cooler and we bought ice blocks and groceries as we went along. Breakfast was cereal and milk and fruit. Lunch was sandwiches. We cooked over the fire in the evening. The first night a kid in the next campsite screamed when his hot marshmallow stuck to his leg. The next night we made a slit in each hot dog, pushed in a long slice of cheese, and wrapped the whole thing with a piece of bacon, held firmly with toothpicks. Yum! The last night of camping we had a can of beans with sausages served over an open bun like a sloppy Joe. That was very filling.

Monday, May 2, 1966

Every night after we blew up the air mattresses and snuggled into our sleeping bags, we finished the day with singing. Mommy didn't know that at school we had learned so many hymns, folk songs and rounds. She didn't know that we could sing in harmony.

Over the years our parents took us so many places: driving to the top of Pikes Peak, hiking in the Garden of the Gods, touring the Mint in Denver, standing on the rim of the Grand Canyon, splashing in the Atlantic Ocean and the Gulf of Mexico, climbing up inside the Statue of Liberty, holding tightly to Oma's white-gloved hand on the viewing platform of the Empire State Building, learning so much at the Museum of Natural History, and of course, family trips to swimming pools, sporting events, camping, parades, live theatre, religious holidays and pageants.

I wonder where I will decide to travel when I grow up?

Freely Give
1978

I did find an isolated place to live in the mountains of British Columbia, Canada. I helped my husband build our tiny log cabin. I learned to grow and preserve our own food. Together we had four children.

I did not learn to drive until I was almost 40 years old!

I did, however, do a lot of travelling.

In Canada, mothers receive monthly 'Baby Cheques' as well as income tax returns. Year after year, I spent that money on travelling. Since all of my extended family lived back east or in the USA, if my children were to know their relatives, I would gladly take them there.

1980

I bundled up our baby daughter in December to trek on a train for four days and four nights, always east, to Ontario to meet her grandparents, aunts and uncles. And again to return to the cabin in April, for four days and nights always west, to British Columbia to be reunited with her Daddy.

1983

Again, to meet the grandparents, I took two tots through airports to Calgary, Toronto, Tampa, Edmonton.

1985

I curled up overnight on the Greyhound bus, trying to coax two preschoolers to sleep, through tunnels, over bridges, winding between mountains, alongside rivers, to visit college classmates who also had small children.

2000

It was my turn to attend an international conference. Amtrak offered 30-day tickets. From Seattle to Chicago, New York City, Philadelphia, then back through Denver, Sacramento, returning to Vancouver.

My husband never complained and rarely came with us. "Tell them that *you* are my gift to them," he would say as we boarded the taxi, bus, train or plane.

To read more about the Eleanor's travels...
... turn to 10 Days in June Chapter 2, page 131.

Chapter 3
Tuesday, May 3, 1966
3-Room Cabin

Simplify your life.
Don't waste the years struggling
for things that are unimportant.
Don't burden yourself with possessions.
Keep your needs and wants simple
and enjoy what you have.
Don't destroy your peace of mind
by looking back, worrying about the past.
Live in the present.
Simplify!
—*Henry David Thoreau*

Freely Receive

"Run over to the cabin before you leave for the school bus," Mommy sent me, "and take this loaf of bread to Uncle Peter."

Uncle Peter lives in the cabin now. He's fixing up the cabin for Oma. We lived in the cabin when we first arrived two-and-a-half years ago. It had three rooms then. Uncle Peter took down the walls so now it will be one room.

Daddy's old Uncle Allan was the first one to live in that cabin. Daddy bought the property from Uncle Allan. Daddy was still in college. He only had $300. He could only buy one cabin and 52 acres. After Daddy married Mommy, they came to the cabin on their honeymoon, then went back to Pennsylvania to get a job. The cabin stayed empty for a few years. Now Daddy is a professor at the college where he used to be a student! We moved into the cabin. Two years later our new house was built.

There used to be five cabins all together. The cabins were built with no foundation. The soil was dry gravel so there were just poles, buried down and standing up. Rough lumber framed the walls. Slabs with the bark still on covered the outside.

Daddy told me there were two main reasons people built those cabins. One was digging for gold and silver! The other was for summer holiday places, up in the mountains, away from the hot city.

The two larger cabins were way farther up on the ridge. Daddy took us there when we first arrived, to go exploring in the empty cabins. I found old knives and forks and spoons in the pantry. The boys climbed around in the dirt cellar. Julie liked the big, screened-in porch. Daddy said, "Be careful not to step in the meadow muffins!" He explained that cattle wandered there to graze. "Stay away from the pits!" He explained about the gold and silver mines in Cripple Creek. People used to dig here and there and all over the place hoping to find

Tuesday, May 3, 1966

more gold. But the sparkly golden crystals that are easy to see around here are actually 'Fool's Gold.' Iron Pyrite.

I like it up on the ridge. The wind is always bringing the smell of the pines and sage brush. The sky is almost always blue. You can see Pikes Peak's snowy shoulders.

The three smaller cabins were down in the valley. Daddy calls the valley 'The Gulch.' All three cabins were empty, too. Until we came.

The furthest cabin was the biggest. There was red trim on the windows and doors, and screens on the windows. Long grass grew all around a Model A Ford. We used to pretend all kinds of fun games in that old car. Cops and Robbers. Exploring. Chauffeur. Running away from home.

The middle cabin had a short bridge across the gully, a shade tree near the porch, and a big window in each room. Grammie and Grampa lived here when Daddy was a little boy! Grampa was working on a very long translation project. He could work at home on the typewriter. Little Daddy romped on the same hills that we play on now.

The first cabin is the smallest. That's ours. I'm glad I got to live in the cabin. Everything was so basic. The road was gravel. The water came off the roof into the rain barrel. I could scoop the tin dipper deeply into the wooden barrel for a drink of the clear, cold water. Who cares about the pine needles?

A few steps away, we had an out-house for a toilet. We covered the bad smell with a sprinkle of ashes Daddy brought when he shoveled out the woodstove. Mommy warmed water on the kitchen wood cookstove and put the children one-by-one into the wide, white enamel kitchen sink for a bath.

The room on the right was the kitchen. We had a pantry instead of a refrigerator. It was a little room with lots of shelves at the back of the cabin on the north side, where the sun would never make it warm. I found a buffalo-Indian head nickle in a crack in the floor! Daddy said I should keep it. It is very old.

In the middle was the living room with the black woodstove heater. It looked like a barrel laying on its side. At Christmastime we asked, "How will Santa fit down the chimney?"

The room on the left was the bedroom. At first, all four of us kids slept across Mommy and Daddy's big bed. Then they got a bunk bed and two cots. We were all in the same room.

We didn't have any closets because we didn't have very many clothes. We didn't need a vacuum cleaner because we had no rugs. Mommy just swept the floor right out the door, off the side of the porch. There was one bare light bulb up in the ceiling of each room with a string to pull to turn it on.

Out the door of the living room was a long porch with a railing made of thin poles that still had the bark on them. I loved that porch. You could see everything. Pikes Peak. Tall trees. Golden aspen leaves. Blue sky.

When we first moved in, the walls had crumpled up newspaper and empty egg cartons for insulation. Now, Uncle Peter is rolling out pink Fiberglas insulation. Oma will be much warmer than we were! She will also have an electric heater, running water and a modern kitchen and indoor bathroom.

We didn't have a TV because we were always playing outside. Daddy made a tee-pee with poles and a tarp. Under the scrub oak bushes we made forts. The empty hen house made a great store, or school, or castle, or pirate ship. Daddy put up a swing and a trapeze bar. Mommy built a pen for my white rabbit. The boys had a hamster in a cage. Julie had a fluffy black and white cat. And Rex was our trusty black guard dog.

Tuesday, May 3, 1966

Now we have a big, new house that was designed by an architect. It is straight and smooth and handsome and modern.

The upstairs has a bedroom for the boys that faces the driveway, then a playroom with a TV and fireplace, a bathroom with a tub, two sinks and the potty, then a bedroom for my sister and I that faces the flowerbed and hillside. There's also a really huge closet. That's where Mommy puts the Christmas decorations, winter clothes and other stuff. She measures each of us every year inside the closet door. You don't actually know that you are growing, but you are!

The downstairs has the dining room with glass sliding doors that faces the driveway. The kitchen has an electric stove, a double fridge-freezer, a big pantry with a washing machine and dryer. The telephone is in the kitchen, too. The stone fireplace is half in the dining room, half in the living room. The living room is huge and the whole front wall that faces the mountains is glass. The sliding glass doors open onto a nice patio. At the far end is Mommy and Daddy's bedroom which also has glass sliding doors. They also have a bathroom and Daddy's study. Since Baby Carol was born, she sleeps in the study.

After school, when I walk up the driveway, I love to see the little old cabin on the right side and the big, new house on the left side.

I think Daddy is really happy now. He bought this property when he was 22 years old. He knew that someday he would live in this place with his wife and children. We all like it here. I will always call this place 'Home.'

May Chapter 3   3-Room Cabin

Last year, while our new house was being built, another family built their house across the road from the cabin where Daddy lived when he was small.

Now, six kids walk down the driveway to the school bus stop. My twin brothers and I meet up with the three new neighbor kids, Karel, Mark and Ernie. Every morning there is a race. We put our lunch boxes in order. That shows who gets on the bus first. Karel has a 'Barbie' lunch box. The boys have trucks and cars on theirs. Mine has 'Mary Poppins'. (I'm not allowed 'Barbie' anything.)

While we wait, the boys like to go back up the driveway a little ways to stir up the anthill. The gritty red sand forms a perfect pyramid. They are red ants and their bite really stings. So you need to find a long stick. It is easy to poke, dig or make patterns in the sand. It's kind of mean to break their home. But, it is also interesting to see the ants hurry, collecting their eggs. I guess it doesn't do much harm. By the time we get back this afternoon, the anthill will be built again. I do wonder what it is like down in their tunnels?

"Mommy said to leave the ant hills alone."

"Well, she's not here."

"You're not my boss."

They don't get it. I'm the oldest. I know the rules. You have to keep the rules, even when Mommy can't see. "I'll tell!"

Usually, I keep a lookout. Not too close to the highway where the cars zip past. Not too far back, in case the driver thinks we aren't coming and drives right by. Sometimes there is fog down in the valley and you can't see the bus until it is almost here.

"Bus!" I yell, and everyone comes running.

The red lights flash, the door opens, we all climb aboard. Our driver is a cowboy! He always wears a cowboy hat, plaid shirt, blue jeans and big, shiny silver belt buckle. And, of course,

Tuesday, May 3, 1966

cowboy boots. I sit by the window, near the front, behind the driver.

At each stop, I like to look at each house.

First, there is a steep gravel road with driveways sliced into the slope for each mobile home. Next, a semi-circle of little, brightly painted cottages to rent. After that, some boys get on the bus, jostling, stomping, joking. They live in a dormitory, not with their parents. At the top of the hill is a red and white sign for Motel-X. I wonder what it is like to live in an apartment behind the front desk? My brothers have a friend who lives at the top of a switch-back driveway above a gravel pit. I don't think I would feel safe with my house so near to the edge. My sister has a friend who lives in a stone house way back behind big pine trees. They have a pasture and four horses.

Across the valley, just before we turn left up the asphalt road to our school, if I look at just the right moment, I can see red and white and green shapes in between the trees. It is a huge candy cane, Ferris wheel and giant Christmas Tree! It's 'Santa's Workshop' at the North Pole, Colorado! Santa lives here during the summer months in a red-trimmed log cabin. All of his elves and storybook folk live there, too, ready to welcome guests who come to sit on Santa's knee.

Of course, Santa has a home in the north for the winter, but, like many people, he comes to Colorado to live in his summer home.

Later

One day I was late for the school bus. The bus was already there when I came around the bend, started to run, slipped on the gravel and fell, hitting my right knee on a rock. I kept running, embarrassed. On the bus, I looked at my knee. Blood. Ouch! But, I could cover it with my dress. I washed it with cold water and toilet paper when I got to school. I didn't want the teacher to see. I knew what would happen. Merthiolate! Youch! That stuff burns! Plus, everyone can see the orange stain. Mrs. Thompson was as careful as she could be, getting the gravel out of the cut. I kept squeezing my leg with both hands when she put the disinfectant on. I didn't want to cry or make any noise. But, it didn't matter. Everybody knew I was hurt. When people were looking at me, I felt even worse.

1968

In Grade 6 Social Studies we learned a lot more about the kinds of houses Indigenous people had all around North America. In the northeast, birch forests supplied supple saplings that bent over the longhouses and waterproof birch bark to shield the roof. In Florida's marshy lowlands the people built their houses up on stilts. On the wide open prairie, the tribes moved with the buffalo herds, bringing their tents made of buffalo hides. Where the sun beats down in the southwest, the thick, clay adobe walls kept families cool. In the northwest, cedar trees split into slabs were used to build longhouses. In the far north, tents in the summer and igloos in the winter sheltered the people.

When Europeans arrived, they built log houses from the abundant forests and sod houses in the grasslands.

Whenever I look at pictures of houses, I wonder, will I ever build my own home?

Freely Give

Whenever I think about how four generations of our family have lived in Colorado on the same property, I also think about some other things that have been passed to me from my family.

From my Daddy I have: wavy brown hair with the sparkle of a copper penny, freckles on my arms, eyes that need glasses, a talent for reading, theatre, music, writing, and everything academic. Daddy likes to say, "We Hinkles are pretty bright!"

From Mommy I have: a talent for music and color, making things with my hands and understanding children. We both like to sing. She makes our house pretty and holidays special.

I want to pass these things on to my own children and grandchildren. These experiences will give them that sensation of 'Home.' They will gain strength when they look back and remember these moments.

1978

I earned the money ($300). Kevin built the log cabin (4 months).[1] We poured our trust and time and talent into the hot days of work and long days of uncertainly. To build our first home, we each gave the other all that we had. Gladly.

1982

Together we built the stackwall house.[2] It was barely bigger, but much warmer than the original cabin. Kevin had a full-time job on the railroad. He earned a living as a night patrolman, cycling along the train tracks alone in the dark. He brought home every cent to provide for his wife and two small children. Without earning a penny, I worked to keep the fire going, bake the bread, nurse the babies, wash the diapers in a bucket. Every two weeks, on pay-day, Kevin drove us all to town. He did all the grocery shopping, while I tended the children at the laundromat. It took three hours to do almost 20 loads of laundry.

1984

We bought a little cottage in town so our kids could go to school, but that year the school was closed! I had a washing machine, but no dryer. Baby Number 3 arrived. Endless cloth diapers! Rain! I hung up laundry inside overnight. There was a tremendous sense of satisfaction in our home. We had a fertile vegetable garden. We made decisions, met challenges, worked as a team. We both set aside our own wishes and postponed personal pleasures to Give, Give, Give to our children.

1987

How could this be? An elderly couple offered us their property! It's part of their original homestead. There are two-and-a-half acres beside the river: house, garden, apple tree, out-buildings, tools... The price tag was so small, it truly is a gift. As we prepared to welcome our fourth child, we experienced a sense of renewal and trust in Divine Providence. We felt rededicated to the original dream and aware of the wonderful ways it is unfolding into reality.

Receive. Give. Receive. Give.

To read more about Eleanor's log cabin lifestyle...
... turn to 10 Days in June Chapter 3, page 149.

Chapter 4
Wednesday, May 4, 1966
3-Room School

The mediocre teacher tells.
The good teacher explains.
The superior teacher demonstrates.
The great teacher inspires.
—William Arthur Ward

Freely Receive

In Grade 1, I had Mrs. Warner. Every year she taught her class the ABCs. She wrote on the chalkboard with shapes to help students remember the letters. 'S' was a snake. 'M' was a pair of mittens. 'T' was a table. She taught us the sounds each letter makes. But, I could already read. So, I was watching my teacher to see how she was teaching more than I was learning anything new.

The other kids teased me. Calling names.

"Ele-a-nor... El-e-phant!"

I told my teacher.

"Just ignore them," Mrs. Warner said. My heart was aching.

In Grade 2, I had Mrs. Van Kirk. She taught us how to do cursive writing. I liked watching my teacher make smooth, round, slanted, perfect letters on the chalkboard for us to copy on our lined paper. She had a custom. Every year, on the first day that it started snowing during the school day, she made popcorn! All the kids were hoping the snow would start on a Friday, during the weekly Spelling test! She also had a year-end tradition: a Science Fair. Last year, I got to be the announcer, introducing each student and their topic: Bees. Volcanoes. Bats. Weather.

I had to sit in the front because I couldn't read the chalkboard. When I got glasses, the other kids teased me. "Four Eyes!"

I didn't tell anyone. My heart was aching.

I'm in Grade 3 now. Mrs. Thompson is my teacher. On my Report Card, I saw her name, 'Ruby.' She always smiles. She is the most round person I have ever seen. And she is the only teacher I know who is so interested in children. It seems like she really wants us to learn things. She's not just telling things to us and we repeat them back to her. She wants us to understand and do well.

Our school is only three classrooms, plus two hallways, a Boys bathroom and a Girls bathroom, and a small library room. The Grade 1 and 2 rooms, on the lower level, are divided by a sliding door, so when it is open it makes one big room. For a meeting. Or the science fair. Or PhysEd when it is bad weather. There are five doors to the outside. Every classroom has a door and there is one at the end of each hallway. Sometimes we practice Fire Drills to go out. Every day we line up to come in. The lower hallway has cupboards for art supplies, a sink, textbooks and bins for balls, jump rope and other PhysEd equipment we are allowed to take outside at Recess. It is three steps up to the

Wednesday, May 4, 1966

door to the backyard. And three steps up to the upper hallway where the bathrooms are on the left. The Grade 3 classroom and library room are on the right.

There are hooks on the hallway walls for our coats and a bench underneath where we put our winter boots and a shelf above where we put our lunch boxes.

I like our school. It is adobe outside, a kind of tan-pink color. The roof is red clay tiles. There are lots of windows. The wooden floorboards creak.

I like our schoolyard, too. The front yard is fenced. There is asphalt paving the flat yard where the playground equipment is. High swings. A metal slide. Monkey bars. The younger kids play here so the teacher can watch out the window.

The side yard has a lot of young ponderosa pine trees. The dry, red gravel is sloped and the tree roots are exposed. At recess, we girls like to play house under the trees. Best friends make a family. "I'll be the big sister. I am sixteen. You be the Mom and feed the little sister with a spoon." We plan which room will be in each place. We take branches to sweep the floor. We find flat rocks for dishes. We sit on the roots. We use our coats to make beds. If the girls can get a few boys to play house, then there can be a son or brother, a Dad or Uncle or Grampa, or even a boyfriend!

Also, the side yard has a basketball court with a high fence. If the ball gets away it will roll way far down to the highway. So, that would be really bad. So, really, nobody plays basketball.

The backyard has three things.

On the left, there is a steep, gravely, dry ditch that gets carved by rainwater and melted snow. No one plays there because the gravel crumbles and you get a skinned knee.

There is a paved, flat space up against the school where the hot lunch truck comes every day. At Recess, we girls like to play jump rope there because it is usually shady.

The main area is a big playing field for baseball, high jump and relay races for PhysEd. No grass grows in the dry, red, bare dirt.

The big playing field is where the boys like to play War. They choose teams. One side has a big boulder to be the hospital. The other side has a short rise with a few bushes. It has good camouflage. If the boys can get a few girls to play, too, then there can be Nurses. We play the 'Red Coats and the Blue Coats.' Or else 'World War 2.' Or else 'Vietnam.' If someone points their finger at you and shouts, "Bang! I got you!" then you have to lie down and count to ten to be dead. Then a Nurse comes and helps you up and the wounded person has to limp back to the hospital and count to ten. After that, you can go out and shoot some more.

Before school, when the bus arrives, there is not much time to play. We line up our lunch boxes at the classroom door to hold our place in line, and take a quick turn down the slide or across the monkey bars. When the Teacher rings the brass bell, we line up and she lets us in.

After school, when we wait for the bus, there is not much time to play. The girls line up at the gate. The boys run to play. The kids who wait at the front of the line can see down the road as the bus turns off the highway. "Bus!" No one wants to miss the bus. There are two buses. One for the low road beside the creek, and the one I take up the slope, along the highway.

Since there is not much time to play before school, or after school, Recess is pretty important. And Lunchtime. That's when I like to jump rope.

The first thing every morning in every classroom, is attendance. The teacher calls every name and each student says, "Here!"

Wednesday, May 4, 1966

The next thing in every classroom is the 'The Pledge of Allegiance.' We all stand up straight, look at the flag and put our right hand over our heart to make a promise. When Mrs. Thompson puts her hand on her huge, round bosom, we all say the words together.

The third thing in every classroom is singing. Still standing, we join in with all the other people who live in our country. *My Country 'Tis of Thee*, or sometimes *O Beautiful For Spacious Skies* or sometimes *God Bless America*. In Third Grade we are learning *The Star Spangled Banner*. My favorite is *This Land is Your Land*. Sometimes I can hear the other classes singing. I like this part of the day. I love to sing. I love my country. I love joining in. I love thinking of all the children in all of the schools in the whole country singing together.

After these morning routines, the school becomes quiet and the students get to work.

Mrs. Thompson has a very good way of doing things. Plans for each day are on the chalkboard. Each day of the week has a time for each subject.

In the morning we study Reading, Spelling, and Arithmetic.

Then Recess.

Then we do workbook pages in the Phonics book or practice other Language skills, or practice Penmanship. Next comes PhysEd (I had to ask my Daddy to find out what that means. It's short for Physical Education. Which means exercise. We also say 'P. E.')

Then Lunch.

The mornings are all pretty much the same. In the afternoon we do different things each day.

Monday is Social Studies. Tuesday is Science. Wednesday is Music. Thursday is Art. Friday Mrs. Thompson reads Literature to us: poems, stories of long ago or far away places, famous people, historic or mythological adventures.

Actually, she reads to us every afternoon. When we have finished the assignments, and the classroom is tidy, there is always a little time until dismissal.

Mrs. Thompson has additional plans for the year: In September, we learned about plants when we collected seeds and pressed autumn leaves. In October, we decorated pumpkins. In November, we did art projects about Thanksgiving. In December there were so many Christmas songs and crafts. January was when we made snowflakes. February, of course, was Valentines. March we did springtime flower projects. In April we made Easter crafts. Now it is May: Mother's Day is coming!

Mrs. Thompson also has a part of the chalkboard that she uses to collect words. At first, we collected Synonyms which are words that mean the same thing like: windy and breezy, or, big and large. That was so we could make our writing more interesting. It was fun to add to that list. Then we collected Antonyms which are opposites like: big and small, or, wet and dry. It was easy to add to that list. Now we are collecting Homonyms which are words that sound the same but mean something different like: tail and tale, or, meet and meat. Sometimes there are even three in a set, like, too, to and two and also there, their, and they're. It is harder to add to this list and it's pretty tricky to remember how to spell each one so you say what you mean!

Today I am having such a good day!
In Reading, we had a poem. The boys and girls took turns reading.

Wednesday, May 4, 1966

> Girls: The Man in the Moon, as he sails the sky
> Is a very remarkable skipper.
> Boys: He made a mistake when he tried to take
> A drink of milk from the Dipper.
> Girls: He dipped into the Milky Way,
> And slowly and carefully filled it.
> Boys: The Big Bear growled, the Little Bear howled,
> And scared him so that he spilled it.
> —*author unknown*

In Science, we already learned about the Moon and the Milky Way. We also know the Big Bear and Little Bear constellations, which are also called the Big and Little Dipper. Everyone knows the poem is a funny rhyme.

Mrs. Thompson divided us into three groups and we went to different corners of the classroom to make up actions to go with the story. It was fun to act. And to see the skits that the other groups made.

Today is Wednesday. This is the day to write sentences using the new Spelling words. We are learning about compound words. Compound words are easy to spell since they are made of two small words. The teacher wants us to underline every Spelling word.

I like to try to make the Spelling sentences into a story. Here is what I wrote.

This <u>afternoon</u>, my brother is having a <u>birthday</u> party. It will be <u>outside</u>. <u>Anybody</u> who comes should be dressed up. So far we have a <u>cowboy</u>, <u>fireman</u>, <u>someone</u> in a <u>raincoat</u>, and a <u>pussycat</u>. I need a <u>flashlight</u> to find my <u>baseball</u> cap. I will go <u>downstairs</u> when I am ready. Later we will have <u>fireworks</u>.

Next: Arithmetic (which is also called Math). We have been learning the Times Tables by heart. We have to say them all together. We have to write them on the chalkboard. And fill in a page that is a chart. The teacher asks one person to stand up and say one whole row. "Three times one is three. Three times two is six..." I'm OK with 1, 2, 3, 4, 5, and 9. The hardest, for me, is in the middle. 6 x 6. 6 x 7. 6 x 8.

The thing I like about Math is that you can check your work by going backwards. Like this: 2 + 5 = 7 and 7 − 2 = 5 It works for the times tables and division, too. Like this: 9 x 5 = 45 and 45 ÷ 9 = 5.

It is almost the end of the school year. We have to know the Times Tables by heart, because Math will be much harder in Grade 4.

Recess!

I join up with five girls to play jump rope. Two girls turn the rope, one jumps, three wait. When it is my turn, I jump. When I miss, I'm out. That's when I turn the rope. The next girl jumps, misses, takes the other end. Next time, I am replaced and I can line up to jump again.

There are so many jump rope songs.

Down by the ocean, Down by the sea,
Johnny broke a bottle and he blamed it on me.
I told Ma. Ma told Pa.
Johnny got a lickin' and a Ha Ha Ha.
How many lickin's did he get?
One. Two. Three...

Cinderella dressed in yella
Went upstairs to kiss her fella
How many kisses did she get?
One. Two. Three....

Teddy Bear, Teddy Bear: Turn around.
Teddy Bear, Teddy Bear: Touch the ground.
Teddy Bear, Teddy Bear: Turn out the light.
Teddy Bear, Teddy Bear: Say, "Good Night!"

Wednesday, May 4, 1966

In Grade 3, one student gets a turn to be the Monitor for a whole week. They get to help the Teacher collect papers, pass out books, get the art supplies out, and ring the bell to come in at Recess and Lunch. The Monitor gets to wear an orange sash. The little kids can ask the Monitor for help at Recess. The Monitor has to stay in at Lunchtime to make sure each student clears off their desk and the classroom is tidy. My turn to be Monitor was in January.

Today it's Tammy. She already thinks she's pretty important. Now she's even more important. But, she can't jump rope today. She has to stay near the door so the teacher can tell her when it's time to ring the bell.

After playing outside, everybody lines up at the water fountain.

What a noise as everyone is opening and closing the lids of our wooden desks. It takes a while for everyone to get out their Phonics workbook. Phonics is my favorite. I like learning to sound out words.

In the Phonics workbook[3] there are two pages for each lesson. First: a poem. Then exercises to make sure we understand what letters make the sounds of the new words.

You can draw a line to connect things that go together or finish a sentence. (Birds fly through it --- air.)

Or make a circle around the two words that mean the same thing. (little stone small)

Next, we notice the sounds that the letters make. In Grade 1 we learned one letter at a time. Now we learn combinations: ee, ea, ay, io, and also, th, sh, cl, gr, ew, un, br, There are *so* many!

Sometimes we make a circle when we see a prefix or a suffix.

Sometimes we read aloud in unison. Sometimes we work silently. Sometimes the Teacher assigns us partners. Sometimes the Teacher reads the answers and we check our own work. Sometimes we trade workbooks with a partner and check their work. Sometimes we turn in our workbooks so Mrs. Thompson checks your answers and also our penmanship.

On most days: first we read, then we write.

In our Phonics book this week, there is a poem for Mother's Day. We have been reading it every day so we can learn it by heart. Today we are writing the poem on lined paper.

In Art class tomorrow, we will paste the poem onto the inside page of a card. Mrs. Thompson will let each student pick out two pieces of colored paper. We can search through the scrap box to choose pretty colors to make hearts and butterflies and flowers to decorate the front of the card. We each have a jar of paste in our desks. The orange lid screws off. The lid has a long white paddle attached so we can dip down into the white paste. I think I will choose green for the card, pink for the flowers, yellow for a butterfly.

Here is the poem. We are using cursive handwriting. My writing isn't perfect. I only got an A- on my Report Card.

> Hundreds of stars in the deep blue sky,
> Hundreds of shells on the shore together.
> Hundreds of birds that go singing by,
> Hundreds of flowers in the sunny weather.
> Hundreds of dewdrops to greet the dawn,
> Hundreds of bees in the purple clover.
> Hundreds of butterflies on the lawn,
> But only one Mother the wide world over.
> —By George Cooper

Wednesday, May 4, 1966

PhysEd is outdoors now. It's Spring!

Mrs. Camel comes to teach PhysEd. We have been playing baseball for a few weeks.

First, Mrs. Camel picks two boys to be the two captains. Then they do this thing to see who picks first. The teacher passes the bat to one boy, who grabs it partway down. Then the two boys climb their hands up and up the bat until the last hand covers the top of the bat. That person gets to pick the first team member.

All the kids line up. First, the two captains pick the boys, from best to worst. Then, they start picking girls from best to worst. When they pick girls, I am often picked near the beginning. I know the rules. And where to run. And where to stand. I can throw and catch and hit, too. And I know what to do. If I am on a base, I know when to move, and when to stay still. If I am in the field, I know where to throw the ball to get the other team out.

We don't have gym clothes or sneakers. I have to be careful since I am wearing a dress. I don't want to get dirty or skin my knees. But, I sure like to run.

We know it is time to go in when we see the Hot Lunch Truck back into the parking place behind the school. Everybody waves at Bob.

While everybody lines up at the water fountain again, then gets their lunch boxes from the bench in the hallway, Bob unloads the truck.

Bob is an old, bald, skinny guy. He wears dark blue overalls. He has glasses and a big smile.

He folds down the tailgate. He slides the ramp down the three stairs. Next, he rolls the stainless steel silver hot lunch box onto the tailgate, pulls the red lever and the whole thing lowers down. He carefully rolls the heavy hot lunch box down the ramp, into the hallway, setting the brake so it will not roll.

Back to the truck, he rolls out the next box of trays, plates and cutlery, and then the refrigerated box full of small milk cartons.

Every day he brings the truck. Every day the students guess what he is bringing by noticing the smells.

Some kids have Hot Lunch every day! We get to read the menu on Thursday. My Mother gives me money on Thursday to pay for one green Hot Lunch Token and five red Milk Tokens. Hot Lunch costs 35¢ and Milk costs 2¢. So, I have to be careful to bring the right amount of money to school. Sometimes I bring two quarters. Then I bring back 5¢ change.

I keep my Tokens in the front right-hand corner of my desk. I spend one red Milk Token every day, and the green Hot Lunch Token on the day I signed up for.

I decided to have my Hot Lunch tomorrow. On Thursday it is spaghetti and meatballs, a bun, peas and carrots, and canned peaches. I like canned peaches.

When the Monitor brings the tray of milk up to the Teacher's desk, I line up with my red Milk Token. Sometimes I take a straw. Sometimes I just drink out of the paper milk carton.

There is a little post inside my desk so I can make my slanted desk into a flat table.

O good. My mother made a peanut butter and honey sandwich for me. I like it when the honey soaks into the bread. I keep the waxed paper wrapping around my sandwich so my hands don't get sticky. Crunchy carrot sticks, an oatmeal and raisin cookie and an apple finish my lunch.

When we're all done eating and have put our garbage in the can, Mrs. Thomson excuses us to go outside and play.

The sun is pretty hot. Since I already had jump rope and baseball, I think I'll go to the pine trees and play house. Mary Lee and I like to pretend we both have babies. We wrap up our sweaters and pretend to feed, rock, talk to, sing and sometimes scold our babies. We say, "My baby is getting a new tooth," and

Wednesday, May 4, 1966

"I wonder if my baby has a fever?" Sometimes we talk to each other on the telephone while our babies are napping.

After lunch, we all take a moment to look at the Science experiment we started last week. It's springtime, so we are learning about plants: roots, stem, leaves, flowers, seeds.

This is the experiment: Mrs. Thompson gave us each a short, clear plastic cup, a paper towel and some beans. After we pressed the paper towel up against the inside wall of the cup, we filled it with dirt. Then we pushed the beans down in-between the paper towel and the clear plastic. If we keep the dirt damp, then we can look through the clear cup to watch the seed sprout. Every day, before our regular afternoon lessons begin, we pause for a moment to water our plants and then draw the changes that we see.

So far, my beans have cracked open, the tiny root has started pushing down. The green stem is curved and growing bigger to get above the soil. I think the leaf will open tomorrow!

Time for Music!

Sometimes we listen to records, so we can hear the different instruments. Daddy plays a lot of classical music on our record player at home, so I know the strings and brass, the clarinet and flute and French horns, the drums and harp. Mommy plays the piano. That sound is easy to tell apart from the others.

Sometimes we have a film strip. There is a record player. A man's voice narrates. There is a 'ding' sound when it is time to change to the next picture on the film strip. We can see the pictures on the big white screen at the front of the classroom. Last week we could see and hear the musicians playing their instruments.

Sometimes Mrs. Thompson uses this special tool that holds 5 pieces of chalk so she can draw the 5 lines of the music staff on the chalkboard. Then she can write the notes of a song for us to learn. My mother already taught me on the piano about whole notes, half notes, and also rests. I know what the five lines mean and how to remember them. E-G-B-D-F. 'Every Good Boy Deserves Fudge.' And the four spaces. F-A-C-E. 'Face.'

Sometimes Mrs. Thompson teaches us to clap the rhythm, or how to pronounce the words, or the history of a song. National anthems and holiday songs, musical theater and nursery rhymes. It is interesting to learn where they came from.

Sometimes we sing from our Grade 3 songbooks. There are folk songs from other countries in French, or German, or Spanish. Once we learned a lullaby that the mothers would sing inside the tee-pees.

Sometimes we learn hymns for Thanksgiving or Christmas, and sometimes Spirituals.

Sometimes we learn silly songs or rounds.

Today we get to make requests!

These are the songs that I like best:

She'll be Comin' 'Round the Mountain
The Happy Wanderer
My Island in the Sun
White Coral Bells
Old Dan Tucker
T'zana

I'm always sad when Music class is over, but, it's time to tidy up, get in line and wait for the bus.

As soon as the bus pulls away from the school, I realize I made the same mistake that I made yesterday. The morning is chilly and the afternoon is hot.

"Sorry, Mommy, I left my sweater at school again."

Later
After Grades 1, 2 and 3 in the little mountain village, I had to take the bus down through Ute Pass to go to school in the city

Wednesday, May 4, 1966

for Grades 4 and 5. Up stairs, long corridors, hundreds of children, special teachers for Art, Science, Music, PhysEd. It was a big change. Recess was in a paved, fenced, crowded area. Lunch was in a large, noisy room with long tables and little supervision. I always felt like I was watching. Observing. Not really 'in' the place, rather looking 'at' it from a distance.

There were special events.

A circus came to the school gym. Tiny white dogs in pink ruffles stood on their hind legs, jumped over and ran under obstacles. A larger dog zig-zagged between poles and then made a barrel roll while walking on top of it. A colorful parrot and a colorful clown had a funny routine with hoops. A sassy white cockatiel with a big, fluffy tuft on its head got a treat when it climbed, hung upside down, rode on a swing and fluttered to a different perch. A sparkly lady did gymnastics and twirled hoops and batons. The host was grand in his red coat and black top-hat with his elaborate gestures and exciting announcements in his booming voice.

I clapped until my hands hurt.

The radio station came. They set up microphones and wires to record our school choir's Christmas Concert.

I announced the newly composed song, *Do You Hear What I Hear?* On Christmas Day, when the concert was broadcast, I heard my own voice through the radio speakers at home.

Our class put on a play about the importance of education. *School is a Useful Tool* was the theme song. I did a solo dance while singing, "I may not be any movie star or a well-known celebrity, but I ask, how can I really care when I'm glad that I'm me!"[4]

One thing I didn't like. Actually, I was terrified. There was a Science experiment about electricity. The teacher (my first male teacher) had a hand-cranked generator. He demonstrated that he could make a light bulb glow. He said, "Electricity can be conducted through the body." And he told everyone to stand up and hold hands. No! I stayed at my desk. My shoulders hunched. My head down. He insisted I come forward and he wrapped the copper wire around *my* little finger so I would be the *first* person to have the electricity pass through my *body*. I do not remember anything after that. Nothing bad happened. I just did not register any sensations, or save the memory. My mind protected me from the intense fear by becoming blank.

Freely Give

One useful result of all of these early experiences: by observing how my teachers were teaching, I began to collect impressions so that if I ever decided to teach anyone anything, I would have ideals to uphold, and also deliberate methods to imitate or avoid.

I began teaching as a volunteer without any training. A big sister. A babysitter. Leading activities at a summer camp. Helping teachers in the classroom. Putting school plays on stage. Preparing Christmas pageants.

I realized: If I am volunteering, I don't have to stay unless I experience satisfaction. The children don't have to stay or come back unless they are enjoying the experience. They stayed. I stayed. I guess I must be doing something right!

To read more about Eleanor's experiences as a teacher...
... turn to 10 Days in June Chapter 4, page 173.

Chapter 5
Thursday, May 5, 1966
"Look What I Made!"

> Every natural power exhilarates;
> a true talent delights the possessor first.
> —*Ralph Waldo Emerson*

Freely Receive

Today is Thursday! Today is Brownies! Today I get to wear my Brownie uniform to school![5]

A 'Brownie' is a friendly little elf. A Brownie likes to dance and sing and make nice surprises for people. Brownies are very helpful.

I love to wear my Brownie uniform! There are little dancing Brownies on each brown button on my brown dress. There are also Brownies decorating my uniform pocket, my belt buckle and my brown felt hat. I even have brown knee socks and shoes. I need Mommy to help me tie the orange necktie and pin on the golden Brownie pin.

May Chapter 5   "Look What I Made!"

In September, every girl in Grades 2 and 3 gets an invitation to join, or return. The invitation tells them when and where the meetings are, who the leader is and where to buy a uniform. Brownies is part of the worldwide group of girls who are not yet old enough to be Girl Scouts. New girls and their parents can visit a meeting to see if they like it.

If you want to belong, you have to make a promise.

> "On my honor, I will try
> to do my duty to God and my country,
> to help other people every day,
> especially those at home."

We have meetings one afternoon every week. Every girl brings 10¢ every week. Dues help to buy the craft supplies we need.

In October, we learned songs and how the meetings begin and end. We learned crafts and games and safety skills.

In November, when the photographer came to school on a Tuesday, I asked Mommy's permission to wear my uniform to school. On Monday night, Mommy tied my long wet hair in rags. In the morning I had lovely curls!

In December, we practised singing Christmas songs and visited the old people's home. We brought boxes of home-made cookies and a great big Brownie smile.

In January, we learned outdoor winter games and indoor sewing and cooking skills.

In February, every year, we have 'Thinking Day' when all of the Boy Scouts and all of the Girl Scouts all around the world learn about the other countries and how we are all part of one big group. I love knowing I have Brownie sisters all over the world.

Thursday, May 5, 1966

In March, the older girls in Junior Girl Scouts and Cadets visited the Brownies to show us their uniforms, tell about their activities, sing, play games, and share refreshments.

Girl Scouts and Brownies sell cookies in April. We raise money for camp-outs. Everybody loves Girl Scout Cookies. When the cases of cookies arrived at our meeting place, we practised good manners with a skit. We always go out selling in pairs. Our Leader showed us how to write down the money and how many boxes of each kind of cookies we sold.

After school, Mary Lee came home with me on the school bus. We put on our uniforms and made sure our hair was combed. Daddy took us up and down the roads of our town in the car. We carried the cases of cookies by the handle and knocked on neighbor's doors. We had to explain the four choices: shortbread cookies with sugar crystals on top, chocolate and vanilla sandwich cookies, peanut butter sandwich cookies, and also chocolate mints. All of them have the Girl Scout 'Trefoil' symbol on them. Daddy waited in the car where he could see us. He wanted to make sure we were safe. We stayed outside while the lady or man went inside to get their money. We had to be careful to count the change. And remember to say, "Thank-you." Then we ran back to the car to tell Daddy the good news.

"We sold three boxes!"

We had to be so careful about the money, counting the change, writing it down, not losing anything, and, on the right day we had to bring back the cookies that were not sold and all of the money.

Now, it is May, we are having a lot of show-and-tell. Our Leader has each Brownie scheduled to bring in the things they have been making. Today is my turn to bring my show-and-tell.

May Chapter 5   "Look What I Made!"

Oma is teaching me how to knit. She learned how to knit when she was even younger than I am now. She went to school in Germany. All of the girls at her school learned how to knit, crochet, sew and do embroidery.

She knits socks and mittens for all of her grandchildren. She also makes afghans with crochet. She always has big bags of yarn, needles of all sizes, projects on the go, a cigarette within reach, and music playing on the radio.

I sit very close. Oma's arms are around me, her hands on my hands. In. And. Out. My needles move slowly, looping the yarn. Pulling it through. One little stitch at a time. Will it ever be enough to wear?

Oma gave me some olive green and light gray yarn. I can make a scarf for my Raggedy Andy. Eight stitches across, then turn and knit another row. Back and forth. It is not very even. Wide and narrow. Tight and loose. But, it is starting to add up.

Oma lets me take my project home. Mommy can help me if I get confused.

Mommy likes to sew. She makes my dresses and the boy's shirts. Also PJs and nightgowns. Sometimes when I get home from school, her sewing machine is set up on the dining room table. If Baby Carol is asleep, and Julie is still napping, Mommy is working on a sewing project. Sometimes I see her pin the pattern on the long, smooth cloth. Sometimes I slide on the dress that she is making for me before it is finished. There are pins holding the sleeve in place. Is it too tight? Is it too long? When the dress is finished, I stand on a chair and turn slowly. I hold a yardstick near my knees. She puts a pin at the same height all the way around so she will know where to fold up the hem.

Thursday, May 5, 1966

Mommy lets me have the scraps of cloth. I try to make clothes for Raggedy Ann, but they don't turn out very well. So far, I can make a bag, a pillow and a bean bag.

I have decided not to bring my knitting or sewing for show-and-tell. It would be better to bring what I made with another Brownie.

Our Brownie meeting is at the Church in the Wildwood in Green Mountain Falls. After school on Thursdays, I take the other school bus, the one that goes down in the valley.

The valley bus leaves a little later, so, there is a little more time to play.

First, we have to decide who is 'It.' Everybody puts their fists into the center of the circle and one person counts while tapping each fist:

One potato, two potato, three potato, four,
Five potato, six potato, seven potato, more.

Whoever has their fist tapped on the last word has to hold their fist behind their back. Then the person keeps counting until there is only one fist left. That shows who is 'It' to lead the next game.

There is another way to do the same thing, fists in the center, tapping and counting:

Engine, Engine, Number Nine,
Going down Chicago line.

May Chapter 5 "Look What I Made!"

If the train runs off the track
Do you want your money back?

The last person says "Yes" or "No."

Y-E-S spells 'yes' and you are OUT!

Sandy gets to be the first leader. She can pick the game.

"Green Light!" Sandy has her back to us. Now we can move forward. "Red Light!" Sandy turns around fast. Now we have to stop moving. If Sandy sees anyone moving, they have to go back to the start line. Whoever gets close enough to touch Sandy will be the next Leader.

Tammy got to Sandy first. I saw Tammy move. But, Tammy is Sandy's best friend, so maybe she let her win? Tammy can keep this game, or change to a different game.

"Next we will play 'Mother, May I'."

"Susan, you may take three Bunny Hops!" Tammy is the 'Mother' now. Whoever goes forward and is the first one to touch her gets to be 'Mother' for the next round.

"Mother, May I?" Susan calls out.

"Yes, you may."

Susan jumps as far as she can. Three times. If she forgot to say, "Mother, May I?" she would have to go back to the start line.

Scissor kicks, giant steps, baby steps, umbrella steps, froggy hops. The list of possible turns, jumps, and steps is unlimited.

"Bus!"

I look for Kathy. She saved me a seat.

The valley bus goes slowly beside Fountain Creek. There are houses close to the road and the creek, and houses up and up along the side of the hill. First through Cascade, then Chipita Park, and then we get to Green Mountain Falls.

One week, I went to Kathy's house after school until her mother drove us to Brownies. She showed me a small suitcase in her closet. It was woven like a basket with red cloth inside. It was full of candy!

Thursday, May 5, 1966

She told me that her grandmother, from England, often sends her these small, round, tins of candy. I saw lemon, blackberry, current and cherry. Kathy told me that she opens the tin, has a taste of one candy, then saves the rest. "In case I run away," she explained to me. She let me have one piece of one kind. She also gave me a tiny, red ladybug with tiny black spots. I think it was made of glass. "Ammmanda is her name. She is very tame. You can keep her and we will always be friends." I agreed. "If one of us moves away, Ammmanda will fly back and forth with messages."

Kathy and I know a lot of hand-clapping games.

Lap. Clap. Slap. Clap. We keep the rhythm while we sing:

Miss Mary Mac, Mac, Mac
all dressed in black, black, black
with silver buttons, buttons, buttons
all down her back, back, back.

This one has extra hand gestures. We salute each time we say "see" or "sea."

A sailor went to sea sea sea
to see what he could see see see
but all the he could see see see
was the bottom of the deep blue sea sea sea!

This one was harder to learn. The hand-clapping is complicated.

Take me out to the ball game.
Take me out to the fair.
Buy me some peanuts and Cracker Jack.
I don't care if I never come back,
For it's root, root, root for the home team.
If they don't win it's a shame.
For it's one, two, three and you're out in the old ball game!

Meanwhile, the boys are singing at the back of the bus.

99 bottles of beer on the wall...

The ants go marching one by one...

This is the song that never ends...

There's a hole in the bottom of the sea...

Nobody likes me. Everybody hates me.
I'm going to the garden to eat worms.
Long, slender slimy ones. Short, fat juicy ones.
Itsy-bitsy, fuzzy-wuzzy worms. Yum, yum!

Once I looked over the back of my seat to watch the boys play 'Rock. Paper. Scissors.' Whoever shows the hand signal for the weaker thing gets a hard wrist slap. If the slapper licks his fingers it really stings.

The girls like to try to figure out who they will marry. There are two ways to do that. You can twist your apple stem and say, "A-B-C..." until the apple stem breaks. The letter you said when it breaks is the initial of the boy you will marry! I think some girls cheat. They hold the stem in and don't tell that it has broken. That way they can make the letter come out to be the boy they already have a crush on.

The other way you can tell who you are going to marry is with a jump rope rhyme. Whatever word you are on when you miss, that is the answer.

Rich man, poor man, beggar man, thief,
Doctor, lawyer, fireman, chief!

Thursday, May 5, 1966

I learned how to play string games on the bus, too. The older girls teach the younger girls. Cat's Cradle. Broomstick. Jacob's Ladder.

Mommy taught me how to fold paper to make another game. Then I could show the other girls. You need a square. Fold the corners into the center. Then flip the paper and do it again. Now you can use your pointer finger and thumb to open this way and that, like a bird's beak. On the outside, you write the names of colors to spell. On the inside, you write numbers to count. Your partner chooses the color, then the number, then they point to which little flap to open. You read the riddle or joke that you wrote inside the flap.

Q: Why does a cow wear a bell around its neck?
A: Because its horns don't work!

Q: What goes 99 clump... 99 clump?
A: A centipede with a wooden leg.

Q: What goes ha-ha-ha-ha-plop!
A: A man laughing his head off.

Knock knock.
Who's there?
Banana.
Banana who?
(repeat this three more times!)
Knock knock.
Who's there?
Orange.
Orange who?
Orange you glad I didn't say banana again!

May Chapter 5   "Look What I Made!"

Every week Mommy phones one of the other Brownie mothers to ask if I can stay there from after school until it is time for the meeting. This is my stop. "See you later!" I wave to the others and step down. The red lights flash and the bus driver waits for me to cross the road.

Today I am staying with the Brownie leader, Mrs. White. She lets me watch TV. I am never allowed to watch TV after school at my house. These are the shows I am not allowed to watch. 'I Dream of Jennie' and 'The Beverley Hill Billies' and 'Gilligan's Island.'

Mommy says the costumes on the ladies are not wholesome. But, in September, she did let me stay overnight with Amy to watch the Miss America pageant. Amy has a color TV.

Since I am with the leader, we get to the meeting room early to get ready. We don't need any chairs because Brownies sit in a circle on the floor.

Here they come! We gather in a horseshoe shape. Stand to say the Promise. Then sing two songs.

> *I have something in my pocket that belongs across my face.*
> *I keep it very close to me in a most convenient place.*
> *I'm sure you'd never guess it if you guessed a long, long while.*
> *So, I'll take it out and put it on. It's a great big Brownie smile!*

I love this round.

> *Make new friends, but keep the old,*
> *One is silver and the other gold.*

When it is my turn, Mary Lee and I hold up the picture of our show-and-tell. It is a little embarrassing, but I explain and

Thursday, May 5, 1966

make everybody laugh. "We could not bring it, because we ate it!" We made our craft when I stayed overnight at Mary Lee's house. She is an only child. She was adopted. Her bedroom is all pink and ruffly. She has red hair and a lot of freckles. And a lot of toys. Her mom got everything we needed to make our project. We explained what we did. "You take a small plate, put on one slice of canned pineapple ring, then a round scoop of vanilla ice-cream. With those red candied cherries you make eyes, nose and mouth, then with shredded coconut you make hair. The last thing you need is a pointed ice-cream cone for a hat. It's a clown!"

Kim used a cardboard box to make a stable for her toy horses. Karen made a braided leather leash for her dog. Kathy brought cookies she made from a recipe from her grandmother in England.

O, good, there is time for one more song.

Little cabin in the woods,
Little man by the window stood,
Saw a rabbit hopping by, Frightened as could be.
"Help me! Help me! Help me!" he said,
"Or the hunter will shoot me dead!"
"Come little rabbit, come inside, Safely you may hide."

There are actions for each part, and every time we sing it again, we are silent for more and more of the song, until the whole thing is silent with only actions to tell the story. It is so much fun!

Now we make the Brownie circle, holding hands right over left.

Day is done. Gone the sun.
From the lake, from the hills, from the sky.
All is well. Safely rest. God is nigh.

Silently, the Leader makes a wish, shows she is finished by putting her right foot into the circle, and then squeezes the hand of the Brownie to her left. Slowly, quietly, we each do the same. When the squeeze has been passed all the way around the circle, we silently step forward, untwist our hands and leave our special time together.

Outside, the parents have gathered with their cars and pick-up trucks. Some of the brothers are waiting, too. Running, jumping, shouting. When the girls come out they call, "Brownies!" They chase the girls, pretending they are chocolate brownies. If they catch one, they pretend to feast!

Daddy came to get me.

Mommy has supper ready.

What a good day.

Later

Mommy and Aunt Barbara decided to be the leaders for the next two years when I was in Girl Scouts! I got to go roller skating in an arena with fancy lights and peppy music, hike from the Rampart Range Road down to our house, cook on a fire, camp with a bedroll, go to a formal cooking class, earn my Collector badge and march in a parade for Memorial Day wearing my green uniform, badge sash, felt hat and white gloves.

Thursday, May 5, 1966

I have always been good at crafts, at least, starting them, not always finishing.

In Grade 9, in Art class, we had an assignment: "Write your name using your craft or hobby." I noticed the boys' art. One used wood burning, another had leather stamps for each letter. One had a board with wires, a switch and a light bulb. It took me a minute to see. The wire was bent to form the letters of his name.

I had so many different projects... unfinished.

I decided that would be how to write my name, with a variety of unfinished projects.

I started with the front of a red dress that I had cut out, but had never sewn together. That would be the background.

E was made with embroidery stitches, a vine with leaves and flowers. It started out with lots of flowers, then dwindled down to just a few petals. Like the blouse I started last year.

L was a bookmark I started stitching on white canvas with cross-stitch when I was twelve.

E was the pink cord I made with spool crochet during the Christmas when I was ten years old.

A was an embroidery of a green maple leaf I planned to finish for my Mom's birthday, but never did.

N was a strip of blue felt, intended to be a headband.

O was the olive and gray scarf I made for Raggedy Andy when I was eight and Oma was teaching me how to knit.

R was long strips of yellow, brown and orange cloth braided together, the beginnings of a rug I wanted to make for my room.

My hands love to make. My eyes love color. I love to learn. There are so many things to try.

Freely Give

Crafty Gifts. I have made so many.

A pinch-pot for Father's Day. Ceramic heart-shaped jewellery box for Mother's Day. Place-mat with beads to make initials for Julie. A soft pillow for Carol. Painted rocks for my brothers. Pottery in high school. Writing on birch bark for classmates in the dormitory. Embroidery for girlfriends. A quilt for my fiancé.

Quilts have become my most often repeated craft. My photo album shows over 70! I just love laying two fabrics side-by-side to enjoy the colour combinations. My eyes are so happy. I also love the math. How big will the finished quilt be? How much fabric is needed? I carefully measure the squares. I love the anticipation as the finished product takes shape. I love hand-sewing to hold the layers together. I love thinking of the person I am making the quilt for, remembering our time together, wondering how life will unfold as the years go by and this quilt will be wrapping warmth around the recipient.

Sometimes the fabric I use is scraps from clothing, or a table cloth. In this way, meaningful memories are preserved. Sometimes I cut up old shirts or dresses. Sometimes people give me pieces of fabric, or I raid the Thrift Store. Sometimes I cut up blue jeans, or soft corduroy, or plaid wool, or elegant silk.

Whenever I make a gift, I can feel the love in my heart flowing out through my hands.

To read more about the things Eleanor likes to make by hand...
... turn to 10 Days in June Chapter 5, page 189.

Chapter 6
Friday, May 6, 1966
Chore Chart

The joy of living is found in work,
no matter what the work may be.
For all who wake each morning with a task before them
know the excitement of a challenge,
the satisfaction of achievement,
and the pleasant feeling of fatigue
that ends a busy day with a night of dreamless sleep.
—Nicole Windsor

Freely Receive

Opa was a hard worker.

He started when he was a young lad. His father was so mean that Opa left home. He slept in a neighbor's barn. He earned his own way by working for shepherds in Germany and Switzerland, way up in the mountains. As soon as he could, he left Europe to come to America. He worked for his uncle when he first arrived until he figured out how to make his own living. Then he was a driver for rich people. Later, he married Oma. He bought half of a duplex and made a laundry business in his basement. He had a regular schedule to pick up dirty and deliver clean laundry to many customers.

Opa hired a worker. The laundry business was growing and he had to be out driving for pick-up and delivery.

Oma wanted a piano. She did the math. If she worked in the basement, Opa would not have to pay the other worker. That would leave enough money for the piano and lessons for the children.

Even with eight children, Oma kept the house neat and tidy. The children could all play the piano. They all did household chores. They all learned to work in the laundry. There was steam, the soapy smell, and heavy baskets. There were many clotheslines outside in the chill and the hot mangle to press the sheets. They had to learn the precise way to fold. All of them left home as soon as they could. The three boys signed up for the Army, Navy and Air Force. The five girls got married.

My mother taught us to do chores. But we don't have to work as hard as she did. How to set the table. How to iron. How to sweep. How to make hospital corners with the bed sheets. How to help in the kitchen peeling, chopping, measuring, stirring. How to crack an egg. How to sift flour. How to test if the cake is done, wait for it to cool, then spread the icing.

Grampa had many jobs. He moved the family from place to place. He was good with words but not so good with people. Grammie helped with Grampa's translating. They were not very tidy, with stacks of paper and books here and there.

Friday, May 6, 1966

Daddy did a lot of odd jobs when he was a teenager: cutting a lawn, painting a fence, moving furniture, babysitting little ones, errands for older ones. He was good at school. He was good at singing. He was in school plays. He decided to keep studying until he could become a professor. Typing. Phone calls. Meetings. Speaking. Diagrams. Chalkboards. Big Words. Books. Books. Books.

My father taught us how to wash the car, start the lawnmower, wash windows.

In our family, Saturday is Room Cleaning Day.

But, I have to clean my room today because my dance class has been moved from Saturday afternoon to Saturday morning, so I won't have time tomorrow. All of the Saturday dance classes are getting ready for the annual recital. So, we need to practice more than usual.

There's not much time after school and before supper. But, I'm pretty quick.

First, I measure exactly half of the room. My sister cleans her half. I clean my half. In the middle of the pine floor we have a purple shag rug. It's the color of the lilac bushes blooming at the church. I step heel-to-toe, counting to measure across, divide by two. To mark the half way point, I make a line with my heel, combing the yarn of the rug to show what is fair. If there is anything on my side of the floor that is hers, I toss it over onto her side. If there is anything of mine on her side, I step over the line to bring it back.

I have a bed, a bookshelf, a closet and a window on my side. She has the same on her side. The bed is attached to the wall. The shelf is built-in beside the bed. Inside the closet there is a string to pull to turn on the light bulb and a shelf up high.

The window is big. I can watch the weather and the seasons change. The top part of the window doesn't open. The bottom part has a crank to open and a screen so no bugs get in.

In the middle, against the wall, is the dresser that we share. I have the top two drawers, because I am taller, and my sister has the bottom two drawers. My socks and stockings and leotards and undies and PJs are in the top drawer. My shorts and pants and play clothes are in the lower drawer. My drawers are pretty empty because it's Friday. Mommy will do laundry tomorrow. Then my drawers will be full again.

I pull the sheets off of my bed and carry them downstairs to the laundry basket.

Mommy brings the vacuum cleaner upstairs and helps me put my clean sheets on.

"Make sure you vacuum under the bed and in the closet. Call me when you're finished. I'm coming back up to check."

I lay on my belly. It's dusty and dark down here. I was wondering where Raggedy Andy went. I make him sit up on the bookshelf with Raggedy Ann. There is just enough room beside my blue poodle and Winnie the Pooh. Some people say that dolls and toys really come alive at night. Maybe that's how Raggedy Andy got down there. He was out playing while I was sleeping. When I woke up, he had to stop moving.

I take all of my shoes out of the closet so I can vacuum. There's also a big box of clothes from my cousin. On the day the box came in the mail, it was fun to try on everything. Most things are too big for me. I really like the pale green dress with bouquets along the hem. There's also a plaid kilt that makes me feel grown-up. That box is heavy! After I vacuum the closet, I set my shoes straight. Sunday: black, shiny patent leather shoes with a silver buckle on the strap. School shoes: brown leather with laces to tie. Play shoes: sneakers (that used to be white). Ballet slippers: black with elastic straps.

Friday, May 6, 1966

The vacuum cleaner reaches to the far corner under my bed. Then I take off the floor attachment and put on the rug attachment. I like to make patterns. Sometimes I brush the shag rug all one way. It looks so smooth. Sometimes I make stripes with the shag going one way and then the other. Even when I walk on it so carefully, the pattern doesn't last very long.

"Mommy," I call down from the balcony, "I'm ready for inspection!"

"Look," I open my closet, "I even put my dresses in rainbow color order!"

The red and black plaid with a white collar was my 8th birthday dress, but I also wear it to school.

Mommy made me a special red dress for Christmas Eve. I love the ruffly skirt and puffy sleeves.

There is also the sleeveless red A-line dress. She added embroidery on the sailor collar to make seashells and starfish.

I put my Brownie uniform next because of the orange tie.

Next is the yellow, sleeveless dress that was my costume for the dance recital last year. Everyone in my class had the same kind of dress. Mommy made four of them. (Some girls have mothers who do not have a sewing machine.) We were dancing a story about evening primroses. The dresses have three layers of ruffles to show the petals.

I have two green dresses. Mommy made them both from the same puffy sleeve pattern with a big gathered skirt. The light green one is too small now. It was my First Day of School dress in Grade 1. Mommy decorated it with brightly embroidered flowers all the way around the hem. She adjusted the pattern and made the dark green dress for me this year. It has a band of lace around the waist and around the sleeves. I love wearing this dress to jump rope or high-jump at recess because the skirt puffs out in the wind.

My blue dress is for church only. The short sleeves and bodice are light blue. From the waist down, the light blue is covered with a layer of white lace. I have to be careful not to sit on a rough wooden bench that might tear the lace.

Last one! For my first day of Grade 3, Mommy made me a light purple dress. It is such a pretty color. She used the same pattern as the other dresses, but she changed it. The other ones button up the back. This one buttons up in the front. Now I don't need help getting dressed.

Mommy smiles, "You pass inspection!"

Supper is ready.

Then it's time for clean-up chores.

I look at the Job Chart. My turn to clear off the table and help Mommy put the leftovers away. Then I have to wipe the counter, high chair and table.

When I'm done, I mark one tally on my Mark Chart. I don't add anything to my Mark Chart for cleaning my room. But for other jobs I earn money.

Mommy made a 'Mark Chart' for each of my siblings. She gives us new jobs every week. Help prepare. Clear away. Wash the dishes. Dry and put away. There are ways to earn more than what is assigned. Clean a cupboard. Fold and deliver laundry. Wash the car.

At first, we were paid 2¢ for every chore. Now we get 5¢. One time Mommy made an extra prize. She taped a big silver 50¢ piece to the kitchen cupboard near the Mark Chart. The picture of President John F. Kennedy made me want to do a good job and even ask for extra work.

Friday, May 6, 1966

The only time I ever have a lot of money is when Oma sends a $1.00 dollar bill in a birthday card. She does this for every grandchild, every year. I watch when my brothers and sisters open their cards. I wait for my card. It is such a huge sum of money. What to do? Spend it all at once? A little at a time? Save it for a whole year? If I wait until next year there will be two dollars! Wow!

There is one thing I have my eye on: silver and turquoise earrings. Each has a silver heart with a perfectly round turquoise stone in the center. They have tiny screws to tighten on my ear lobes. $3.00.

When my eighth birthday came, that meant I would have my birthday $1.00 from Oma. She often wears silver and turquoise. She has a ring, necklace, bracelet and a hatpin. Some of her earrings are clip-on. Some have screws. I have never had earrings. I haven't told anyone how much I want them. Maybe they will be sold before I can save up enough money?

Is there a way for me to get two more whole dollars?

Good News! Daddy wants to hire me to do an extra job. He has written a book. I can read the manuscript aloud while Daddy is proofreading. He said he would pay me, too! A-Penny-A-Minute! Daddy's book is about Economics. I am an excellent reader, but this is hard to do! I don't know what some of the words mean: Gross National Product, Wage and Price Controls, Inflation and Deflation, Tariffs and Import Duty, Taxes and Investments.

Also, when the cases of books arrive, Daddy will have to sell them. He is writing letters to other professors. James and Andrew and I are hired to stuff envelopes for 1¢ each.

It is possible! Someday I will have enough money to buy the earrings! I want to wear them to church.

Later

Daddy earned the money. Daddy paid the bills. Mommy kept a budget for food and clothing, shoes and gifts, school supplies and outings for five children.

As a teenager, I earned 35¢ per hour for babysitting (which I loved) and 50¢ per hour for housework, window washing and weeding (which I did not enjoy).

I did not have a clear idea about money as I approached adult life. My mother and aunts stayed home. My father was a teacher. Some of my uncles were in the armed forces. One ran a gas station. One was the milkman, delivering door-to-door in the very early morning.

I read the ads in the newspaper. Help Wanted: Male. Help Wanted: Female.

It looked to me as though women could be teachers, sales clerks, bank tellers, nurses, secretaries, factory workers. Cleaning. That was a job that everybody needed and nobody wanted. Those jobs were for females. Unless you wanted to be a dancer, singer or actress. Or a stewardess on an airplane.

Drudgery. Repetition. Glamor. Those are the choices for women. Ugh!

While I was a teenager and still lived at home I took low-skill jobs. I measured and stirred in a bakery. I set tables, made toast and poured juice in an old folks home. I always washed dishes.

Earn. Save. Give. Spend.

I earned a little.

I saved almost nothing.

Friday, May 6, 1966

I brought my offering to church.

I spent my money on pretty paper and envelopes to write letters, birthday and Christmas presents for my friends, posters for my room.

It was unspoken, but expected, that I would finish college, be a teacher, get married, have children. In the 1970's, as I approached adulthood, loud voices were shouting for equal pay for women. And for women to get an education. And for women to use contraception and abortion to stay in their career and not be stuck at home. Women were entering previously unattainable roles: army, navy, air force, medicine, science, politics... all kinds of professions.

I quietly watched. Listened.

I tried to sort through my own interests. I got good grades. All of my teachers had positive things to say. I had so many choices. What was most interesting? What would be worth pursuing for my whole lifetime? How could I use my talents to be of service to others? What do people need that I could provide? What do I love?

I yearned for something. Shall I share this? Keep quiet? My heart was pounding. I could dream of the satisfaction, the sacred calling, the bright future. All of my skills could be focused in this one precise way. Reading and writing, learning and teaching, listening and speaking, music and art, theatre and storytelling, reverence and silence, celebration and customs, research and academics, children and families, ethics and decisions, guidance and leadership.

I wanted to work in the church, become educated and ordained. I wanted to be a minister.

Blocked. Silenced. Impossible. Entirely denied.

The church I was raised in forbade women to enter the clergy. Period.

That left me with two options. Marry a minister.

Or change religions.

Or a third option: Leave.

Freely Give

I left.

If they don't want me, and I simply must follow this 'Calling,' then I will find a place, a time and people who are hungry to learn about the Lord.

That decision has led to a lifelong satisfaction: listening to questions, finding resources, developing themes, creating curriculum, designing projects, directing plays, leading songs, searching the Scriptures for clues. I keep asking myself, 'What is the kernel?'

Somebody made me. Somebody loves me. Somebody sees and hears me. Somebody is guiding me.

When a person knows this deep in their heart, like a blossom opening to the sunshine, they become curious and eager, bright and beaming, blessed and grateful.

I have been given a Gift. I gladly share.

Unpaid work is what I do. Volunteer effort makes a lot of worthwhile projects possible.

To read more about how Eleanor earned money doing domestic work...
... turn to 10 Days in June Chapter 6, page 199.

Chapter 7
Saturday, May 7, 1966
Born to Dance

Enjoy what you do
and do it because you have something to give.
The joy in having something
is sharing it with other people, especially those we love.
A person needs to be inspired to create beauty
and challenged to grow as a human being.
Although other people can encourage you
the motivation to work at whatever you do
has to come from within yourself.
—*Marianna Tcherkassky*
American Ballet Theater

Freely Receive

Did I look back to wave good-bye? Or did I only look at what is ahead?

As Daddy pulls away in the station wagon, I climb up the wide stone stairs, out of the sunshine, into the broad, echo-filled hallway. Like a wishing well, the wooden banister wraps around the circular balcony. Downstairs is a mystery to me. I continue along the wooden floor, around the curve, into the long hallway.

Am I early? Am I late? No other girls are coming or going. I can never be sure. Daddy is not always aware of the time. Plus, it is a long way to drive from our home, down Ute Pass, through the city, to arrive on the college campus. My dance studio is in one of the college buildings on the same campus where Daddy teaches Economics.

I can hear the piano music, muffled through the door, echoing down the corridor. The farthest door on the left enters directly into the studio. Timidly, I push it open a crack. The girls are taller than me. I am early.

I enter the dressing room. My shoes go under the bench. My dress onto a hook. I am already wearing my short-sleeved black leotard. As the other girls enter and prepare, I feel awkward. Most of them have the same leotards, but many also have smooth, pink stockings. Mrs. Gray likes students to have bare feet, so the mothers have cut off the feet of the stockings. My legs are bare. I feel undressed, chubby and realize my parents have less money to spend on extras.

In a moment the room is filled with more little ones entering and the older girls leaving. My classmates greet each other. The older ones have been silent for the whole hour of class. Now they can talk. So many voices!

I push the door to enter the studio. It is so quiet. The wooden floor is smooth and golden, to my right is a wall covered with a huge mirror. In the far right corner, the pianist is shuffling her papers, ready to begin. Behind the piano, out of the way of dancers, is the resin box. Since we are barefoot, we don't need it. When I am strong enough, I will press my toe-shoes into the resin to prevent slipping. The sunshine streams in through the full length of windows along the far wall. A single row of chairs is always there,

Saturday, May 7, 1966

although parents are only invited to stay and watch once a year. To my left and along the far left wall are the ballet barres.

Mrs. Gray stands near the door, greeting each child by name. Her long black skirt, black tights, long sleeved black leotard and bare feet are the same every Saturday. Her soft gray curls frame her smiling face. Her daughter, Sharon, studies at the college, and today she is here to help. I wonder. How old is Mrs. Gray? She must be in her 50s to have an adult daughter? I didn't know that old people could move so gracefully, have such stamina, leap with energy, teach others to dance!

Here come the other girls. I can't help it. I notice so many things. Gretchen has such long, thick, blonde hair in a French braid. Susan has pretty barrettes holding back her abundant, dark curls. Patty is so slim. Karen has beautiful black eyelashes. Mary Lee has red hair and freckles. She's more chubby than I am, but also has more friends. I glance into the wall of mirrors. I look so plain. Until I start to dance!

I like to practice at home. I stretch. I try to remember the French names of the exercises at the barre while I stand with one hand on the balcony banister. I dance while my mother plays the piano. I turn on my Daddy's records: Giselle, Nutcracker, Sleeping Beauty, Hansel and Gretel, Coppelia, Swan Lake. When night falls, the dark sky turns the glass sliding doors in our living room into a mirror, so I can see my own performance. I can imagine the huntsman entering, the battle with the Mouse King, the Prince searching for his true love, the gingerbread children awakening, the dollmaker's astonishment when Coppellia begins to move, the brilliantly white swans and the grieving Prince swirling into the dark lake.

When I dance, I don't know where my parents are. I don't know where my siblings are. I don't know how much time goes by. All I can see are the eerie willies, the bright sugar plums, swirling snowflakes and red Russian boots, the generous and jealous fairies, the witch's swirling cape, the mechanical doll, the courtiers and swans, the male dancer's dramatic sleeves, brocaded vests and fabulous leaps, the prima ballerina's lifts and spins, the colorful costumes, sequins and tiaras. All I can hear are the rhythms, melodies and harmonies, the richness of the instruments, each and together.

It is time for the class to begin. We sit, spaced apart, facing the windows. All eyes follow her as Mrs. Gray joins us, at the front, showing us how to do each exercise, speaking encouraging words, counting to the beat as the piano music fills the room with rich chords.

"Point and flex" to strengthen our feet. "In and out" to develop turnout. "Sit tall. Reach forward" to lengthen the tendons along the back of the legs. "To the left... to the center... to the right" with feet far apart, we stretch forward, preparing to someday be flexible enough to do the splits.

Repetition. Familiar.

After the floor exercises, we move to the barre. Sharon demonstrates, while Mrs. Gray moves to correct each student. Again, there is repetition. Again, it is familiar. Again, the piano keeps the rhythm so we move in unison. The positions all have French names: plié, relevé, tendu, battement, port de

Saturday, May 7, 1966

bra, ronde de jambe. Posture is important. The eyes follow the hands. Simple movements, yet, expressive.

The warm-up is over. Now the fun!

There is a rush to line up in the corner. "Now we will cross the floor." On a diagonal across the empty space, we move towards the mirror. Then line up again to cross the floor again, diagonally, one-by-one. We can watch ourselves in the mirror during the first trip towards the piano, but not on the return trip. The row of empty chairs under the windows helps to remind us that someday we will be dancing for the audience!

There are so many ways to travel across the floor. Mrs. Gray demonstrates. Hop is from one foot to the same foot. Leap is from one foot to the other foot. Jump is from both feet to both feet. Slide, first with right leg leading, then with the left leg leading. There are many ways to walk. We communicate our intention with our posture, the gestures of our hands and arms, and how we hold our head and facial expression. Piano music sets the pace: erect marching, heavy shuffling, lightly on tip-toe, knees up high, with an energetic kick forward, painfully dragging one leg behind.

Crossing the floor while turning is much more difficult. Mrs. Gray separates each part of the movement. Hands on shoulders (to keep an upright posture). Eyes on the desired destination (to keep direction). On the diagonal, we begin. Step right. Cross left. Quickly turn clockwise. It's hard to balance. There is much to concentrate on. Watching the others. Being watched. Patiently Mrs. Gray speaks her special combination of correction and encouragement.

Now she calls everyone back to the center of the floor. While we are seated, Mrs. Gray tells a story, her hands express the meaning of her words. "Under the snow, the seeds are waiting. Waiting for the warmth and light as spring returns. Slowly uncurling, slowly reaching, the sunshine calls to the new plants. Roots seek nourishment, stretching downwards, thick and long. Stems seek sunlight, reach upwards, tall and strong. Leaves open. Buds uncurl. Glad to be alive, the flowers sway gently and share their colors for all to enjoy."

Now, we gather in groups of three. While the piano suggests how the story develops, each group quietly cooperates to make a creative interpretation of the story. Exploring possibilities, watching each other, moving in harmony, each group creates a short routine based on this theme.

"Come to the center," Mrs. Gray signals. Each group performs. Each group watches. Each group applauds.

Next, we need to practice for the recital. It will be soon! At the end of May!

Last year our class composed a routine about the opening flowers. We were yellow primroses. We wore sleeveless ruffled yellow dresses. We learned a few folk dance steps, some graceful arms, simple jumps, and combined them with the story of the springtime sunshine awakening the blossoms.

This year we made a story about Frost Fairies decorating the forest by night. Each Fairy carries a long silver paintbrush and a small silver bucket. Four dancers at a time come into the center from each corner of the studio. (When we have the recital, we will come in from the wings, between the huge, tall, black curtains on either side of the stage.) One group tip-toes cautiously. One group swirls and turns. One group skips and hops. One group takes sliding steps. Then we form a big circle. Like many folk dances, we move together: eight counts to the left, eight counts to the right. We end in a straight line across the front of the stage. When we hear the music change, we pretend to dip the paintbrushes and spread frost on all the leaves and branches. We make the whole forest sparkle with silvery glitter. The high, twinkly notes shift into deep, low chords, representing the sunrise. It is time to quickly scurry away.

Saturday, May 7, 1966

It is the kind of dance that changes every time you do it. Creative, interpretive dance. That's what Mrs. Gray likes to teach her youngest students. Her older students learn folk dance with more exact steps and planned routines. I like it this way, but someday, I also hope to learn real ballet.

Of course, we end every class and our dance on stage with a curtsy. Three times we curtsy. It means "Thank-you" to our teacher and the pianist, "Thank-you" to our parents, and "Thank-you" to the audience.

We all stay after class today. The costumes for the recital are already here! The metal coat rack looks like a princess' wardrobe! Long gowns, puffy sleeves, formal tutus, soft capes. Aqua. Lavender. Rose. Pastel and bright. Soft and bold. Flowing rayon. Shimmering gauze. Rich velvet. Stiffly gathered tulle. Each costume has a label naming the dancer who will wear it.

Today we get to try on our Frost Fairy costumes. Everyone is excited. It is hard to wait!

All of the Frost Fairies will be wearing black leotards and tights and bare feet. There are three new parts to our costumes. While we sit quietly, Mrs. Gray demonstrates and explains each piece. A short, soft, flowing, white skirt will swirl as we twirl. A little jacket with the body made of thick, white felt, trimmed with silver sequins and little white pom-poms will sparkle like the frost. The puffy white sleeves are real silk! Mrs. Gray shows us the headpiece. It is a white hairband made of swan's down! So soft. So fragile.

Now, the mothers help us try them on, to be sure of the size and length, then put each name on each hanger. I want to twirl and spin and leap and dance! But, not today. Next week is the dress rehearsal!

May Chapter 7   Born to Dance

The best part is: we get to keep our costumes when the recital is over!

There is one more special thing about today: I am staying after class with Karen and Mary Lee. A photographer is coming to print an announcement for the recital in the newspaper! It's my first time to be in the newspaper.

Next week we will practice on the real stage at the real theater! The week after that is the real performance!

I'm tired. On the way home I remember the past and imagine the future.

When we lived in Pennsylvania, on my 4th birthday, my parents gave me a record with music telling the story of Peter Pan. Also a pink tutu with silver sequins! That summer, when my cousins came, we acted out the story in the backyard. Mommy helped me find costumes for my brothers and sister and boy cousin to act out Peter Pan, Captain Hook and the Lost Boys. Mommy was Wendy. I let my girl cousin wear my tutu so she could be Tinkerbelle. I was Tiger-Lily and also the Narrator.

Whoever had to fly would 'think of a happy thought,' then put their tummy on the seat of the swing, pull it back and run forward, to be lifted up off the ground. "We can fly! We can fly! We can fly!"

When we lived in the cabin, Daddy played his records. He put on classical music. I swirled colorful scarves, wore my mother's jewellery, tapped with my patent leather shoes, and made grand gestures while spinning and bowing. I felt beautiful and strong, blissful and elegant.

Saturday, May 7, 1966

I did not know that my three-year-old sister idolized me. Focused. Vain. I thought a chubby toddler would just be in my way. I did not include her, did not praise or encourage her. I turned away, ignoring.

I liked praise. I did not share my dancing with her because I did not think there was enough praise to share with my sister!

Later

I continued with Mrs. Gray for three years. When I was in Grade 5, I also enrolled in a ballet class with Mr. McCormick. All the other girls were older, ready for toe shoes, tall, lean, beginning to show womanly curves.

Mr. McCormick used a cane to correct the students. Lifting a chin, pressing a back, shaping the hands, extending the height of a leg. I felt humiliated when he came to me. Speaking to correct, the cold cane was a surprise to me. The expectation was so much more serious than the creative dance interpreting, exploring, pretending. The formal discipline felt intense.

On visiting day, my mother couldn't come. She had to stay home with the baby. I invited Aunt Barbara. She was my Girl Scout leader, a nurse, *and* had been a ballet dancer! I thought I would die of embarrassment when Mr. McCormick corrected me. After all, I was a beginner, the youngest, the other girls had so much more training than me. But, with my head hanging, on the way home Aunt Barbara explained, "He wouldn't have spent time with you if he didn't think you were capable. He can see that you have excellent qualities. Now you need to carefully learn technique." My heart soared.

That Christmas, I was in 'The Nutcracker Suite Ballet.' I was one of the tin soldiers battling the Mouse King. I was the only Drummer Boy, moving alone, dodging here and there, signalling the attack, retreating, sounding the alarm.

When I was ten years old, my mother let me stay up late to watch TV. 'The Red Shoes Ballet' movie was based on Hans Christian Andersen's story. The magical red shoes compelled the young girl to dance and dance, at first with abundant joy, then wandering in loneliness, until, exhausted, she collapsed in death. The movie also portrayed the agony of the ballerina herself, who was forced by the director of the ballet company to choose between either her dancing career, or marriage to her sweetheart.

Daddy bought the record of 'The Red Shoes' ballet music. Over and over again I listened, danced, and imagined the tension. I wondered: would I ever have to choose: *either* marriage and children, *or* a career? Do men get to have both, but women have to choose one or the other?

Just as I was about to begin learning toe shoes, we had to move. Mrs. Gray gave me a tiny German doll, wearing a dirndl and straw hat. (I still have her!) I knew that Mrs. Gray's name was 'Ursula' so I named my doll Ursula, too.

No classes when we moved to Florida, nor in Ontario. I did choreograph a simple routine for the Sugar Plum Fairy for a school Christmas Concert when I was in Grade 7.

In high school, I choreographed one piece in our year-end play, 'Where's Charlie.' In college, I traded babysitting for dance class. But I never stepped on stage. Never got past barre exercises. Never felt the thrill of those three years with Mrs. Gray. Never again felt beautiful and strong, blissful and elegant.

Saturday, May 7, 1966

Twice I have seen a world-class ballet performance.

One Christmas, the family I was babysitting for took me to Toronto to see the 'Nutcracker.' It felt kind of strange to see the way the music was interpreted after the many times I had imagined the whole thing while I danced alone at home. Uncle Drosselmier looked scary. The mouse king was grotesque with several heads! Graceful snowflakes were replaced with silly, round snowmen. I felt uncomfortable. Who was I to gauge this performance? Who were they to tamper with my vision?

During the year I took off between high school and college, I lived with my aunt and uncle and cousin Janet on Long Island while they had Grammie and Grampa living with them. Everyone else went to work. I stayed home. I took dictation for Grammie's many letters and read aloud. I fixed lunch, helped my elderly grandparents into and out of the bathroom. I felt pretty lonely, yet privileged to care for the people who had cared for me when I was an infant.

One special night, Aunt Madeline drove Janet and I into New York City. We attended a performance of the National Ballet Theatre. Peter Martins and Suzanne Farrell were the Principal Dancers. Every nerve of my being gathered sensations. Every movement, melody, meaningful gesture was significant. O! This is the Path that I did not take!

Just before Kevin and I were married, my mother took me to the movies to see 'The Turning Point.' Anne Bancroft played the aging ballerina. Shirley McClain played the mother. She had given up her dance career to become a parent and then open her own dance studio in a small town. They met again when the daughter became a pupil of the ballerina. While I watched, I grieved the life I would never have.

When I moved out west, I left behind the sound of my Mother playing piano, scores of my Daddy's classical records. I knew I would never belong to a choir or band or dance troupe or have an opportunity to participate in performing productions prompted by musical expression.

I sold my clarinet.

Although I was greatly excited to leave the city, I also wondered. What will I find when I go out west? How will I find a creative expression without this facet of life that I enjoy so much?

Freely Give

At home. At school. At church. In the choir. In school plays. In the school band. Music has always been a part of my life.

I learned to play the guitar so I could lead singing as a volunteer in schools, in church, as a Brownie leader, around the campfire. I have hundreds and hundreds of songs in my notebook, hymn book, on cassette tape, records, CDs and spinning in my head day and night.

Music is like vitamins to me!

I am not the Mom who sews costumes. I am not the Mom who raises money or sells tickets. I am not the Mom who drives the kids on field trips. I am not the Mom who runs for office or writes letters to the editor or speaks up at the PTA meetings.

For me, volunteering often means music, teach a song, lead a round, create a dance, bring sounds from other cultures, share a singing game, encourage rhythm and rhyme.

I have been given so much. Music does not become less when you give it away.

To read more about Eleanor's choreography...
... turn to 10 Days in June Chapter 7, page 213.

Chapter 8
Sunday, May 8, 1966
Mother's Day

> If there is beauty in the character,
> There will be harmony in the home.
> If there is harmony in the home,
> There will be order in the nation.
> If there is order in the nation,
> There will be peace in the world.
> —Confucius

Freely Receive

Daddy gently tugs at my foot. "Come on, Eleanor. Wake up. Let's get the breakfast started!" He quietly calls each of us and we tiptoe down the stairs.

Mommy is usually the first one up. We know it is morning because we can smell the coffee and hear the dishes and pots and pans while she makes us breakfast and gets the school lunches packed.

May Chapter 8   Mother's Day

But, not today! Today is Mother's Day! *We* get to make breakfast in bed for *her*!

Daddy buckles Baby Carol into her high chair and gives her a handful of Cheerios on the tray. Then he measures the coffee grounds into the peculator and fills the pot with fresh water. Julie knows how to make the toast. Andrew stands on a chair to get down the dishes. James cracks the eggs. I am the oldest. I know what to do, so I arrange the tray.

Using a cookie sheet as a tray to carry the breakfast, I decide to use the red, white and blue place-mat. "Use these egg cups," I point out the white duck, the red rooster and the blue bunny. "They will look nice together." Andrew is scooping raspberry jam and strawberry jam and honey into the egg cups. I choose the cutlery and use the blue and white striped plates, bowl and coffee cup. Daddy is cutting the grapefruit. Julie has the margarine ready. James stirs the spatula through the scrambled eggs.

"Do you have your presents? and cards?" Daddy prompts us to tiptoe back upstairs for the things we made at school.

The tray is ready. The parade is in order. Using the Happy Birthday tune we enter her room. "Happy Mother's Day to you!"

"O!" she's so surprised! "Well, isn't this lovely!" While we perch on the sides of the bed, careful not to bounce, Mommy admires each feature: the colors and tastes, the choices, the care.

Early Childhood Memories are so very hard to recall with accuracy. However, if the fragments can be pieced together, interviews with parents, a house, a room, a color, a sound, a photo, a little research into the place, the date, the day of the week, the weather, current fashions, world events, and slivers of other factors, it is possible to fill out a sketch and give it a fuller story than the little glimpses first suggest.

Sunday, May 8, 1966

One day I do remember!

A yellow room. The family smiling. We are all on Mommy's bed. She is eating. I am eating. I take a bite and sweet juice dribbles down my chin. Something feels strange. I look. And see my own tooth embedded in my apple! A little blood. A grin!

I have lost my first tooth. Instructed to wrap it up in a tissue and place it under my pillow, I will try to stay awake to see the Tooth Fairy sparkling into my room.

But little children fall asleep.

In the morning, under my pillow, just as foretold: a bright silver penny!

I remember that silver penny so clearly... arguing with my Daddy who said it was something called a 'dime.' He told me that there were in fact ten copper pennies inside that one silver 'dime.' But that seemed wildly impossible to me. I saw no slit, no hinge, no opening. Even if the pennies were somehow made small, like a deflated balloon, there was no way for me to get them out! It was easier to believe that in my hand I held a rich and rare treasure: a silver penny!

Now, remembering, I ask myself: Where was the yellow room? Why was Mommy eating in her bed? Daddy and I, my twin brothers and little Julie were all so happy. Mommy wasn't sick in bed. Why, indeed, was *I* eating in her bed? It was a big bed. Iron bedstead. Squeaky springs. It was my parents' yellow bedroom. The morning sun streamed into the window. We were happy because... it must have been Mother's Day!

How old is a child who loses their first tooth? Usually four. I turned four in the fall of 1961. So, this moment must have been: the second Sunday in May, the 13th, 1962.

If I was only four, the twins had just turned three and Julie was barely one year old. Daddy must have done most of the breakfast-in-bed preparations. Daddy would have carried the tray. The apples might have been something I had brought up the stairs. Something that would not make crumbs. Something the children could eat while Mommy enjoyed her Special Day.

There are no photographs of this day, although my Daddy almost always had his camera ready. I know this is my own memory. I have not heard stories retold. This is one of my earliest memories.

My first memory includes: A husband and a wife, smiling. A Mother and a Father, their healthy children gathered 'round. A safe, warm, sunlit, comfortable home. An annual family tradition. Each person taking a role to be of service. My own turning point as I grow up. Believing in fairies.

How many significant details wrap around this one experience. It is a foundation upon which I see myself standing, stable, secure. It is a flashing glimpse of the future. I see how I will build my own family someday. This memory is like roots drawing nourishment from these early days.

What stands out clearly is the sensation of admiring that silver penny in my little palm.

Four years have gone by from then until now. I am eight now. I have lost lots of teeth. Placed them under my pillow. Slept through the visit of the Tooth Fairy.

Mostly I cannot remember anything else about Mother's Day, except last year. We were still living in the cabin, but we had running water. So, in the place where the rain barrel used to be, we planted a lilac bush. Daddy was hoping that the rain water would be enough to keep it alive in the dry, gravel soil. It seems so amazing to have the prickly pear cactus, yucca plants, lichen growing naturally, and suddenly this green leafy bush with so many fragrant flowers!

Sunday, May 8, 1966

"This is for you, Mommy," and we each present our treasures.

James and Andrew are in Grade 1. The Teacher asked each child to bring one favorite recipe from home. Then she typed them out, including the name of each student and their mother, and used the Ditto machine to make copies. Now each mother has a recipe book made by the whole class.

The boys also made cards. They are kind of a combination of a Valentine and a Birthday card. The Teacher showed the students how to make a big, round, red 'M' shape into a heart to begin the word "Mother." Then they drew flowers all around the edges.

Daddy bought flowers for Julie and Baby Carol to give to Mommy. That's a present he always gives her on Mother's Day. He also picked out a big, colorful card for all of us to write our names in.

"Open your mouth and close your eyes. I have for you a big surprise!" Daddy coaxes Mommy to play the game, and pops a chocolate into her mouth! There's a great big box that she will share (after we have breakfast).

I hold my present behind my back. It is such a strange shape I could not wrap it. I grin and say, "Pick a hand!" Then I show Mommy what I made at school. In one hand is the card I made. In the other hand is a decoration. The teacher showed us how to use green florist's foam, put it in the toe of a high heel shoe and stick plastic roses into the foam. Then we went outside, spread out newspaper on the paved area behind the school and used spray paint to make everything gold! It's kind of beautiful and kind of ugly at the same time! And, I have one more thing in my bathrobe pocket. "We made these in Brownies." It is a red heart-shaped pillow, stuffed with pine needles. "It is a sachet. For your sweater drawer. To make them smell nice."

May Chapter 8 Mother's Day

Now we have to hurry-scurry to eat breakfast, get dressed and get to church on time.

I am so happy. I want to wear my brightest clothes. My yellow ruffly dress from the dance recital last year. My red knee socks. Mommy thinks they don't go together, but I like it. Plus, there is no time to go back and change.

Since I can get dressed and brush my own hair, I am dressed first. Mommy likes it when I can look after Baby Carol on her big bed while she gets dressed.

I like to play with the Baby, but I also watch Mommy. Ladies have so many things they have to do to get ready. Girdles don't look very comfortable, but they make her look smooth and she needs the little button latches to hold up her stockings. Her black shiny shoes have pointy toes which is not the shape of her feet, but it is the fashion. Her bra is covered by her smooth white slip.

Curlers aren't very comfortable, either. You have to wear them overnight while your hair gets dry. I know. Mommy curled my hair that way at Christmastime. They are bristly and poky and you can't put your head any way on the pillow without itchy jabs. When Mommy brushes out her hair it looks fluffy and round and poof-y. Nice. Hair spray! Close your eyes! Hold your breath! Nasty smell!

Mommy's dress is blue. I zip her up. She has sparkly clip-on earrings and a matching necklace. The earrings pinch tightly so they won't fall off. Mommy isn't going to wear a bracelet because she might scratch the Baby when she carries her.

Last of all is lipstick. Mommy rubs a tiny bit onto her cheeks and makes her lips all red.

Now Julie needs her hair brushed and braided. The boys come, for inspection. Daddy has the car ready.

Sunday, May 8, 1966

Mother's Day is kind of a small holiday. I mean, it only lasts one day. Every family just celebrates it at home. There are no parades, or decorations, or special clothes, or certain foods. But, it's kind of the biggest holiday of all, too! Every single person in the whole wide world has a Mother! No matter if there are fireworks, or music, or parties, or glittering gowns... it would never really be enough to thank Mothers for all that they do.

Who gets up first to make the food? Who takes care of the money and makes sure there is enough of everything? Who keeps the house and clothes and children clean and cuts their hair and fingernails? Who reads and sings and sends Christmas cards and picks up the mail and makes playdough and birthday cakes and even sews our new dresses and PJs? Who takes care of us when we are sick or hurt? Who crushes the vitamins and aspirin and mixes them with honey so we can swallow them? Who makes us be good and spanks us when we're bad, or washes our mouth out with soap if we say bad words? Who teaches us how to take care of the cat and dog and bunny and feed the hummingbirds? Who can plan the whole day Sunday, after church, playing games, or sledding, or going on a picnic, or having a friend over, all fitting together so that we get ready in time for Lassie and Walt Disney?

Who?

Every single question on that list has the same answer: My Mother!

Later

After many Mother's Days as a child, it became my turn to be the Guest of Honour.

What a strange sensation to hear early morning footsteps and whispering. Pots. Water. Toaster. The refrigerator door. Eggs. It's hard to not get up, to peek, to offer suggestions.

The kettle whistles.

Now it is my turn to be surprised, admire the tray. Sample the pancakes (underdone), eggs (runny), toast (overdone) smiling all the while.

Smell the flowers. Share the chocolate. Praise the artwork. Cherish the gifts.

Mothers shoulder an impossible task! Time drags. Time flies.

One morning every year, there is a pause. Deliberate appreciation.

Yes, families are complex, and, being a Mother... is how families begin!

Freely Give

I believe that Mother's Day customs are a significant moment for children. They become aware of all that their mother has given to them and the small creative ways they can give something from their heart to their mother.

Breakfast in bed is one custom. It implies that the children have learned domestic skills, planning, cooperation and careful delivery. My own Mother's Day breakfast-in-bed tray was often decorated with white blossoms from the crab apple tree and fragrant lilacs in full bloom.

Homemade cards and gifts are another custom. Is a shiny store-bought gift of higher value than the lumpy, crooked, smudged offering from a child? I treasure the last macaroni necklace my youngest child made, the wooden box the son in high school made, the red felt pine needle sachet from my daughter and the card our son's children send each year.

To read more about Eleanor's parenting style...
... turn to 10 Days in June Chapter 8, page 233.

Chapter 9
Monday, May 9, 1966
I love to Read

> Don't put off for tomorrow
> what you can do today
> because if you enjoy it today,
> you can do it again tomorrow!
> —James A. Mitchener

Freely Receive

It's Bookmobile day!

My desk is in the middle of the classroom, so I can't see out of the window, but I can hear the engine as the driver pulls into the flat space behind the school where the lunch truck usually parks. There is a stir of excitement as we hear the younger children line up.

The big bus-shaped van comes to the school every three weeks loaded with shelves of books. Each student is allowed to take out three books. The Teacher supervises five students going in at a time. It takes a long time until everyone has had a turn.

I brought back my three books:

'Mrs. Piggle-Wiggle,' by Betty MacDonald
'Just So Stories to Read Aloud,' by Rudyard Kipling
'The Adventures of Reddy Fox,' by Thornton W. Burgess

I pick out three new books:

'The Little Princess,' by Frances Hodgson Burnett, illustrated by Tasha Tudor
'Inky: The Seeing Eye Dog,' by Elizabeth P. Heppner
'The Fox Went Out on a Chilly Night' Traditional, illustrated by, Peter Spier

Grammie gives each of her grandchildren a new book every year for their birthday and also one for Christmas. I like to see her handwriting in my books. My name, the date and her name are in each one.

The church in Bonnie Hills sends each of us a book about God every year. We open the shiny red paper on Christmas Eve. Sometimes my Mommy and Daddy or an aunt or uncle give me a book. At Sunday School, we get an attendance award at the end of the year. It is a Gift Certificate for the Chinook Book Store!

I have my own Library at home, on the shelf beside my bed.

Just like on real library books, I taped a small slip of paper into the front inside cover. I also have a chart on a big piece of

Monday, May 9, 1966

paper: Name. Title. Date Borrowed. Date Due. Date Returned. I allow my brothers and sister to come and look, one at a time. They can sign out one book at a time. I write the details on my paper and the due date on the slip inside of the book so they will bring it back.

I have tried arranging all of my books in alphabetical order by title. I tried arranging all of my books in alphabetical order by author. Either way, they looked kind of messy. So, I tried arranging all of my books by color: all the red, yellow, brown, green, blue in groups. I know that real libraries arrange books by topic. So, I tried that for a while. But, I think I like the way it looks best when I arrange all of my books from tallest to shortest.

These are the titles I have in my library, from tallest to shortest:

'The Doll and the Kitten,' by Dare Wright
'The Christ Child' illustrated by Maud and Miska Petersham
'Mouse House,' by Rumer Godden
'David' illustrated by Maud and Miska Petersham
'The Fairy Doll,' by Rumer Godden
'Tatsinda,' by Elizabeth Enright
'Little Bear's Friend,' by Maurice Sendak
'The Twilight of Magic,' by Hugh Lofting
'Nobody's Girl,' by Hector Malot
'Charlotte's Web,' by E. B. White (a Scholastic book, I bought with my own money)
'Helen Keller's Teacher,' by Mickie Davidson (a Scholastic book, I bought with my own money)
'Strawberry Girl,' by Lois Lenski
'Judy's Journey,' by Lois Lenski
'Mary Poppins,' by P.L. Travers
'The Little Leftover Witch,' by Florence Laughlin
'When We Were Very Young,' by A. A. Milne

May Chapter 9   I love to Read

'The Adventures of Bob White,' by Thornton W. Burgess
'Jerry Muskrat at Home,' by Thornton W. Burgess
'Racketty-Packetty House,' by Frances Hodgson Burnett

In the afternoon, when our school work is done, before dismissal, Mrs. Thompson has been reading to us. Every year, for every Grade 3 class, she reads 'Little House in the Big Woods,' by Laura Ingalls Wilder. This year she finished before the school year ended, so she is continuing with the second book in the series, 'Little House on the Prairie.'

We are on Chapter 11, 'Indians in the House.'

Pa had to go away for a while so he tied up Jack, the dog. He told Laura and Mary that they must not untie Jack, no matter what.

Laura and Mary knew that Jack didn't like to be tied up, so they stayed near the barn to keep him company. But then they saw something that was not quite right. Two of the people who lived in tee-pees across the creek were coming to their house! Then they went inside!

Laura and Mary were so frightened about the two men being inside their cabin with their Ma and Baby Carrie. They started, stopped, turned around and finally got up their courage to go inside. Laura watched what was happening while she hid behind some lumber that was leaning up against the wall. Laura had never seen people with brown skin and black eyes, men who wore moccasins and fur, almost no clothes, hair so long, feathers and beads, and a knife. They were speaking to each other in ways she did not understand.

Ma was very still. And she was very brave. When the men pointed at the fresh cornbread Ma was baking, she quietly gave the visitors what they asked for.

Laura's heart was pounding. The men went away and Ma sat down. Pa came home. The girls told him that they had almost decided to untie Jack! But Pa was very glad they did not do that. Jack might have started trouble.

But, in the end, everyone was safe.

On the school bus, I leaned my head against the window. I kept thinking about the danger, the hiding, the waiting, the risk of having strangers come into your house.

When we got off the bus at our stop, the other kids started to run up the gravel road, but I was walking slowly, still thinking, remembering the story, wondering what I might do.

When I got up past the bend, I heard a car behind me. I ducked behind the small trees. I lay down in the ditch. My heart was pounding, just like Laura's.

A dark purple, almost black, car was driving up our road. I had never seen any car like that except on TV. Bad guys in movies drove those kinds of cars. Big bulging fenders. Big shiny grill. Big chrome bumpers. Four doors for the whole gang. Big trunk in the back for guns and booze and dead bodies!

It looks like in the movie, with Jimmy Stewart and Doris Day... and their little boy got kidnapped!

That car turned into *our* driveway!

Someone was getting out!

A man was going into our house!

O!

I was just like Laura. The same danger. The same fear. The same courage. My mother, my little brothers and sister and baby sister were in there! What was going to happen?

I carefully climbed the slope, staying in the deep grass, hiding behind bushes, quietly getting closer to the house, until I could peek into the glass door. I saw the man!

It was Daddy!

I was shaking, but I went inside. I heard him talking to Mommy. He decided to drive that car home to see if he wanted to buy it!

Like Ma in the book, I let out a big sigh of relief and sat down, holding tightly to my Baby Sister. In the end, everyone was safe.

Like Doris Day in the movie, I thought, "the future's not ours to see."

Later

Christmas Day, 1966: I know by the shape that my present from James is a book.

Look! It's Mary Poppins, from the Walt Disney movie. All the words to all the songs are here! The drawings of the children match the characters in the movie. Admiral Boom with his cannon to tell time. Bert with his chimney brush. Uncle Albert with his tea party on the ceiling. The Bird Woman at the cathedral steps. Mr. Banks ready to fly his kite. And Mary Poppins with her umbrella, lifting up into the clouds, ready to find a new family who needs her.

So glad for the movie, the songs, the book, the gift.

Monday, May 9, 1966

So sad when I learned that on December 16, 1966, Walt Disney... died! How is it possible? What will happen? All of his old movies. All of his new ideas. All of the people who work together to make the movies and TV shows and Disneyland and books and toys... the songs and costumes and cartoons and... well... everything?

First, it was President Kennedy. Now, Walt Disney.

What happens to the world when someone so important dies?

In the 1970s, when I started to babysit, I always brought a book to read:

'Poems,' by Robert Louis Stevenson
'The Brave Cowboy,' by Joan Walsh Anglund
'Make Way For Ducklings,' by Robert McCloskey
'Andersen's Fairy Tales,' by Hans Christian Andersen

When I was 14 years old, I asked Grammie if I could take home these books from her attic:

'Every Girl's Annual' (1883) by Routledge
'The Outline of Mythology' (1913) by Thomas Bulfinch
'From Manger to Throne' (1889) by Rev. T. DeWitt Talmage
'The Story of the Other Wise Man' (1895) by Henry van Dyke
'The Romance of a Christmas Card' (1916) by Kate Douglas Wiggin
'Mother Play and Nursery Rhymes' (1878) by Frederich Froebel, translated from the German

And, best of all, Grammie gave me my own copy of the book that she wrote in 1964!

'The Shining East' by, Cornelia Hinkle

One good thing about books: even after the person who wrote them dies, the books are still there, so you can still know what the author was thinking.

Freely Give

"The thing about books," my fiancé told me when we were in college, "is that you get to take them with you after you die."

Thinking of the pyramids and tombs in Egypt, mummies wrapped, boats, food, gold, all manner of household necessities, mummified animals, all at the ready to accompany the deceased to provide for the Journey to the Underworld... Thinking of the great warriors, their shields, swords, helmets and insignia, ready to attack or defend whatever lies beyond the grave... Thinking of the Time Capsule, photos and letters we buried with a favourite dog... I do not understand what Kevin is talking about.

"I've never heard of anyone getting buried with their books?" I look at his face, puzzled.

"You get to take the knowledge with you," he replied.

And so we continue to buy, borrow, trade, loan and often search for 10¢ books at the Thrift Store. And give. A book is such a great gift to give.

To read more about how Eleanor earned wages by reading...
... turn to 10 Days in June Chapter 9, page 249.

Chapter 10
Tuesday, May 10, 1966
Of Course I Can Write

> When you reach for the stars,
> you may not get one,
> but you won't come up with a handful of mud either.
> —Leo Burnett

Freely Receive

I'm going to write a book.

Not now.

When I grow up.

It will be just like how Laura Ingalls Wilder wrote 'Little House in the Big Woods.' She wrote a true story of her life. She told all about her mother and father, her grandparents, aunts, uncles and cousins. Mostly she told about herself and her sisters and their dog. She told about their house and the seasons, what they play with and going to town, what books they have and the food they eat.

She told about the work her Ma and Pa do and the way they have different things to do at different times of the year. Even Christmas. And she loves to hear her Pa play the fiddle when she falls asleep. She told about what scared her and what made her laugh. She got in trouble and she was also helpful.

I can write about those things, too.

I already know how to print and spell and I can even write in cursive. I read a lot of books, too, so I think I could write one.

So far I have made this story. I wrote it when I was seven. I used Daddy's typewriter. That's how he is writing his book. For me, right now, the typewriter seems slower than writing with a pencil, but Daddy goes pretty fast, so I guess I can learn, too.

Eleanor's first story — 6/1/65 age 7½

```
              THE BIG BIRD

ONCE upon a time there was a big bird he aced like the king
        He bosed every boty aroumed . Now there was a tiny bird he
        bosed the big bird around ..The big bird caled the tiny
            bird a pesed wenthis ha pend. One day the tiny bird
        gatherd a hole flok of tiny birds then one day thay all
        swooped down    on the big bird .

OWW   WWWWWWOW WWWWWWWWOWWWWW
        Yelled the big bird and floo out of the big wood.
            And never came bake agen .
        And the tiny bird live h a pp ly ever after
              TH E END
```

But this story won't be part of my book, because this story is pretend. I want to write a true story of my life. I'll have to remember where we go and what we do and how I feel and what I decide while I am growing up. I don't know if I will have any adventures. It won't be like a TV show or a movie with bad guys and running from danger. At least, I hope not. I will write about my own, true, real life. Like Laura did.

Tuesday, May 10, 1966

Mrs. Thompson said that Laura was more than 60 years old when she started to write her books. I am eight years old now. O, my! Will I wait 50 years to start?

Mrs. Thompson said Laura started by writing for the newspaper. Mostly, she wrote about farming information to share her knowledge, but sometimes to tell about the old days. I could do that. You can even earn money when you write for the newspaper! Plus it's short. You don't have to write pages and pages. Some authors write their books this way: one chapter at a time. Every week there is another chapter in the newspaper. Then they gather them all together to make the whole book. I think that is a great idea.

Mrs. Thompson makes sure that we know the author of all the books, poems and stories that she reads to us. I know that when Mommy goes to the library she likes to find books by the same author. Daddy knows the authors of a lot of books, too.

Helen Keller wrote a book. More than one. And she was blind!

When you write a book, your name is on every copy. I think it would be wonderful to see my name on my book!

One thing about writing is: it's different from being a movie star or famous singer or dancer. You don't have to be the only person on the stage. You don't have to be 'the best.' You just have to write the story! There are millions and millions of books. They each have an author. Maybe the author only wrote one book. Maybe, like Laura, they wrote a whole bunch. Maybe you get famous. Maybe you only tell your friends about it. The main thing is: you wrote down what you were thinking about. Maybe it will be the same as someone else. Or, maybe it will be way different. It's a good way to save what you know so other people can learn. Maybe it will help someone?

I can be one of the millions of people who write a book.

May Chapter 10   Of Course I Can Write

Another thing: the book lasts. When the dance is done or the music stops or the curtain closes, the performance is over. The only way to see or hear the show again is to do it again. A book is different. Some books are more than 2000 years old. The Bible is one. There are other people like Aesop who wrote stories way back in time. And other people like in China and India have books that are even older.

Rock carvings and cave paintings are older than books. Those people didn't use words, they used pictures to tell about their lives, danger, food, the sun and stars. The people who made them are long gone, but what they wrote is still here!

I have already made three books.

The first one was called 'Textiles.' I made it at home. I cut pieces of paper in half. Then folded each piece to make pages. I asked Mommy for little pieces of fabric. I sorted them out. I asked Mommy to tell me how to spell. I glued the pieces of cloth on the pages. I wrote the labels. Linen, cotton, wool, velvet, rayon, nylon, silk. Plaid, polka-dot, stripe, print, gingham. Lace, braid, ric-rac, bias tape. I made a green cover and put my name on the front. I stapled it together.

The second book I made for school. It has big pages and lined paper. The front cover is green paper. With my crayons, I drew a happy sunshine, a tree and tulips and a girl jumping rope. The back cover is blue paper. I drew with my pencil. There is one cabin, three tepees, two trees and three hills. The title page says 'Health Word List,' my name and the date, Nov. 5, 1965. Then there are two pages of my best printing. On the first page, I made the word extra dark with my pencil. On the second page, I made the word underlined. I'm not sure which I like better. Then I wrote the definition.

Appetite – Your liking and want for food.
Courteous – Being polite and thoughtful of others.
Disease – Sickness caused by harmful germs.
Eyestrain – Tiredness of the eyes.

Tuesday, May 10, 1966

Margarine – A fat taken from vegetables. It is used instead of butter.
Microscope – A glass that makes things larger than they are.
Molars – The large flat teeth that grind your food.
Observed – Obeyed or paid attention to.
Odor – A smell or scent.
Organs – Parts of the body. The eyes are organs.
Permanent – Made to last a long time.
Perspire – To lose water through the pores.
Prevent – To keep something from happening.
Regular – Steady happening as always.
Regulate – To make regular. To make happen as usual.
Respect – To pay attention to and be careful of.
Responsibility – To take duties and care upon yourself.
Temperature – A measure of heat in a body in the water or air.

The third book I made for Daddy's birthday.[6] I folded whole pages in half. Blue for the cover, white for the pages. I drew 36 of each thing: candles, music notes, books, balloons, and I taped on pennies. I stapled the whole thing together when it was done.

Of course I can write a book!

My great-great (times seven) grandfather was a minister. He wrote sermons and magazine articles. He traveled a lot and gathered the people together to teach them.

My grandfather translated Latin into English. He also is writing a booklet called 'Rite Riting'. He wants to teach everyone to spell English phonetically.

My grandmother wrote a book about what she thinks it is like to wake up in heaven. She gave me my own copy. Here's how she explains it.

"Some time or other we must all leave this world. It seems to me that our lives will be better here, and our necessary partings with friends will be less painful if we have an idea of heaven that makes it seem a desirable habitation. If my story *The Shining East,* makes heaven seem worth trying for here and now, the story will be fulfilling its purpose."[7]

My father, his uncle, brother and sister also write. So? I can, too!

Some did research and wrote textbooks. That seems really hard to me. Some were more creative by writing poetry or a play. That seems really tricky to me.

Here is something I like that Grammie wrote in the front of her book. It is real, ordinary, but it is like you get to go there, see everything. I feel happy to know about another person's life. She is telling about *her* life in the cabin! Just like I want to write about *my* life in the cabin!

"We were in a sunny, narrow valley, dropping steeply toward the south and the road through Ute Pass near Green Mountain Falls...

"From our cabin we had a constant view of the sharp point of Pike's Peak, rising over the steep, wooded foothills across the creek. There are almost no cloudy days...

"While I lived among the mountains, I made a business of looking at them and enjoying them every day...

"Housekeeping in the cabin was simple. We had a bedroom, which just held Bobby's crib, a large twin crib for Grace and Madeline, our bed and a tiny white bureau. Our living room was more ample. It held a wood stove with an oven in the chimney, a trunk which Grace sat on at meals, two highchairs for Bobby and Madeline, a couple of chairs for us and a rocking chair. The tiny kitchen, up two steps from the living room, held a tiny wood stove we seldom used, a sink, shelves and our pail of fresh water. Refrigeration was no problem. A cupboard underground, reached by a trapdoor in the living room, kept things cool. We finally dug a well across the road in the dry creek-bed, but much of the time our only water was the five-gallon can my brother-in-law brought up – each day he went for his mail – from the free spout of water on the pole downtown near the Green Mountain Falls post office. The fresh water went into a pail for drinking and cooking, the leftover water into the storage tub for washing.

"Whenever it rained, which was seldom, we caught the water from the roof. All through the winter I melted snow and heated it for the washing, which I did outdoors. It was always comfortable outdoors in the sunshine, if you were sheltered from the wind, which we were, as our cabin was in a steep, narrow valley facing the south. We often heard the wind howling overhead.

"The snow melted within a day or two, where the sun hit it, but enough for washing remained for months, frozen in back of every ridge or tree trunk. It seldom snowed. The only really heavy snowfall during our two winters came late one April.

"Life in the cabin was delightful in many ways: no expense except for a tiny rent, a little kerosene for the lamp, and our food. Fuel we cut for ourselves. Each Saturday, my husband and I took turns going with Uncle Allan, seventeen miles down the road to Colorado Springs to do the shopping. Besides our food, we always selected from the excellent public library the books we wanted to read but never had had time for. There were always books for the children – 'Heidi', 'Alice in Wonderland,' 'Dr. Doolittle' and so on."

I want to be like Grammie.

She reads. She writes. She sings. She has a husband and kids. She volunteers. She makes plays for Sunday School. She travels. She gives books as presents. She isn't loud or the center of attention, but she makes friends wherever she goes, writes them letters and encourages people.

She is not tall or slim, and has kind of a plain face, gray hair, glasses, and not much interest in fancy clothes or jewellery, but she looks beautiful to me with her soft blue church dress, wedding ring, and kind eyes.

I like to watch her bend over, comb her long hair, twist it and wrap it in a bun. With four hairpins, she fastens the bun, then uses four wire combs to hold her hair in place. Last is the hairnet. That's Grammie. The same. Every day.

This is the song she often sings to me:

I think when I read that sweet story of old,
When Jesus was here among men,
How He called little children like lambs to His fold,
I should like to have been with Him then.
To think that His hands would be placed on my head,
And His arms would be thrown around me,
And to I think I could hear His kind words when He said.
"Let the little ones come unto Me."[8]

I know that Grammie had a good idea for her book. And she had a typewriter. She knew how to tell a good story, but she didn't have much time. She told me that she started writing her book in the 1930s and didn't publish it until 1964. Four kids, washing by hand, helping Grampa with his translating, writing all those letters. Plus, they moved so much. Once I asked her and she said she 'self-published.' That means her book didn't go to a big company. She paid for the printing herself. I guess that's a good idea. If you want your book to turn out the way

Tuesday, May 10, 1966

you decide. You might not get famous, but you get to see your name on the cover!

I like to do a lot of the things that Grammie likes to do. So, that's probably how I will publish my book, too.

Later

I read a lot. I get good marks in school. When we have a writing assignment, I do extra.

While others train for sports, I wrestle with words.

While others study living things in the field, farm or forest, I find fascination in lives preserved in ink.

While others develop expression through music and drama, I choose expression through rhythm and rhyme.

While others twist tools, I turn a phrase.

While others focus on microscopic detail, I seek specific sounds.

While others study what is really there, I work with things that only exist in my imagination.

While others wait for phenomenon to photograph, I wait until a word arrives.

While others travel, seeking adventure, I stay still, and Journey within.

While others deliberately plan and construct, I build a plot.

While others scribble a sketch, I use words to describe a scene.

While others master the precision of mechanics and technology, I struggle to learn the skills of my trade... or is it art? or a profession? or a vocation?

Freely Give

A love letter to my husband, a thank-you note to GrandmaD, a cheerful memory to a widow, a page of poetry to Mom,

"The fat cat sat on the mat" for my little daughter, an email of encouragement to my grown son, annual Christmas letters to relatives. I have written all of these, and more. I wrote to my doctor, my counsellor, my priest in gratitude when they each helped me along the way. I wrote to the newspaper, local government, the school board to point out problems and offer solutions.

Words seem to pour into my mind, flow through my pen, spill onto the page.

Does one person make a difference? Writing. Preserve a thought. Touch a heart. Convey meaning. Share ideas. Explore. Remember.

To read more about how Eleanor earned money by writing...
... turn to 10 Days in June Chapter 10, page 265.

EPILOGUE

"Kevin?"

"Hmmm?"

"I know I spend a lot of time with all of this volunteering... and all of this writing... I wish I was doing more things each day *with you.*"

"You are reaching towards your goals. We both are."

"So... even if we are working apart we are still Twogether?"

"Yes. We do different activities but we share a common purpose!"

>Each of us is called to be unique and unrepeatable.
>Creative choices are our birthright.
>Creativity is the glory of being human.
>—John Bradshaw 'Homecoming'

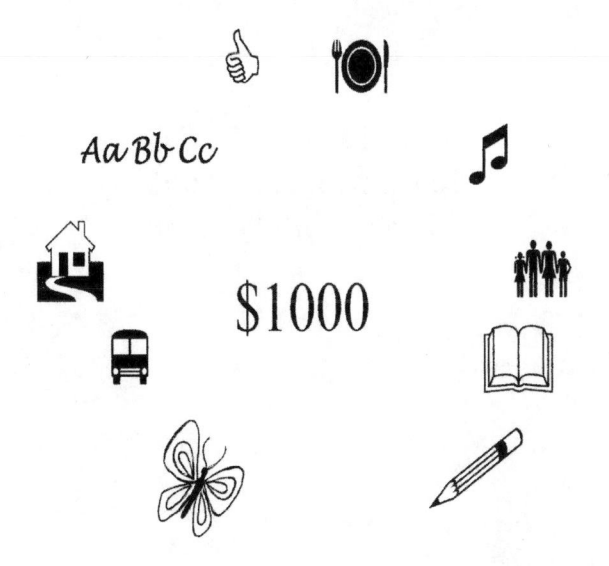

10 Days in June, $1000
... BONUS: 10 Seminars

I want to get married,
go out west,
build a log cabin,
have a bunch of kids
teach them about the Lord,
volunteer in my community,
and then write a book about it.
—*Eleanor Deckert*

a memoir by
Eleanor Deckert
BOOK 7

Table of Contents
10 Days in June, $1000
... BONUS: 10 Seminars

Introduction   115

Chapter 1
Saturday, June 17, 1978
We Make a Plan: Get Married
Gift : $1000   117

BONUS: Seminar #1
7 Healthy Habits
... since 1999   129

Chapter 2
Saturday, June 17, 1978...
Wednesday, June 11, 2014
Departures... Arrivals : $1000   131

BONUS: Seminar #2
Canada Name Game
... since 1996   144

Chapter 3
Monday, June 2, 1980
Log Cabin Lifestyle
Three Pay Cheques : $1000
First Loan : $1000   149

BONUS: Seminar #3
14 Economies for Tough Times
... since 2008   162

Chapter 4
Wednesday, June 7, 1995
A Talent for Teaching : $1000   173

BONUS: Seminar #4
Home? School?
... since 1995   180

Chapter 5
Saturday, June 7, 1997
Barter : $1000   189

BONUS: Seminar #5
Question Quilt
... since 2005   197

Chapter 6
Tuesday, June 9, 1998
$100 per day for 10 days!   199

BONUS: Seminar #6
H.O.W. 2
Home Organization Workshop (what's the 2 for?)
... since 1992   208

Chapter 7
Tuesday, June 3, 2003
Learn... Teach... Dance... $1000?   213

BONUS: Seminar #7
Teach Dance
... since 1998   227

Chapter 8
Thursday, June 2, 2006
Parent Educator : $1000   233

BONUS: Seminar #8
Mommy Matters
... since 1998   241

Chapter 9
Tuesday, June 28, 1988
Tuesday, June 17, 2008
"You will pay me $1000 to read?"   249

BONUS: Seminar #9
What do Fairy-Tales tell us
about Child Development?
... since 2001   261

Chapter 10
Thursday, June 25, 2015
$1000 : Ink   265

BONUS: Seminar #10
"Eleanor Deckert's
Memoir Writing Method"
. Title . Theme . Topics . Tips .
... since 2018   272

Epilogue   281

INTRODUCTION

I'm not as interested in "Where did I come from?" or "Where am I going?"

Reincarnation? I leave that to Shirley McClain and others.

Heaven and Hell? I leave that to Billy Graham and others.

I am less interested in the invisible past nor the unsearchable future.

What I am interested in is this: *"What am I here for... now?"*

It is poetic to say, "We each have a purpose" or "Each person is unique" or "Just be yourself."

I can see for myself that there are infinite variations.

Flakes of snow. Flowers. Feathers. Fingerprints.

This myriad swirl of newness is at the same time reassuring ("I *am* unique!") and dizzying ("So... what?")

Next question: "Can I know my purpose?" And from there, "How will I know? Am I told? Led? Do I go exploring? Do I experiment? Trial and Error? Could I spend a lifetime on Earth and *miss* the whole reason of why I am here?"

If, as I thought in my youth, I must set a goal and achieve it, I am woefully a failure. Every project I begin with great enthusiasm soon fizzles out. Every eager dream withers and bright clear vision fades. Stacks of unread books. Incomplete course requirements. Piles of papers. Sewing left unattended. Yes, dishes in the sink.

Is my purpose inevitable? Will I arrive at the right place at the right time and make the right decision to change the trajectory of history in some small or mighty way?

June INTRODUCTION

Am I doing it without knowing it? Just by 'being me' am I radiating some splash of colour to the human portrait that would otherwise not be there?

Is it 'Random Acts of Kindness?' Helping a little old lady across the street? Rescuing a kitten in a tree?

Is it noble and grand? Words? Actions? Single? Married? Birthing? Attending the dying?

Is my purpose fulfilled as a once-in-a-lifetime significant stand-alone moment? ... or somehow woven into the tapestry with others? ... is my lone thread humble or splendid? ... unique? ... yet, somehow, needed?

None of this I can answer. All I can do is share my own path, listen to your story, become aware of others who are sensitive to these questions, explore literature, observe turning points, watch for crossroads, try to discern my own decisions and believe that, yes, I have a purpose. I may grope in the fog. I may glimpse it. I may only see it in hindsight, or not at all, or only after I leave this Earth and enter what ever lies ahead.

> Each man has his own vocation;
> his talent is his call.
> There is one direction
> in which all space is open to him.
> —*Ralph Waldo Emerson*

Chapter 1
Saturday, June 17, 1978
We Make a Plan: Get Married
Gift : $1000

> Without Divine assistance
> I cannot succeed;
> with it
> I cannot fail.
> —*Abraham Lincoln*

Before we begin

So: If God has a Plan... and I am made in His image... then... it seems to me... that I should have a Plan, too...

If God has a Plan, how will I know what it is? where to go? what to do? whether I am getting closer? Am I even capable of following it?

If I want to make a Plan, I can collect some clues.

"God created mankind in his own image, in the image of God he created them; male and female he created them.

"God blessed them and said to them, 'Be fruitful and multiply; fill the earth and subdue it. Rule over the fish in the sea and the birds in the sky and over every living creature that moves on the ground.'

"Then God said, 'I give you every seed-bearing plant on the face of the whole earth and every tree that has fruit with seed in it. They will be yours for food. And to all the beasts of the earth and all the birds in the sky and all the creatures that move along the ground - everything that has the breath of life in it - I give every green plant for food.' And it was so.

"God saw all that he had made, and it was very good. And there was evening, and there was morning - the sixth day."
Genesis 1: 27-31

"...a man leaves his father and mother and is united to his wife..."
Genesis 2: 24

"I have set before you life and death, blessing and cursing: therefore choose life."
Deuteronomy 30:19

"One thing have I desired of the Lord, that will I seek after, to behold the beauty of the Lord and to inquire in His temple."
Psalm 27:4

Saturday, June 17, 1978

"The mountains shall bring peace to the people."
Psalm 73:3

"Cease to do evil. Learn to do well."
Isaiah: 16-17

"'For I know the plans I have for you,' declares the Lord, 'plans to prosper you and not to harm you, plans to give you hope and a future.'"
Jeremiah 29:11

"Jesus said, 'I have come that you may have life, and have it more abundantly.'"
John 10:10

So, it seems that there is A Plan, and it might be a good idea to stick with it.

Eat plants. Get married. Be fruitful. Seek the Lord. Live in the mountains. Cease to do evil. Learn to do well. Live an abundant life.

Sounds like a good plan!

Plan

'Homesteading'
'Back-to-Basics'
'Back-to-Nature'
'Self-Sufficiency'
'Back-to-the-Land'

My fiancé, Kevin, and I have been dreaming, collecting, planning. There is so much to learn. Could we really become 'Self-Sufficient'? Build our own log cabin? Drink water from a clear flowing river? Cultivate a vegetable garden? Store food for the winter? Gather enough firewood? Live the 'Simple Life'?

If we learn to do things ourselves, then the less money we need.

If we need less money, then we can live on one wage.

If we live on one wage, then I can stay home.

If I can stay home, then we can teach our children how to do things, too.

I learn how to make bread, pickles, jam, yogourt, quilts, clothing. Kevin learns how to fix machinery, build with wood. We collect tools and books, winter clothing and sleeping bags, a first aid kit.

We knew that if we stayed in Ontario we would be able to find excellent farmland, a good growing season and Farmer's Markets to sell our produce. But, since I loved Colorado so much, I also knew I just had to live in the mountains. That meant searching for land in western Alberta or British Columbia.

It took a year to get ready.

I quit college and lived at my parents' home. I worked at the warehouse of a large department store for minimum wage: $2.25 per hour. Every day I unpacked cases of trendy clothing, pallets of cosmetics, electric appliances. There was nothing in this mountain of merchandise that would be necessary in our future. Every day I checked off the packing slip, printed the price tags, sent the shipment off to the store. I paid my room and board at home, rode the city bus, paid for our winter-ready Cannondale sleeping bags, a down parka, an alpaca wool sweater, and a gorgeous, brown, hand woven poncho. I saved up for the camping fees, food and necessities for our long journey.

Kevin worked at a textile factory for $3.85 an hour. He paid rent on a basement apartment and prepared his own meals. He bought a 1971 VW van, and the tools he needed to set about the task of repairing and outfitting it for the journey west. He bought

Saturday, June 17, 1978

a Cannondale tent and camping gear, a small chainsaw, CB radio and a camera, books, first aid kit and a mattress and pillows. Kevin set money aside for repairs that might be needed along the way.

There were two bridal showers!

First: Kevin's Mother invited all of her sisters, daughter-in-law and friends. They gave us essentials. Sheets and blankets, pots and pans, towels and silverware, camp stove and cooler, all were highly valued. Pretty things like a pink table cloth, a glass cake plate, and silver-plate serving spoons were packed up to be mailed to us later. The electric kettle, toaster and coffee pot were left with my sisters.

Second: My Mother, invited the ladies from church to a 'Money Tree' shower! $5, $10, $20 bills were attached to a little tree. It was enough to pay for gas for the entire trip from Kitchener, Ontario to the mountains of British Columbia.

The guests asked, "What are your plans?" They expected me to say that we would stay in or near the church community. But, there was a plan which had been developing between Kevin and I in our private conversations. The time had come. I was finally brave enough to say it out loud to everyone's surprise. "I want to get married, go out west, build a log cabin, raise a bunch of kids, teach them about the Lord, volunteer in my community and then write a book about it."

Now everyone knows that we are leaving right away. Everyone knows we are planning this 'Back-to-the-Land' life-style. Everyone knows we have no need of electric appliances.

$$ $ 1000 $ $

It's time. We are planning our wedding. We will make our vows outside on a grassy hill with the view of the rising sun far across the valley.

Meanwhile, we compared plans with five other newly-wed couples. More traditional Tom and Laurel were still finishing college, and stayed on in the church community in Pennsylvania with extended family. Laurie married a newly ordained minister and was sent off to a place she'd never been. Trey and Lanna tried to make it as self-employed children's entertainers. Cam and Freida bought a tandem bicycle and lived in a tepee in Maine. Jim and Alison hesitated, waiting for their first baby to arrive, and never really made it to the 'out-west' lifestyle they had dreamed of.

Our plan: Get married. Leave.

Although I intended to abide by religious traditions, there were a lot of things I didn't know about being a bride. I didn't realize that our wedding was the only one in our church community that would be performed outside, so even the guests did not know exactly what to expect.

The night before the wedding was the rehearsal inside the church. Who enters first? What about the music? Where to stand? What to say?

After the rehearsal we requested a worship service that included Holy Supper. Kevin and I sensed it was important to dedicate our future to be of service to the Lord, ask for His guidance and pledge to trust His Plan.

Then we all walked across the soft lawn, through the church community, up the hill to my parent's house for the rehearsal dinner. We were surrounded by aunts and uncles and cousins, siblings and grandparents. Since Kevin and I were vegetarians, my mother made quiche. Kevin and I passed out the thank-you gifts for our wedding party.

Our relatives brought gifts for us. My Aunt Caroline and cousin from Vermont brought a cut glass serving bowl and set of glass salad bowls. My Aunt Barbara from Colorado sent six lovely pottery mugs. My Oma made her traditional granny square afghan, each brightly coloured woollen square was outlined with a black border. My parents gave us a set of copper bottom Revere Ware cooking pots, and a pressure cooker (for the beans we vegetarians depend on).

Afterwards, Lisa, my maid of honour, so gently tucked me in, listened to my nervous chatter, assured me that the to-do list would be complete by morning, and left me relaxed on my last night in my parents' home.

$ $ 1000 $ $

The wedding was scheduled for early in the morning and the weather forecast was fair.

I had already recruited our friends to decorate. "I want daisies. Lots of daisies." So, very early on the day of the wedding, my friends waded into the fields gathering armfuls of daisies. Then they added yellow and orange day lilies offered from our neighbours gardens.

Our wedding reception would be a breakfast in the church meeting hall.

Della has been baking banana, apple, and pumpkin muffins. Lanna went shopping for every kind of fresh fruit for fruit salad. Lori composed a Psalm to play on her guitar. My brother, James, composed a piece for his classical guitar accompanied by Jeff and Len, who will play their flutes. My brother, Andrew, will be the photographer. My sisters, Julie and Carol, and my best friend, Lisa, are the bride's maids. Their dresses have been made by my mother's friend, Judy.

All together, with so many homemade and volunteer projects, the wedding costs were small. Our honeymoon, too, will be short and simple. We want to use the money we've saved to leave Ontario and seek land in British Columbia as soon as possible.

$ $ 1000 $ $

Was I breaking tradition yet again by popping in early to see how things were progressing?

The church kitchen was a bustle as ladies were cutting strawberries, melon, pineapple, apples, oranges, peaches, bananas, and grapes to fill the enormous punch bowl with fruit salad. The baking was being set out on the long white tables. Water was coming to a boil to make herbal tea. Two five-gallon boxes of grape juice and apple juice were ready.

Carl and his helpers were outside setting up the chairs. The flat lawn behind the church, shaded by an ancient beech tree, at the top of a hill, was the perfect size for the 150 guests.

Inside, a rainbow mural covered the wall where Mr. and Mrs. Kevin Deckert would hold the reception line after the ceremony.

The wedding guests will be arriving in about an hour. They include the children I babysit and volunteer with, Kevin's Mennonite relatives, my Oma, aunts and cousins who have travelled from afar, and Grampa, who lives with us now, since Grammie died.

$ $ 1000 $ $

I hurry back home to get dressed.

I have stitched my dress by hand. White cotton gauze is pleated to form a bodice with a loose fitting gathered skirt.

Instead of a veil for the bridegroom to lift, I have made a softly draped hood for Kevin to lower, and golden circlets for both of us to wear in our hair is our symbol of virginity.

Kevin will be wearing blue corduroy pants and the white linen tunic that I stitched by hand.

Kevin made our wedding rings. Bands of gold were cut and made smooth with a file and emery paper. On the inside surface, he used the fine point of a swiftly spinning Dremel tool to engrave our initials, wedding date and two birds flying.

Breaking yet another tradition, I wanted Kevin to see me coming down the stairs in my wedding dress. I wanted to see him waiting for me. We were ready to leave my parent's home and begin our lives 'Twogether.' We stepped out of the known and into the unknown. We walked the two blocks, hand in hand, all the way to the church.

I heard harmonies and arpeggios of the two flutes and guitar like a swirling dance conveying a heart-felt message within the sweet sounds. I saw my bridesmaids carrying small bouquets of daisies while singing *Morning Has Broken* accompanied by Lori on guitar. I smiled at the children, seated in front on picnic blankets. I watched my parents' faces as they watched me transformed from a daughter to a wife.

I carried no flowers. I wanted to hold Kevin's hand. And, breaking another tradition, we both carried the rings ourselves.

Exchange

Now we stand facing the white robed priest. Seven crystals sparkle in the wide spreading beech tree. The slope downward to the east gives everyone a wide vista, of the dawn, the fields, the forest, the places Kevin and I had explored on our hikes.

We make our vows outside on the grassy hill. The rising sun feels like a warm blessing for a bright future.

"I promise to love, honour and comfort you and cleave unto you alone, that we may dwell together in holy state of marriage, according to the ordinance of our God." These are the traditional vows. It was breaking custom to repeat the whole thing, not merely acknowledge with, "I do."

Exchange vows. Exchange rings. Exchange a simple kiss. Exchange life. I give him mine. He gives me his.

June Chapter 1   Gift : $1000

$ $ 1000 $ $

Such a short ceremony. Such a huge change. Now we are married!

Children pull wild flowers from the long grass and bring me a bouquet of weeds. Didn't I know every bride carries a bouquet?

Childhood friends, classmates, elderly neighbours, some guests have come from so far. The reception line is long. The greetings are special. These faces are dear. I collect hugs. Lori serenades us with Psalm 129 which she composed for our betrothal.

> *Blessed are they that fear the Lord and walk in His way.*
> *Thou shalt eat the labour and the fruit of thine own hand.*
> *Thy wife shall be as fruitful as the vine beside thy home*
> *with children like olive plants around.*
> *The Lord shall bless thee and happy shalt thou be.*

Yes, please. This is our prayer. These blessings I ask for and strive to accomplish.

Now for the food!

The long tables have long lineups. Our guests seem pleased to have so much variety for such a healthy breakfast.

My mother and I made the three-tiered wedding cake together. It is richly generous with jewels of dried cherries, pineapple, currants, dates, apricots and plums. There is a mini-miracle on top: someone out in the fields this morning noticed a double centred daisy. It is a sign! A blessing for us that 'Two shall be One.'

Then the toasts. To the Bride! To the Groom!

Now, the cards. Lots and lots of cards. Somehow, I didn't know I would be opening cards on my wedding day. Doves and bells, silver glitter and pastel swirls, churches and romantic photography, couples in embrace, brides like soft ice-cream swirls. The cards are full of cash and checks. I didn't know.

But, wait. There's more.

What is this? Have I read this correctly? Unexpected. My parents have given us a check for $1000.00! I have never had such a thing.

"Mom?" I look at her, my face full of questions. "How is this possible? One thousand dollars!" I cannot quite understand this wealth. That's nearly three month's pay! My parents have already hosted the rehearsal dinner, covered the church rental and made a gift to the priest, and given us the pots and pans and pressure cooker... now more?

"I asked you to pay $20 per week for room and board while you were working this year. This is the total. This is from saving $20 per week."

Value

My mind overflows with meaning. Purpose. Determination. A little bit at a time combined with commitment brings such results.

With the $1000 wedding gift set aside, we now have something to offer as a down payment when we find a piece of land.

Kevin and I walk back to my house, gather my things and prepare to leave for our honeymoon. My heart is struggling to adjust to the changes this day represents. What is left behind forever? What is collected and preserved? What resources will I draw on later? What lies ahead?

One More Thing

That first day of our marriage, when we had the gift of money and how we decided to manage it, was so significant that

I pledged to do the same for each of our children. I wanted to give them each $1000 twice.

First: I put $100 into the bank from age 9-18 so that each young adult could make a dream come true. I told them it was coming, so they could dream and hope and plan.

Elise went to France on a high school student exchange trip. She saw the Louvre, the Notre Dame, the Eiffel Tower.

Michael went to England on a high school student exchange trip. He saw Stonehenge, a Shakespeare play, Big Ben.

Nicholas and Toby went to France on the same high school student exchange trip, but they each had different host families and very different experiences. Nicholas shared a room, while Toby had his own suite. Nicholas took public transit, while Toby had a driver. Nicholas had to sink-or-swim with his limited French, while Toby practised amusing attempts at French on the family dog because his hosts were fluent in English.

Second: I planned to make a $1000 gift for each newly-wed couple. Off, away, into their own adventures, they would have the same blessing my parents had given to us.

To read more about how Kevin and Eleanor's Plans withstood the pressures of the Covid-19 Pandemic...
... turn to 10 Days in July Chapter 1, page 287.

But Wait! There's More
How did practical Kevin and idealistic Eleanor develop healthy habits?

Here is the seminar Eleanor delivers on this topic.

BONUS: Seminar #1
7 Healthy Habits

... since 1999

(1) opposites
(2) water
(3) food from plants
(4) sunshine
(5) movement
(6) air
(7) rest

Prepare: Cut 7 circles of stiff paper about 6 inches across (trace around a saucer or salad plate)

Supplies:
scissors
glue
old magazines to cut up
needle and thread

First: Tear pictures out of the magazines to represent each of the 7 Healthy Habits.

Next: For each of the 7 Healthy Habits: collect several pictures, trim, arrange to make a collage, glue onto the front and back of each circle.

Finish: Using the needle and thread, either make a loop to hang each of the circles separately, or one-after-the-other EITHER 'top-to-bottom' OR 'across' in a long row. Display them where you can see them often, encouraging you to make healthy choices throughout your day.

7 Healthy Habits

(1) opposites (find pictures showing things you don't want to do: smoking, alcohol, fattening foods, dreary or sad emotions)

(2) water (find pictures showing water in nature, washing, toothbrush, splashing, soaking, drinking, pouring, having fun)

(3) food from plants (find pictures showing fruits and vegetables, gardens, variety, salads)

(4) sunshine (find pictures showing people enjoying the sunshine, summertime and wintertime)

(5) movement (find pictures showing exercise, walking, stretching, cycling, etc)

(6) air (find pictures showing birds, butterflies, flowers, wind, hair blowing, weather)

(7) rest (find pictures showing lounging, sleeping, relaxing, comfort, contentment, peace and quiet)

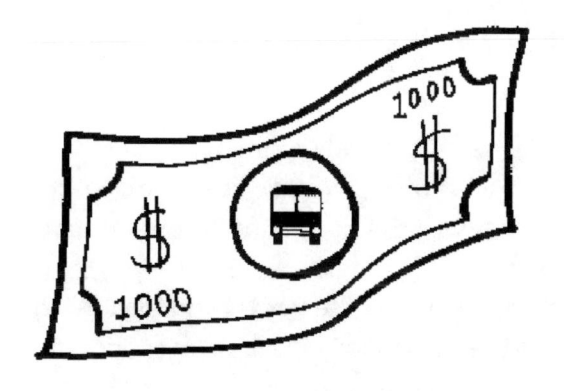

Chapter 2
Saturday, June 17, 1978...
Wednesday, June 11, 2014
Departures... Arrivals : $1000

The journey of a thousand miles
begins with a single step.
—*Tao*

Before we begin
The thing about travel is this: You are sad to leave what is behind, but you are glad to see what is ahead. It happens to me every time. Depart. First I look back, wave and cry. Arrive. Then I lean forward, eager to see what is around the bend.

$ $ 1000 $ $

June 17, 1978

The wedding ceremony and reception are over.

We laugh as we offer Lisa a ride home... it's only two blocks!

We laugh as we drive Lori to the Toronto Airport and walk her to her gate.

When I can no longer see her, I am suddenly overwhelmed. This 'Good-bye' is symbolic of all of the 'Good-byes' we are saying. We are leaving behind every single person, place, memory, every single familiar anything. Everything. I am overcome with weeping, Kevin guides my steps while I cannot see to navigate through the airport, back to the VW van.

$$\$\$\$1000\$\$\$$

We newlyweds are not alone. We pass through small towns and pass by rural churches. It is a beautiful Saturday in mid-June. We are not the only bridal couple today! Seven times we pass families entering churches, families throwing confetti, families posing for photographers, brides in fluffy gowns, flowers being tossed, cars bedecked with garlands.

And then, we newlyweds *are* alone. In a tiny cabin, beside a quiet lake, warmed by a wood stove, feasting on left over wedding fare, snuggled under a quilt, we enter the newfound sweetness of the physical union we can celebrate now.

He is my husband. I am his wife. Twogether.

$$\$\$\$1000\$\$\$$

June 11, 1996

Once, I stood on Ellis Island, which is just beside the Statue of Liberty in New York City. It was the exact place where my Oma stood, alone, 17 years old, leaving Germany, entering the USA.

Saturday, June 17, 1978...Wednesday, June 11, 2014

I studied the display, a huge world map, a list of dates, a pathway of little lights showing when large groups of people came to the USA from various parts of the world.

There has to be something you're leaving that you want to get away from.

There has to be something up ahead that you want enough to take the risk.

Plan

1962
West!

The first time I was almost five years old. My Daddy and Mommy took turns driving the light blue Ford station wagon, switching drivers every two hours from Pennsylvania to Colorado.

1978
West!

Now I am twenty years old. My husband drives the red and white VW van. It is our first home. Leaving southern Ontario after our wedding, we go north the whole first day, around the Great Lakes. Then west. Mile after mile. Highway #1. Prairies for 3 days. Then we explore BC and find the land we have been dreaming of.

Get Married: check!
Go out west: check!
Build a log cabin: check!

But, the extreme cold of that first winter seizes the engine. With no means of transportation of our own, we have to hitchhike for the rest of the winter, spring, summer.

1979

Kevin gets a job on the railroad! His first paycheck is enough to buy a bicycle!

He leaves our cabin at 6:00am, cycles 2km of gravel road and 10km of highway. Works on the railroad from 7:00am-3:00pm. Heavy tools. Digging ballast. Lifting 100 pound kegs of spikes. Cycles home.

Hot, dirty, boots still on, he lies on the floor, asleep.

All summer, in the heat of the afternoon, I have to light the wood stove to make his supper, and something for him to eat for lunch the next day.

Exchange

In September, I join a team of five to go pine-cone picking.

Fellers with buzzing chainsaws drop tall trees laden with pine cones (fir and spruce) so that they fall onto the gravel road.

Climbing through the maze of branches, we pull off the tightly closed cones, filling gunny sacks. Each sack holds one-and-a-half bushels. Each sack is worth $50. The cones will be dried, burst open, the seeds planted in a greenhouse. Next spring the seedlings will be planted by more teams of young adults to reforest the wide cut-blocks of land where the timber has been cut for lumber.

Mosquitoes swarm. Repellent stinks. Sun is fierce. Hands get sticky with fragrant sap. Exhausted, yet, when the day is done, I must carry the water, light the fire, prepare some food for both Kevin and I. We both have an early exit the next day.

I can fill two or three bags each day. I earn $1000 in a week. It is enough to buy a green Chevy pickup truck.

It is worth the effort. Suddenly, we are finished with that first chapter of poverty. So begins a new chapter of our life story.

Value

Transportation means Kevin gets to work in 15 minutes! And comes back home! He's not exhausted!

Transportation means I don't have to carry water! I'm not exhausted!

Transportation means we can bring firewood, get groceries, go to the laundromat, go for help, even go places for fun!

Transportation means we can start the next part of our Plan. Have a bunch of kids: check!

Family Travel 1981-2003

Plan

Kevin likes to explore locally. Our children benefit from hiking and snowmobiling, swimming and canoeing, hunting and long drives up in the mountains.

I like to travel afar. Our children also benefit from airports and subways, museums and city sights, taxis and tour buses.

Exchange

In order for our children to know their grandparents, aunts, uncles and cousins, I have to pack them up and trek across the continent. I budget so the total for transportation evens out to $100 per day. We stay with relatives, enjoy their hospitality, accept their invitations to the pool, zoo, beach, and movies.

Kevin's wages can't stretch that far. I have a secret stash: every month, I get a 'Family Allowance' check in the mail from the Canadian Government. It is meant to be used for the benefit of the children. Then there is a sizable annual check from the Income Tax return.

Every penny I own is set aside for an annual jaunt. It's a worthwhile exchange.

And away we go!

$ $ 1000 $ $

And then there were gifts to provide for travel.

1987
An anonymous donor paid for me to attend my sister's wedding with Elise, who was a flower-girl, and Baby Toby, who was still nursing.

1995
My Dad, upon retirement, was given an unexpected bonus which he gave to me, which immediately transformed into tickets for all four children and I to visit all of the grandparents. It was the last time we saw Daddy alive.

$ $ 1000 $ $

Sometimes I was invited to travel. When one of my siblings planned a trip to Spain, or Africa, or Armenia, or Hawaii, or Italy, I was recruited to provide child care for their children at their home. In exchange all of my travel expenses were paid. I was eager to agree!

Value
Toronto. Tampa. Philadelphia. New York City. Colorado Springs. I have lived in each of these places. I have relatives in each of these places. I have taken our children to each of these places. We board planes, feast on new experiences, collect memories and souvenirs, phone Kevin at home, and make memories while knitting the family together.

There are benefits. When the grandparents and other relatives come visit us, the children are comfortable, eager, connected. When the generous gifts arrive for birthday and Christmas, the children know who the gifts came from and who their thank-you notes are going to.

Even in their school studies, all of this travelling yields another benefit. The children can better understand the history and geography of the places they learn about. They have seen oceans, deserts, farm lands, mountains, canyons, dams, forts, skyscrapers, statues, museums. Each ecosystem supports different kinds of animal and plant life and the resulting resources are available to meet the needs of the aboriginal peoples.

Perhaps the best benefit of all, when the time comes for the children to travel alone, they have experience, confidence and safety skills to last a lifetime. Away to Europe! Sailing on the Caribbean! Zig-zag across North America. And even back home to visit us with the grandchildren.

Another generation begins the tradition. Hurrah for Travel!

40-Day Cousin Quest 2014
Plan

January 1, 2014.

Wait. Let me think.

1934 to 2014.

My mother is turning 80 this year!

We have to plan a family reunion!

My brother, James, lives in England. "Will you be coming to the USA any time in 2014?"

"Yes! I can be in Colorado on May 15th."

Let me look at the calendar. Our youngest son, Toby, is graduating from university with a degree in architecture on May 8th in Atlanta, Georgia! How in the world could I get

June Chapter 2   Departures... Arrivals : $1000

from Avola, BC, to Atlanta, Georgia and then to Colorado Springs, Colorado?

Exchange

"Kevin," I informed my husband, "If I can do it for $1000, I'm going to go."

I used to make an appointment with a travel agent to arrange flights. Now I know how to look for flight information on-line. It looks like it will be well over $1000. Ouch!

What if I take Amtrak? Or Greyhound? I could stop along the way. See all the relatives I said good-bye to when they came to our wedding so many years ago?

I used to ask the price of a train or bus ticket by talking on the telephone with an automated voice. Now I can gather information and make all of my own arrangements, book tickets and even pay for everything with my computer.

I make maps and lists, phone calls and charts. Tally up the money. Late night connections. Ideal rendezvous. Look for shortcuts. It seems like the puzzle pieces just might fit together.

"Kevin! I think I can do the whole thing for just over $1000!"

Email messages. Phone calls. Is this exchange worth it? For me? For them? Of course!

I am going on a '40-Day Cousin Quest.'

I know how to pack. I want to be able to carry all of my own luggage. I use an old trick: wear a bulky sweater and puffy vest and my raincoat when boarding the plane, bus or train. Then I won't need a larger backpack. I can use the puffy vest as a pillow and the sweater as a blanket when I nap while I ride.

I have neither a cell phone nor portable digital music, but I do own a digital camera. When I get home, I will be able to show my husband where and what and who I have seen.

My husband draws me close when it is time for me to leave. "Although I am not coming with you," he repeats his

Saturday, June 17, 1978...Wednesday, June 11, 2014

usual blessing, "make sure they know that *you* are my gift to everyone. And here," he hands me a beautiful, blank journal. The cover is decorated with silver and turquoise swirls. "Each person you meet can write a greeting. Then you can give this to your Mom for her birthday."

Treasure!

Value

How can I possibly remember the people, places, events, sequences and emotions of this 40-Day Cousin Quest? How can I synthesize what I have heard, observed, pondered, become aware of? All of the life-stories I have been told, the complexity of decisions, interactions, successes, grief, celebration, new branches on the family tree.

I challenge myself to write a column for the local newspaper.

> Date: June 2, 2014
> Column: "It Seems to Me"
> Title: "Cousin Quest"
> by, Eleanor Deckert
>
> At some point one becomes aware of one's mortality.
>
> For me, that moment is now: my Mother is turning 80, my Dad is already gone. My husband has outlived his Father. I am older now than photos of my Grandmother. Several aunts and uncles have left this world... It all makes me want to be with my extended family, to reminisce, to laugh, to catch-up, to better understand my own Family Tree.
>
> And so, I embarked on a 'Cousin Quest.' Booking Greyhound, Amtrak and airplane tickets online, whipping out my Visa card, paying it all off with online banking.

June Chapter 2   Departures... Arrivals : $1000

Through 21 states, making 22 stops, sleeping in 29 different beds, for 40 days, I collected hugs from 58 relatives.

Interesting Family History: Oma emigrated from Germany when her older sister became ill and gave up her ticket! Opa was a chauffeur when he first arrived in the USA. Grammie buried her mother, daughter and sister within a year. Grampa moved the family again and again looking for translating and editing and proofreading work.

Many of my cousins (like Opa) are self-employed. I was able to tour and pester them with questions. I trimmed bamboo in Washington to feed the elephants, toured a maple sugar bush in Vermont, gathered eggs and held baby turkeys in Colorado. In North Carolina I helped corral horses who knew the electric fence was off.

Physical fitness is high on the to-do list of many cousins and together we: hiked Haystack Mountain in Vermont, Pilot Mountain in North Carolina, and to the Cascade Falls in Colorado. I attended Silver Sneakers, NIA and Tai Chi classes.

Food! We had Mexican, Sushi, Italian, Tacos, steak, grilled veggie wraps, BBQ, family favourites, cheese cake (I don't know how many times), peach cobbler, and a fabulous Mother's Day brunch prepared by my son in Atlanta.

I laughed with my first grandchild, cried when my youngest child graduated with a degree in architecture, filled my heart with choir music, remained silently still in the Adoration chapel, and cheered while my Mother blew out her 80 birthday candles.

Visiting widowed Aunts and an Uncle who will be leaving the world soon drew me closer to the cousins I share sweet memories with.

It seems to me that cousins are my favourite people. Generous, skilled, focused on faith and family traditions, bonded through our story, name and character qualities. Each and together I love them all.

Saturday, June 17, 1978...Wednesday, June 11, 2014

$ $ 1000 $ $

A contented man is one who enjoys the scenery along the detours.
—George Herbert

On a more personal level, over many days, I turned the bits and pieces of individual stories this way and that, recognizing and connecting similarities and seeing the patterns in the collection of details.

As a child I asked my mother and father, "Our family is pretty special. We have no physical deformities, no one is in jail, no tragedy or danger. Right?" They assured me, "Yes."

But, now, decades later, veil pulled back, listening to more open communication, I see:

Beyond the blushing bride in the wedding portraits there is also violence, adultery, divorce, step-families, half-siblings. Beyond the bright children's faces there are some with disabilities, mental health issues, flashes of genius and depths of depression. Beyond the robust health and excellent fitness for some, others are dealing with accidents, surgeries, obesity, alcoholism, drug addiction, Parkinsons, Alzheimers, diabetes, cancer. Beyond the musical talent, the artistic paint brush, the embroidery, knitting and crochet, there is also isolation and grief. Beyond the holiday traditions and family customs there are also sons who left home slamming the door behind them, daughters who do not speak to mothers, divisions among siblings, Christmas dinners with empty chairs, and, perhaps saddest of all, Oma's funeral could not be held because of religious differences, her ashes scattered from a favourite high place overlooking a green valley.

And yet, we are bound together! Each of my cousins walks along their own Path, comes to a crossroads, makes a decision and faces whatever consequences come. Each individual searches their heart, fills their mind, looks back at their own youth, looks ahead to the horizon, takes practical daily actions and seeks guidance from a Higher Power.

Somehow, all of these stories weave together. Somehow we are each doing the best we can with what we have. No one gets up in the morning intending to cause damage, and yet, there is hurt. Hopefully, somehow, maybe, there will be progress, reconciliation, acceptance, blessing.

Beyond the photos of bounding children there are doctors and lawyers, professors and health care workers, army, navy and air force members, entrepreneurs and authors, speakers and coaches, labourers and adventurers. Talents were inherited, developed and put to good use. Couples wed. Children were born. Families thrived. The cycle continues.

One More Thing
One-Way Trip
June 11, 2014

No matter how clearly you know it will happen, it is still a shock to get the phone call.

Uncle Ronald has died.

When I was four years old, he brought me a pair of wooden shoes from his trip to Europe. His face and voice and mannerisms are forever in my eyes and ears and heart.

I'm so glad I got to see him on my Cousin Quest. I'm so sad that he's gone.

And yet, there is an angel choir resounding within me, too. The iceberg that seemed to be permanently lodged between Uncle Ronald (the youngest rascally brother) and Aunt Grace (the straight-and-narrow-way eldest sister) simply vanished. When he realized he was ill, he asked if he could come and live out his days under her roof, she opened wide her door. It was not easy. But, the distance, cold and silence that has been between them, shifted into the warm reality of the family.

I will say this about the '40-Day Cousin Quest'. I travelled many miles and saw many people, all to rekindle and carry home with me that precious sense of belonging.

And, like every other trip, there is the loss of what you leave behind and the gain of what lies ahead. Uncle Ronald has made that last one-way trip. I believe that somewhere in the 'Great Beyond' he has found what every seeker strives for: that satisfying sense of belonging.

To read more about how Covid-19 impacted Eleanor's travels...
... turn to 10 Days in July Chapter 2, page 291.

But Wait! There's More
Eleanor shares a family-friendly game about travelling in Canada.

BONUS: Seminar #2
Canada Name Game

... since 1996

a traditional rhythm game for 2 players
(of course you can play with names from any country)

Canada Name Game
This is a game for two people.
Seated or standing, face each other.
Clap with this rhythm:

    1 (palms face and clap with the other person)
    2 (each person clap their own hands together)
    1..2..1..2

While keeping this clapping rhythm, they take turns, each says the words using the same letter to tell each part of the story.

Start with "A" and continue, taking turns. Next person speaks with "B" and so on.

Here are the words:

"My name is ___. My husband's name is ___.
We live in ___. And we sell ___."
Example:
"My name is Alice. My husband's name is Allan.
We live in Alberta. And we sell apples."

A
Alberta
Armstong British Columbia

B
British Columbia
Bona Vista Newfoundland

C
Coppermine Northwest Territories
Corner Brook Newfoundland

D
Drumheller Alberta
Dalhousie New Brunswick

E
Edmonton Alberta
Emerson Manitoba

F
Flin Flon Manitoba
Fort Good Hope Northwest Territories

G
Gander Newfoundland
Goose Bay Newfoundland

H
Head Smashed in Buffalo Jump Alberta
High River Alberta

I
Indian Head Saskatchewan
Iroquois Falls Ontario

J
Joliette Quebec
Mont Joli Quebec

K
Kamloops British Columbia
Kapuskasing Ontario

L
Labrador
New London Prince Edward Island

M
Manitoba
Moose Jaw Saskatchewan

N
New Brunswick
Nova Scotia
Northwest Territories
Newfoundland
Nunavut

O
Ontario
Ottawa Ontario

P
Prince Edward Island
Prince George British Columbia

Q
Quebec
Quebec City Quebec

R
Regina Saskatchewan
Red River Manitoba

S
Saskatchewan
Saskatoon Saskatchewan

T
Twillingate Newfoundland
Tuktoyuktuk Northwest Territories

U
Unity Saskatchewan
Ugava Bay Quebec

V
Fort Vermilion Alberta
Valleyfield Quebec

W
White Horse Yukon
Westpoint Prince Edward Island

Y
Yellowknife Northwest Territories
Yukon

Z
Zoar Newfoundland

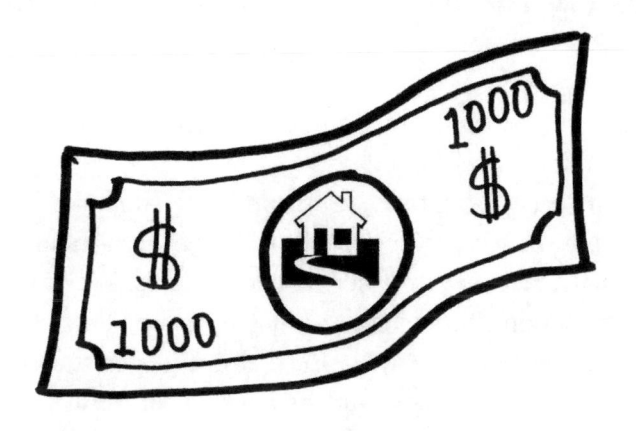

Chapter 3
Monday, June 2, 1980
Log Cabin Lifestyle
Three Pay Cheques : $1000...
First Loan : $1000

> I went to the woods
> because I wished to live deliberately,
> to front only the essential facts of life,
> and see if I could not learn what it had to teach,
> and not, when I came to die,
> discover that I had not lived.
> —*Henry David Thoreau*

Before we begin
'Home'
    Now, there's a topic!
    Does 'House' mean the same thing as 'Home'?

During those early years, and even to this day, I often say to Kevin, "*You* are my 'Home.'"

By the usual definition, Kevin and I were 'homeless' for the first 6 months of our marriage, living in the VW van and when it got cold, sleeping in other people's houses. When we had the satisfaction of moving into our tiny cabin, it was barely a shelter to keep out the snow. The cracks between the logs and floor boards did not keep out the merry breezes! Although we had deliberately decided to build a one-room log cabin with no running water, no electricity, no telephone, we did not expect the bitter cold to result in the temperature indoors dropping well below freezing day and night for three weeks.

Plan
1978 How hard could it be?

How the west was won includes that first, primitive structure to live in, built by a lone man, using materials found on the land. Soddies on the prairie. Log cabins in the forest.

In the autumn of 1978, while I earned $2.57 an hour as a waitress at the truck stop beside the highway, Kevin worked in the mountains alone, felling dead standing cedar trees left from a previous forest fire, shaping the notches with his axe, wrestling the logs into place. We paid cash with my earnings bit-by-bit as we went along, to buy spikes and nails, lumber for the roof and floor, tar paper and a chimney. The whole thing cost $300 and took 4 months to build.

But that first harsh winter told us the truth. As romantic as a log cabin is, we needed to build a better house if we were going to provide for little babies.

$ $ $ 1000 $ $

April, 1979
Dear Lori,

I am alone in the cabin. Kevin got a job! It is such a long day to be home alone, but now I have time to write letters to my family and friends back east.

Let me start here: On March 27, 1979, everything changed. All winter, Kevin has been hitch-hiking to town every week to get the mail and phone the railroad boss asking for a job. Last month, Steve, the Road Master, drove his big orange 4x4 CN truck along the road near our cabin. Kevin was nearby, cutting brush. The boss stopped when he saw Kevin, rolled down the window and in his Polish accent call out, "Are you the fellow looking for work on the railroad?"

"Yes!"

"Are you a hippy or a farmer?"

This question came because there are lots of hippies in BC. Some 'Back-to-Nature' people grow their own marijuana and brew their own beer. Poor work performance means that the Road Master hires and fires men pretty fast.

"I'm a Farmer."

"Then come to work Monday at 7:00."

"I have no vehicle."

"We'll come get you at the crossing. Be there. We'll pick you up."

What a huge change! A steady income! We had to wait 2 weeks while he worked, then 2 more weeks to process and mail the cheque. His first pay cheque arrived at the same time as his unemployment cheque and also his income tax return. $1000!

We could pay Howard more of what we owe him for the land. We can buy FOOD! Kevin also bought two essential things: a chain saw and a bicycle!

This morning, very early, I made biscuits on the frying pan with cheese melted inside for Kevin's lunch. While he is gone to work, I will continue to clear brush with my hatchet. I'm dragging the branches into a huge pile to burn. I am also removing obstacles, like rocks and bushes and fallen logs so I don't trip when I am carrying water buckets up from the river.

Just a minute. I hear the dog barking...

You will never believe it! When I went out to see what it was, there was a bear! They are coming out of hibernation now. I thought, "I will test myself and see if I can remember how to use the gun when I am nervous." I loaded and aimed for a small sapling. I got a good shot at the tree and the bear ran away from the noise of the gun.

Whenever I go outside, I always whistle, sing, or talk loudly to myself. So far I have only ever seen the rump of a bear, never one walking towards me.

All winter it was easy to get water. I just stepped outside with my pots and pans and scooped up clean snow to melt on the wood-stove.

Since all of the snow has melted now, I need to go to the river for water. I made a good path along the flat place through the brush, then it gets very shady and dark through the cedar forest, then down, down, steeply to the river. There are fallen, rotten logs overgrown with thick, damp, slippery moss. Not good footing. So I made steps. The river is shallow there with lots of big rocks so I am safe. It smells wet and mossy and the mica makes silver sparkles in the sand. My big dog, Sam, is with me. So I feel perfectly safe.

I have two plastic water buckets, both with lids. One bucket is 3 gallons, from the delicious honey we bought. The other one holds 5 gallons, which is way too heavy if it is full, so I take what I can carry. I scoop up water, snap on the lids, grip the handles, swing the buckets up left, step up... right, step up, so I'm not actually carrying their weight, but swinging them, using the weight of the water to my advantage. Keeping a steady rhythm all the way up and pausing at the top while I catch my breath.

When it gets to be summer, I'll have to stop to swat mosquitoes, but now I just keep going to get the water to the cabin.

On the way back, the hot sun gets me thinking. "I am like women all over the world, all through time, and even today who have to carry their water and walk so far. Women's work. Men's work. Someone has to go out. Someone has to stay home. Who will carry the water, tend the fire, make the food, care for the children, and keep the house safe? The woman is the one to stay home."

Then I thought, "I'd better not get pregnant while I have this heavy load to carry every day. I sure don't want to have a miscarriage!"

I am very thrifty with water. Of course we need to drink and cook. But, when I wash dishes I am careful to start with the clean things (cups and silverware) then bowls and plates, last the pots and pans. Usually I wash off the sticky, oily stuff and wait to wash them again next time to get them really clean.

When I wash my hair, I let the water drain into the basin, then use that to wash myself. I decided to take the laundry to the river. But I pour the soapy water up onto the land, not directly back into the river.

Well, that's about all for my daily life.

Good News! My Mom and Dad and little sister, Carol, are planning to come in August. And I might get a job in September. Us hippies get hired to pick pine cones. You can earn $1000 in a week! Then we can buy a truck!

June 2, 1980
Dear Lori,

Here's another homesteading story I can tell you. Sometimes a specific moment is crystal clear. I will always remember exactly where and when and why Cheryl and Kevin and I were standing in the dark, damp cellar and what we were doing on June 2, 1980.

It was just getting to be twilight. I was up at Brooksong (Cheryl and Fran's place in Avola). I always have to stay with other people anytime Kevin was away because I am largely pregnant (for the first time) and due at any moment.

Kevin went out hunting for the first time since we decided not to be vegetarians anymore.

Just as the day was closing, Kevin drove in... with a BEAR!

I was so large in the belly and really shouldn't be lifting anything, so Cheryl and Kevin wrestled the heavy load out of the truck, across the kitchen, through a trap door, and down the stairs to the dirt cellar. Kevin found a way to hang the carcass up-side-down from a beam in the very low ceiling.

Kevin was like: "I'm a hero. I brought food for my family. I am successful. This is important."

I was like, "Wow, I said I was going to eat meat again. I said I was going to eat meat that was hunted. I said I was going to eat whatever wild animal Kevin brought in... but really? a BEAR!?!"

Cheryl was like: "OK these are my friends. I can hardly say, 'No.' I have to help, obviously. (yuck) Here goes! Be brave!"

So, I stand around in my white hand-embroidered maternity blouse saying, "Wow!" and "O my!" and "Isn't this wonderful!" (Meanwhile, trying not to be grossed out by my first look at a whole, raw, red, body of hanging meat...)

Kevin is struggling with nails and rope and hooks and making a plan that will work.

Cheryl is trying to seem like this is no big deal.

I am trying to both remember every detail (for the book I will write someday and someday I will tell the child I am carrying about this pre-birth adventure). Meanwhile, I am trying *not* to see, hear, look, or remember *anything* as the body of the bear (after the fur is removed) looks almost exactly like a human! The shape of the rib cage, the proportion of the arms and legs, the joints and even feet! We are all having a nightmarish anatomy lesson down in this creepy basement!

Cheryl goes up to 'check on the children' who are in bed. She is gone for awhile, so I go check to see if everything is OK. I find her out on the porch gaining a little courage from a few puffs of... well... I can't really say!

That, indeed, is an especially memorable homesteading moment.

And yes. I ate it. And yes, bear meat was actually good!

Exchange
First Loan : $1000

I sure have mixed feelings about taking out a loan.

1980

While I was pregnant, we started to build the larger, warmer house so that when the baby came, mid-summer, we could make it through the winter in comfort.

It is a 'stackwall' house, which means that the walls will be over a foot thick! Kevin cut slender poles of pine. I peeled off the bark with a draw knife, then marked the lengths with a yellow wax marker. He cut them with the chainsaw, and we stacked the pieces ready to use. Kevin bought two gas powered water pumps and 400 feet of hose to bring water up from the river. We borrowed a gas powered cement mixer. There was the right kind of gravel close by that we shovelled into the pickup truck. Every payday we bought more bags of cement. When all the supplies were ready, we made a few rounds every day, cementing the layers of wood as the walls slowly got higher. We left gaps open for the window and door frames.

June Chapter 3   Three Pay Cheques : $1000... First Loan : $1000

After Elise was born, we kept working on the house all summer. The downstairs floor joists were all cemented into place and Kevin made a way to hold the upstairs floor joists in place by nailing them to up-right poles.

But, in the autumn it started to rain. We covered everything with black plastic, but it never got dry enough to continue. I had to go back to Ontario with the baby to stay with my parents for the whole winter.

$ $ 1000 $ $

Kevin survived alone. He worked on the railroad all day, came home to the frigid cabin, made himself a fire and supper, then let the fire go out while he slept. That cold cabin was the start to another day. I honestly don't know how he made it.

$ $ 1000 $ $

1981

In April, I returned with the baby. That summer, my brother, James, and Matthew, a neighbour from the church community back east, came to work for us. The walls are done and the floor joists fit in just great. The floor boards make it feel like a real house! The framing is ready for the barn roof. We bought sky lights which will be fantastic to provide light upstairs. Kevin has built the window frames and door. We have Plexiglas from an old hockey rink for windows.

There is just one problem. So far it has worked out just fine to buy what we need as we go along. But, this won't work for the roof. We have to put up the tin roof and insulation all at once. And the summer is rapidly turning to fall. Winter is on the way... and so is another baby!

Monday, June 2, 1980

We decide to take out our first loan. We need $600 for the sheets of tin roofing, and $400 more for lumber and insulation. $1000. In debt!

It is a strange sensation. But, the house is ready as the snow begins to fall.

DIY
Homesteading
Food

The original dream to 'build a log cabin' also included the idea of growing our own food, and as much Do-It-Yourself as possible. It took awhile for city-girl Me to learn. But, eventually, I made it happen.

The soil near the cabin and stackwall house was kind of gritty. Our vegetable garden didn't amount to much. Plus, we didn't intend to raise a family so far from other people. And to finally tip the balance, we found marijuana growing on the property we shared with others. Sad, but true. It was time to leave.

We moved into town so our kids could go to school.

We rented a little four-room place from a kindly old man for $150 per month, 'rent-to-own' and eventually paid off the $5000 the owner was asking. The soil was great and my gardening skills yielded a significant amount of food for the freezer, jam, canning jars and root cellar.

In 1987, an elderly couple who lived down by the river offered to sell us their house and two acres for only $7000! Yes, please!

$ $ 1000 $ $

By now we had four kids, all learning, all helping, all knowing that our food comes from the chickens, pig and garden. Elise raised rabbits and learned to roll out pie dough. Michael gathered the eggs and fetched supplies from the root cellar. Nicholas hilled the potatoes and experimented with cookie recipes. Toby picked berries and measured ingredients for bread, pickles and jam.

Yes, we have electricity now, running water (gravity feed from a fast flowing mountain stream), TV, a telephone, computer and washer and dryer. So, there are bills to pay.

And yet, I think it is safe to say that the homesteading lifestyle has been a success.

1996

When my Daddy died and his Will was read, we learned that all five of us siblings had inherited the house and land in Colorado that we loved so dearly. Although our family had left nearly 30 years ago, we still called Colorado 'Home.'

My sister, Julie, took action, moved her family there to live permanently, and divided the value of the property equally with each of us siblings.

2000-2001

With my share of the inheritance, I made a few improvements to our home (new bathroom and kitchen), and decided to use the bulk of the money to go back to the church college in Bonnie Hills, Pennsylvania for one year. I paid my tuition and also the full year's rent for a small basement apartment. Elise and Michael had already been provided for through generous grants, and were already living in the college dormitories. It was good to interact with them on campus. Nicholas and Toby lived with me and went to the church elementary school. Their tuition was magically waived. Kevin stayed home in Canada, sending frequent emails, phone calls and wishing us all well with our endeavours.

I mention this interruption because one of the courses I took was a combination of: Psychology, Sociology, and Anthropology, all focused on family and the 'Home.'

My final project was to write about a series of photographs. Family homes had been emptied of their contents. All of their belongings were on display in front of the camera. A wealthy Texas rancher, a tiny Japanese apartment, a yurt in Mongolia, a shepherd's hut in the Sahara, a Norwegian reindeer hide tent, a New York City high-rise, an inherited country estate in the green hillsides of England.

Who is 'wealthy'? I had to choose one family and write a 3000 word essay to demonstrate my understanding of the facets of the meaning of 'home.'

Anthropology How does this home provide what all people need? shelter from the climate, safety, places for family members to sleep, disposal of waste, provision for birth and death, privacy for sexual activity, source of heat for cooking and warmth, food storage, food preparation, supply of water, resources for the future, defence.

Sociology How does this society compare status symbols such as the materials used in the construction of the home, and the monetary or cultural value of the furnishings?

Psychology What is the meaning of this home for these family members? Look at details such as colours, decorations, keepsakes. What emotional pressures might family members have in this home? What adjustments have been made to accommodate for gender, child development, generational connections and ethnic customs? What kind of stories might these family members tell about their home?

This experience gave me a view of my own life, decisions and priorities. I felt a strong sense of satisfaction for the domestic work I had been doing to make a 'Home' for myself, my husband and our children since I first made curtains for the VW van as a young bride so long ago.

One More Thing
My Tiny Cabin
2020

How quickly the children grow up and leave home. How much our house seems too big, too quiet and soooo empty. Soon Kevin retired. What new projects will we find to occupy our time and make use of our talents?

"How would you like me to build you another cabin?" Kevin asked with a twinkle in his eye.

Gradually, using found, made and salvaged materials, he has built me a small version of our first cabin. The upright cedar logs and moss in the cracks were just like the old cabin. The tin roof was pieces a neighbour gave us. The mis-matched windows were found here and there as neighbours offered items to help with the project. The skylight we already had. The only expenses were the plywood floor, insulation, and lumber ceiling. And one more thing: Kevin made the porch with a skylight from clear sheets of roofing. What bliss to enjoy the forest and sky! All together, we estimate it cost under $1000. And, in a flash, I realized another delicious detail.

I ran inside, and returned with the hand made woven brown poncho. I bought it when we were engaged. But in 42 years, I have rarely worn it. (Autumn, the perfect time for a poncho, is also hunting season. I didn't want to be strolling through the forest paths all dressed in brown!)

So now, I can be cozy in my poncho, relaxed in the chill, bathed in sunshine, at home in the woods.

Thank-you, Husband.

You are my home!

And I love my cabin!

I go there in the afternoon to read and Journal. I enjoy the forest from the screened-in porch. The skylight shows me the stars when I sleep there. I soak in the sense of satisfaction as I time-travel in my mind, scanning the years, pulling forward happy times, dwelling on details, hearing voices and seeing faces in my memory.

After a quiet hour, I return to the house, our Home, and continue to type type type, focused on finishing this memoir.

To read more about how Eleanor's lifestyle changed in 2020...
... turn to 10 Days in July Chapter 3, page 295.

But Wait! There's More

> The price of anything
> is the amount of life you exchange for it.
> —*Henry David Thoreau*

Since our wedding in 1978, I have rarely earned money. A few hours a week. A few months a year. Here and there. Start and stop. Fortunately, my husband has had steady employment.

Sometimes I was paid by the hour. Sometimes I was crafty and sold things I made. Usually I found ways to get what we needed without using money at all.

After years of building a house, making it a home, having a family, strengthening traditions, and volunteering, I have developed this seminar which I would like to share with you!

BONUS: Seminar #3
14 Economies for Tough Times

... since 2008

> People, for the sake of getting a living
> forget to live.
> —Margaret Fuller

I have always found the topic of 'money' rather confusing. How can one hour of my time and effort be worth such-and-such amount of money, and yet, this valuable project I am focused on, spending hours of my time and talent, have no measurable value at all? Keeping this quandary in mind as I started my adult life, I have noticed many kinds of exchange and ways to obtain what is needed.

People ask me, "How can you raise a family on just one wage?"

I started to think about that and I realized that I do fourteen deliberate things that make me feel wealthy and supply all of my family's needs, satisfy my creativity and provide stimulating opportunities.

During forty years of homemaking with a husband and four kids I have learned from the wisdom and experience of 'little-old-ladies' who have taught me many practical skills, short cuts and thrifty habits while raising a family.

I gladly share what I have learned so that others might benefit from my trials and errors, successes and accomplishments.

Economy #1: Second Hand

Clothing, furniture, appliances, dishes, pots and pans, and almost every household item you need is OK to use 'Second Hand.' Every car and truck we have ever had, snow pants, skates, toys, books, tools, TV and other equipment...yup... it was all acquired after some other person bought it brand new. Cameras, snow-blower, hobby equipment, musical instruments... the list goes on-and-on.

Where does one find such marvellous Second Hand items? I look in Thrift Stores. How fun to find the exact shirt to match with the rest of an outfit! How clever to stash items for a hobby project or next year's winter clothing.

Now, with the internet, almost every object you can find brand new is also available through 'Buy and Sell' sites.

Sometimes you have to wait. But it saves enormous amounts of money and it makes sense to 'Reduce. Re-use. Recycle.'

And then there are friendly neighbours who pass things along. Say, "Thanks!" In a world which loudly encourages consumerism, it feels bold and independent to reach for 'new-to-you' items and by-pass standing in line at the mall.

Economy #2: Gifts

Giving: It feels pretty easy to give things away when you have plenty. However, the most generous people I have ever come across are the people who have the least. Examples: Overnight hospitality from a person who lives in one room. Meals offered by a person who walks to the grocery store.

'Enough' and 'not enough' seem to be a state of mind more than what is in the cupboard.

Asking: Is it OK to ask for what you need? A hug? Time? A favour?

When my Dad phones to ask "What are the children interested in? What would they like for Christmas or a Birthday?" He appreciates it when I answer with a list of current hobbies, studies, projects and questions they are asking. With so many advertisements pulling their attention this-way-and-that, it is helpful to aid Grandparents in their quest to find ways to convey affection to their grandchildren. And when the gift giving is satisfying for both parties, the bond is strengthened in the giving and in the receiving.

Receiving: Can you remember a day when you forgot to bring your lunch to school? How dreadful! Do you remember how wonderful it was when someone offered to share what they had with you? 'Pay it forward' is a way to live. 'Re-Gifting' is a trend.

Economy #3: Learn From Others

Does having knowledge save you money? Let's think of some examples: If you know a short cut, then you can save gas. If you know a recipe and can make something yummy from scratch, then you don't have to pay more for store-bought. If you know how to cut hair, change a tire, fix a bicycle, knit or mend or sew... then you won't have to pay others to do this work for you.

So how can you add to your knowledge?

To learn more there is: research, trial-and-error, a friend can show you... or you can pay someone to teach you the skill.

I learned homesteading skills by working side-by-side with women who were more experienced. Knead bread. Pluck a chicken. Sterilize canning jars. Dry fruit. Flip pancakes. Freeze popsicles. Transplant seedlings. Milk goats. Cut meat.

I have also paid for courses to teach me skills which would bring in money or save money. Self-employment. Driver training. Quilting. Computer skills.

After you know how, you won't have to pay for that work ever again.

Economy #4: Do-it-Yourself

Recently the influx of 'Back-to-the-Land' and 'Off Grid' folks renewed the interest in learning how to do things with your own hands. Muscle. Wits. Experience. Problem Solving.

We cut our own grass. We haul our own firewood. We repair, maintain, renovate our own home and vehicles. I cut the kids' hair and make bread, jam and gifts. My husband does the snow removal and many other tasks.

There is a satisfaction that money can't buy. I love teaching my children to work in the garden, look after the animals, repair and bake and sew and mend. It starts when they are so young with bringing the kindling.

Economy #5: >FREE<

Once I was so broke at Christmastime that I went to the library and took out two books for each of my siblings. I wrapped them and put them under the tree! (and returned them to the library on time)

There are SO many free things to enjoy if you look around.

Look at these 'coupons' my son made one Christmas.

Let your imagination bring you new ideas! For free!

The coupons in this book allow the holder to cash in any of the advertised products any time between 8am and 7pm	Feeling down? FREE COMPLIMENTS! Two compliments will cheer you up in moments!
100% off ALL IN-STOCK HUGS! Hugs for any occasion! (use only once)	FREE IDEA Catch an excellent brain-wave right from the source!
FREE SIGNATURE One day, when I'm famous, that signature will be worth $Fifty-Grand$	One Item of Trivial Knowledge! ABSOLUTELY FREE! Use anytime you want to: ask, and an amazing, astonishing, pointless fact will be given.

Economy #6: Belong to a Group

When you are alone, you do the same things the same way. When you belong to a group you hear new ideas, ask, learn and do new things. No money is gone but much is gained.

I've been making quilts since I was 17 years old. But as soon as I joined the quilt group, I started to learn so much just by walking around looking, asking, sharing. Preparing the cloth, tools to use, even how to iron properly.

And they learned from my tips, too!

When you are alone, some problems are too much to solve. Some projects are too big to do. Some work too difficult. When you belong to a group there are many hands. The load is lighter. 'Great minds' offer suggestions. The experience of others speeds progress. You didn't hire but the job got done.

Lifting while building, digging a water line, clearing land, rushing to get firewood after a season of recuperation. These are times when we need the neighbours or the friendly assistance from a group we already belong to. When several people 'lend a hand' everyone benefits from a job well and cheerfully done.

When you are alone how much fun are you having? You pay out money for entertainment, comfort food and pretty things.

When you belong to a group laughter is contagious, fun is spontaneous. You feel enriched without making your wallet any thinner.

It feels a bit awkward to join an existing group. But with a little experimentation, it will be possible to explore or start a new collection of people you like to be with.

Remember, this is a part of your thrifty thinking. Look for ways your family economy will benefit from group participation and working together.

Economy #7: Do Without

Yipes! Did I really say that?

Well, yes I did!

Consumerism drives us into thinking we need x-y-and-z... Really? Someone is manufacturing 'stuff' so that you will buy it - so that it will go out of fashion - so that you will throw the first one away - so that you will line up to buy another, newer one!

I remember giving my sons a lecture on this topic. It went something like this, "See those t-shirts, slippers, towels, toothbrushes all with the guy from the new TV show or movie? Someone made aaaallll that stuff with that guy's picture on it ahead of time to be ready so that as soon as the movie came out then aaaalllll of the 4-8-11 year old boys who *begged* to see the movie would also *beg* to buy the stuff with that guy's picture on it... They are reaching into your pockets and trying to tug out your money!"

Tweens (children aged 8-14) have an enormous amount of buying power at present. With single, divorced, re-married, blended, two-pay check families, these kids have four parents and eight grandparents (maybe more) all offering gifts and/or spending money. This demographic of kids has more money coming towards them than at any time in our history. Marketing is something to think about and talk about in your family.

Meanwhile: what are some of the things we can 'do without' to stretch our dollar and leave unnecessary purchases behind? I watched a talk show about budgeting. One lady saved $100 per week by learning how to decorate her own fingernails instead of going to the salon!

Processed food and eating out, fancy coffees and other drinks are luxuries which we can 'do without' or learn to make from scratch.

Can you discipline yourself to 'do without' the newest gadget or improvement and wait until the price goes down? Can you 'do without' vacation expenses and have a 'stay-cation' this year? Plan a holiday to explore where you live.

Economy #8: What do I really need?
You've already seen this chart, no doubt.

The point is: only the bottom two rows are concrete, physical things that you need to buy. Everything else is a state of mind. Invisible, real things that we need. More money does not always equal more 'value.'

No matter how much more 'stuff' I buy, I won't actually be meeting those intangible, invisible needs. Spending more and more money isn't the way to get those higher needs met. I have to go 'inside.' How do I do that? Build and strengthen relationships. Learn. Give. Believe. Try. Join in. Risk caring for someone. Do some 'soul searching.'

Maslow's Hierarchy of Needs

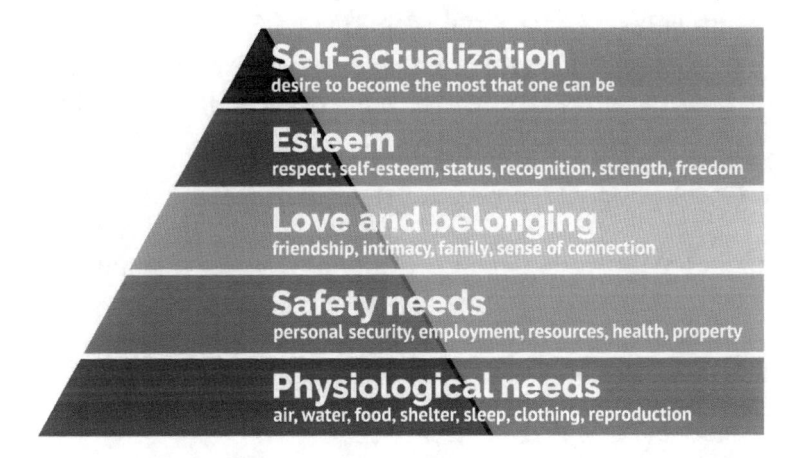

Self-actualization
desire to become the most that one can be

Esteem
respect, self-esteem, status, recognition, strength, freedom

Love and belonging
friendship, intimacy, family, sense of connection

Safety needs
personal security, employment, resources, health, property

Physiological needs
air, water, food, shelter, sleep, clothing, reproduction

Economy #9: Keep the Family Together

Keeping the family together. This in itself is an economic advantage. Struggles, problem solving, compromises, stress, doubts, disagreements and hard times: these are all a part of the journey as we grow and change.

All families go through hard times. Staying together, helping each other, knowing you can do it makes you brave enough to 'keep on keeping on.'

Economy #10: Share an Experience

We all wish our wallets were a little thicker for gift giving. We express how much we value our family and friends through the gift we choose. Yet, no matter the price tag on the object *the invisible thing inside the gift is the real value: Love.*

What if we decided to express the intangible love in some other way besides a store-bought gift? What if we planned a Shared Experience together?

Shared Experience (face-to-face play) is how babies learn. Shared Experience (a snow day or a picnic) is how children and youth know we care about them. Shared Experience (a games night) is how families stay together. Shared Experience (a date) is how sweethearts show they are dedicated to each other. Shared Experience (a cup of tea) is the thing most highly prized by our elders and seniors.

Think of someone you know who might go on a fun outing if they had a ride. Pick up the phone. Make a connection. Giving your time and sharing the experience will bring you both a sense of wealth that no amount of money can buy.

Economy #11: Family Traditions

Family Traditions are Shared Experiences we deliberately repeat. Traditions come from customs passed from previous generations or from a religious or cultural heritage. Make memories. Highly valuable. No price tag. Smiles.

Celebrations might include lights, colours, sharing food, music, decorations and symbols. We tell stories. We go to great effort to make special days and bring people together.

Shared Experiences and Family Traditions are a lot of work. But it is all worth it!

Economy #12: A Steady Income

Well, the goal we all have is to establish a steady income we can rely on. Then you can make some solid decisions.

Whatever amount that steady, reliable income is: that is the amount to use to pay for those steady, predictable expenses.

To me it is sort of like the Serenity Prayer: What is the part that cannot change? What is the part that can change?

I use the wages that do not change to pay for the expenses that do not change. I use the flexible part of my income (let's say selling a craft item) to pay for an optional item (let's say more crafting supplies).

In this way a predictable balance is put in place.

Economy #13: Volunteer

Volunteering? How can giving away my time be a Thrifty thing to do? That seems like a contradiction. What could I possibly 'gain' by ignoring my 'per-hour' worth?

Let me tell you about some of my experiences.

I have volunteered with Moms and Tots by reading at the library and preparing a craft project. I didn't have to pay for anything (using the space, books or supplies) but I gained a very fun morning, made new friends and enjoyed the little ones.

I have volunteered as a Brownie leader. I didn't have to pay for anything (the leader's manual, craft supplies, camping gear, music, games, equipment) but I gained training (including my First Aid ticket), over-night outings to interesting places, respect from the girls and their parents and the Girl Guide community.

I have volunteered in a community choir. I gained fabulous friends, deeply appreciated the pieces of music, and did not pay for a ticket to the rest of the concert.

I volunteer in non-profit groups. It takes time. It takes commitment. But what might I be doing instead? I might *pay* for a class, or I can learn in the group. I could *pay* for a ticket to live entertainment, or I could make entertainment with the talent in the group. I might *pay* for a restaurant meal, or have fun while we prepare, enjoy and clean-up together.

I volunteer at church. I gain counsel, benefit from the music, enjoy the friendships, accumulate knowledge from the on-going instruction. I am blessed and bless others as we volunteer.

Yes, volunteering is a big part of my life and I am all the richer for it.

Economy #14: Barter

Time, talents, and objects all work as trade goods.

My hubby traded carpentry time with another fellow to pay him for improving our driveway with his machinery.

I've traded babysitting for furniture.

I have traded quilts for weeks of child care, a chest-of-drawers, and, best of all, I made a custom quilt to trade for my first car!

Neighbours do it all the time: you give me a ride and I look after your dog. You give me a haircut and I pass along fabric for your project. I have extra berries and you have extra peas.

It's fun. It's quick. It's surprising. It builds bonds. It builds trust.

The object, experience or service you obtain is linked to the person you traded with. A kind of tapestry is woven as you pass back and forth in the exchange. Bartering is so much more meaningful than a purchase from a store or catalogue.

Look around. What can you part with? What do you need? Who do you know? Interactions and connections and bartering can be part of your Thrifty Economy.

Chapter 4
Wednesday, June 7, 1995
A Talent for Teaching : $1000

> Great intelligence, vigour, strength of will,
> however marvellous
> produce nothing unless they are harnessed
> and given direction.
> Harnessing means restraint,
> and restraint means obedience
> and obedience means respect,
> perhaps love for someone or something
> other than one's self.
> —Robert Russell

Before we Begin
Time for a check-up on our 'Back-to-Basics' lifestyle.
- Get married: check!
- Go out west: check!
- Build a log cabin: check!

(Learn all of those 'Self-sufficiency' skills: check!)
Have a bunch of kids: check!
(Two so far... two more in the near future)
Teach them about the Lord......

Plan

1983

Since we decided to live in the middle of nowhere, I assumed there would be no church and therefore it would be up to me to give our children instruction. I had volunteer experience as a teenager teaching Sunday School, so I felt qualified.

Planning for this, I practised my guitar and learned Sunday School songs, ordered binders of lessons (the same ones my mother used to teach my siblings and I in Colorado when we were small), and kept my eyes open for puzzles and crafts suitable to illustrate Bible story lessons.

I decided to offer to teach all of the children in our wee little town. Somehow, people in seven different denominations from churches further down the valley heard about my attempt, and sent boxes of workbooks, flannel board figures, craft supplies, crayons, scissors, paint and paper. I also had permission to use the ditto machine at the school.

Voila!

I developed each lesson on the same format. After all, the instructions God gave to Moses are pretty precise.

> "Hear, O Israel: The Lord thy God, the Lord is one. You shall love the Lord your God *with all your heart and with all your soul and with all your strength.* These commandments that I give you today shall be on your heart. Teach them diligently to your children. You shall talk about them when you sit at home and when you walk along the road, when

Wednesday, June 7, 1995

you lie down and when you get up."
Deuteronomy 6: 4-7

... and Jesus repeated the same idea:

"Jesus said unto him, 'You shall love the Lord your God *with all your heart, and with all your soul, and with all your mind. This is the first and great commandment. And the second is like unto it. You shall love your neighbour as yourself. On these two commandments hang all the law and the prophets.'"*
Matthew 22: 37-40

I made sure that each lesson plan had nourishment for the mind (facts, vocabulary, maps), heart (music, art), soul (reverence, trust in God), body (5 senses, activities, acting).

First I told the story, added a song, and highlighted a memory verse. Then we acted it out. Next the children had a take-home page and we also worked on a group project (a book, mural or diorama). Now that the story was firmly and pleasantly fixed in their minds, the last thing we did every week was a more formal, short worship service with quiet behaviour, reading the story directly from Scripture, reciting the memory verse, singing the song, the Lord's Prayer and brief spontaneous prayer asking for the Lord to help each of us to apply what we learned into daily life.

Sunday School lasted two whole hours!

Every child in the little village, from age 3-12 came at least once!

I led Sunday School regularly for more than five years!

Meanwhile, I was surprised by what *I* learned. As I prepared to teach these familiar Bible stories to rural children for the first time in their lives, I always wondered, "What do they hear? What do these stories mean? Why have they been preserved?

What does a person over 2000 years ago in a foreign land have anything to do with these children of loggers in Canada?"

I watch the children as the story unfolds. Their eyes go wide, their breath slows or quickens, their questions indicate the impact, closeness, reality. There *is truth* within each story. Even if my inexperience does not accurately convey 'doctrinal' truth, or 'historical' truth, or 'scientific' truth... they are gleaning the internal truth, the reality of their inborn sense of 'right and wrong,' and the reality of human experience as we make the Journey that we all have in common: "Who am I? Where did I come from? Where am I going? Is there Someone who cares?"

$ $ 1000 $ $

1984

We left our wilderness cabin and stackwall house, to move into the town of Avola. Now we have a four-room house. (Actually, while setting jars and buckets to catch the leaks, I learned that it was built of three shacks dragged together, without enough care taken to join the roofs!)

$ $ 1000 $ $

1985

The year after we moved into town, the two-room public school closed.[9] A school bus came to take children over a mountain pass to the nearest school, 40km (25 miles) away. Some families decided to enrol their children with the BC Government correspondence school. I did, too.

In the kindergarten box of supplies I found every single thing provided: elastic bands, colourful tissue paper, Plasticine,

Wednesday, June 7, 1995

water paints, etc. There were also teacher's notes, children's activity pages, and beginner books to read.

Soon, with the growing popularity of the homeschool movement, the law changed. Formal participation in a recognized program was no longer required. I could make up my own curriculum!

Homeschooling support groups sprang up. My children and I had permission to ride the school bus once a week to participate with other families. Parents learned from each other. Children learned from each other. Art, math, drama, music, sports, culinary, language arts, all kinds of creative activities sprang up. It was Bliss! We even made a 'Home's Cool' weekly newspaper!

May 18, 1991

Our homeschooling friends planned a year-end event when students could demonstrate something they had enjoyed learning about.

I was thrilled to watch Elise act out the Teacher, Annie Sullivan, while a younger girl took the role of her student, deaf and blind Helen Keller, in the famous 'tantrum at the dinner table' scene.

We were all enriched by the years we spent homeschooling. All of our children and many of the others returned to public school at some point. The awards ceremony at the high school was almost embarrassing. Again and again previously homeschooled students stepped forward to accept awards to recognize their achievements.

Special people. Special times.

Exchange

Children don't stay young forever. Grown. Graduated. Gone! How might I spend my talents, experience and creativity now that homeschooling is over? Are there people who need what I know how to do? Is there any part of what I know how to do that might have a monetary value?

My reputation as a volunteer teacher spread. The academic achievements of my own children was evidence of my skill. I found clients and provided after school tutoring.

I was able to earn what was needed to send my own children to the church high school and later college in Bonnie Hills, Pennsylvania.

Value
Wednesday, June 7, 1995

Since I was successful while teaching children, a few at a time, I wondered how I could make a bigger impact on even more children? Perhaps I could teach their parents and their teachers? Maybe I could distill my philosophy and method and express it to others so I would reach larger audiences, thereby benefiting more children?

First with five, locally. Later, across the continent with hundreds of participants, I shared not 'what' I taught, but 'how' I taught. Not even that. It was more like 'what I am thinking while I teach.'

By pairing fleeting ideas with simple symbols representing seven patterns found recurring in nature, the participants could remember and apply what they learned.

A newsletter. A seminar. A video. A Pro-D Day. Magazine articles. Newspaper interviews. Yes, the Seven Predictable Patterns® seem to resonate with people of varying educational, cultural, religious and socioeconomic backgrounds.

Wednesday, June 7, 1995

Since 1995, I have presented the Seven Predictable Patterns® training seminars in these places:

> Ontario, Alberta, British Columbia, Pennsylvania, New York, Illinois, Ohio, Michigan, Arizona, Colorado, California, Washington.

to these groups:

> Women's Retreat, Parent Support Group, Pastor's Council, Professional Development Day, Homeschool Conference, Community Services, Individuals, Couples, Child and Youth Care Association, Fund Raiser, Educational Farm.

One more Thing

Following in a long line of ancestors who are educators of one kind or another, Elise graduated with a Bachelor of Education, Magna Cum Laude, went on to earn her Masters Degree, and then took special training in Scotland, equipping her to teach in any of the Commonwealth countries.

To read more about school and homeschool during the pandemic...
... turn to 10 Days in July Chapter 4, page 301.

But Wait! There's More

After years of volunteering with children in educational settings, and also homeschooling for a total of 15 years (often creating our own curriculum), I have developed this seminar, which I would like to share with you!

BONUS: Seminar #4
Home? School?

... since 1995

> That action is best
> which provides the greatest happiness
> for the greatest numbers.
> —*Francis Hutcheson*

Homeschooling How To

Homeschooling has always been available: in ancient cultures, in modern times.

If you are new, or need renewal, here are three keys that will bring you and your children balance, strength and enthusiasm.

The **First** key:
Too much... Too little... Just right.
Imagine two intersecting circles.
One is full of all the things you already know, familiar, easy.
One is full of the things you don't know, confusing, difficult.
Where the two circles intersect is The Sweet Spot.

The easy, familiar things will be too boring if you repeat them with your child.
The hard, unknown things will be too frustrating if you jump into them too soon.
The ideal learning is in the Sweet Spot.
Not too hard... Not too easy... Just right!

The **Second** key: The Serenity Prayer.
What are the things that CANNOT change?
What are the things that CAN change?

How does the Serenity Prayer apply to homeschooling?
First of all, weigh in all of the reasons why you might be considering homeschooling.

What are the factors you can / cannot change if you decide your children will attend school this year?
What are the factors you can / cannot change if you decide your children will stay home this year?

There is a lot to sort out. There is a lot of potential.

Secondly: once you decide to homeschool, you get to decide every day:
What are the solid things that will stay the same? (ie: 'things that cannot change' such as routines, resources, behaviour expectations, goals)
What are the creative variations? (ie: 'things that can change' such as resources, outings, interests, artistic, explorations, adventures)

The Serenity Prayer can help you make decisions, solve problems, figure out each student, each lesson, each day.

The **Third** key:
1/3 + 1/3 + 1/3[10]
If you remember and use just one idea, let it be this!

This method will keep your family in a balanced lifestyle and avoid 'burnout' while you are homeschooling.

1/3 Academic (what you think of as school work... Reading, Writing, Spelling, Math)

1/3 Family Business (chores and skills, learning about and participating in your work from home, building a business such as baking, lawn care, paper route, etc.)

1/3 Community Service (participating in celebrations and traditions, helping someone, supporting a fund raiser, using your skills to benefit others)

Here is an example from our family. When our son, Michael, was between 9-12 years old, he looked after the chickens.

1/3 Academic: Math about the number 12. Add, subtract, multiply, divide.
1/3 Family Business: He kept records about the cost of feed, how many eggs we used, how much we sold. When he delivered, he earned 25¢ per dozen.
1/3 Community Service: Springtime: Easter eggs donated to event. Summer: donated to egg toss and egg-on-a-spoon race. Autumn: donated to bake sale. Winter: donated to baking Christmas cookies.
Truly. This 1/3 - 1/3 - 1/3 approach is a wholesome plan for a healthy, balanced, sustainable lifestyle. No matter which curriculum you use, no matter the age of your children, no matter how formal or relaxed your day is, no matter your politics or religion or colour or creed... You will find confidence in the ways your children are progressing, and a sense of satisfaction during the homeschooling experience.

Seminar developed by Eleanor Deckert:
Seven Predictable Patterns®[11]

Seven Predictable Patterns®
#1
→
←
OPPOSITES

IN. OUT.
That's all education really is!
What knowledge is going 'IN' to the student?
What will the student to do to show that they understand?
What is the 'OUT'?

Together: Opposites make a Whole.

Seven Predictable Patterns®
#2

CIRCLE   CYCLE   CENTRE

It is easy to see examples of Cycles in Nature.
Spring / Summer / Autumn / Winter
And... What is at the Centre? That is the Purpose.
Example: We plant and work all spring and summer with the autumn harvest in mind. The central goal is having enough food to last all winter.

This is the Cycle of each homeschooling lesson:
Preparation / Doing the task / Results / Rest

June BONUS: Seminar #4

Get out the books and supplies.
Study the lesson.
Now you know how to use new skills.
Take a break.

Focus: What is the central Purpose of the learning?

When we keep this perspective, the day runs more smoothly. We are less anxious about 'not doing enough.' We can keep going. We realize that 'Rest' is part of the Pattern.

Seven Predictable Patterns®
#3

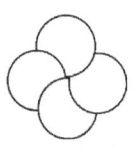

SPIRIT
MIND HEART
BODY

It is easy to see examples in Nature.
Make a list!

SPIRIT... GRATEFUL... HONEST... TRUSTWORTHY
MIND... LANGUAGE... NUMBERS... MEMORY
HEART... FAMILY... FRIENDS...CREATIVITY
BODY... NUTRITION... STRENGTH... REST

How can keeping this Pattern in mind help you with homeschooling?
No matter what the topic, find ways to include each part of the child, stimulating curiosity, nourishing, challenging, allowing for exploration.

Seven Predictable Patterns®
#4

TENDING THE FIRE

Tending the fire in Nature is similar to tending the student while they are learning.

Provide ideal conditions for a new fire, build on a bed of coals, control the air flow.
>Provide ideal conditions for new learning, recall previous knowledge, welcome curious questions.

Add more fuel, harness the fire for a useful purpose.
>Add new information, apply new learning for a useful purpose.

I am more quickly able to move away and return moments later to a strong blaze.
>I am more quickly able to step back and the students will continue to learn on their own, strong and sure.

June BONUS: Seminar #4

Seven Predictable Patterns®
#5
☑☑☒
NEED. NICE. NEVER.

It is easy to see how 'Food' is an example of this Pattern.

Need: What is needed for the growth, health and maintenance of the cells and systems in your body?
Nice: What is mostly for flavour or fun or surprise?
Never: What will actually harm the cells in your body?

How can keeping this Pattern in mind help you with homeschooling? Think of examples of music, art, TV shows and jokes, fashion? What about ways that we express our emotions? What is necessary? Fun? Dangerous? By using this Pattern, your children will be able to make decisions as they grow up and face new situations.

Seven Predictable Patterns®
#6
P
L
→ D
A
N

PLAN→D

In Nature, look at plants or animals, birds or even rocks. There are myriad variations.
How can keeping this Pattern in mind help you with homeschooling?

P = POSSIBILITIES: What are the possibilities? What things *can* change?
L = LIMITATIONS: What are the limitations? What things *cannot* change?
D = DECISION: Bring limitations and possibilities together.
A = ACTION: Planning is over. Time to take action.
N = NEXT TIME: Look back. Measure success. Look ahead. What could be better next time?

Whether planning a lesson, outing, art project or meal, **P L A N ➔ D** is a Pattern well worth mastering.

Seven Predictable Patterns®
#7
DECKERT'S INDEX

It is easy to see examples of this Pattern in Nature.

SPIRITUAL
MOTIVE , PURPOSE
SACRED , IDEALS
CHARACTER QUALITIES

FUTURE
PLANS , GOALS
DESCENDANTS

HEART	**PRESENT**	**MIND**
FAMILY		"OTHERS"
FAMILIAR	**PAST**	UNFAMILIAR
ART	MEMORIES	NUMBERS
MUSIC	ANCESTORS	LANGUAGE
EMOTIONS	FAMILY OF ORIGIN	FACTS, LOGIC
BEAUTY		CHARTS, MAPS

PHYSICAL
BODY, 5 SENSES, EARTH

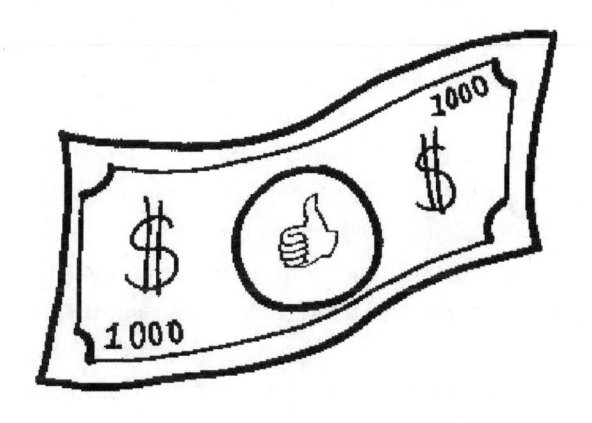

Chapter 5
Saturday, June 7, 1997
Barter : $1000

> Whether you think you can,
> or you think you can't,
> you're right.
> —Henry Ford

Before we begin

I just love to make things with my hands.

In Grade 2, when we lived in Colorado, I made a potholder for my Mother.

In Grade 6, when we lived in Florida, I used a special paint that would form frosty swirls to decorate a glass jar. I put a flickering candle inside it. I gave it to my parents for their 14th wedding anniversary.

In Grade 8, when we first moved to Canada, Mommy often took me to the Farmer's Market early on Saturday mornings. It was my first experience absorbing the sights and smells of

June Chapter 5   Barter : $1000

abundant, locally grown produce: succulent peaches, shiny apples, bright pumpkins, cheerful plums. Specialized booths offered fresh bread, meats, cheeses, jars of jams and jellies like jewels. What caught my eye were the Mennonite ladies who wore plain black dresses with white gauze bonnets. They made afghans, mittens, quilts, cushions and all manner of brightly decorative domestic items.

I wanted to be like them. Domestic. Traditional. Creative.

I wanted to find a way to earn money with the work of my own hands, my own way, not employed to do work that someone else told me to do.

Plan
1973

In high school, I was allowed to spend time by myself in the Mall. Sometimes vendors were featured along the central aisle. Glass blowers made poodles, swans and unicorns. Potters made mugs, planters and casserole dishes. Candlemakers worked with warm wax, sliced long, thin strips through the many layers of colour, then twisted and re-attached the strand in fascinating shapes.

I went home and drew some sketches, made some lists, and did some math. I could sew aprons, pot holders, drawstring bags, pillows, stuffed toys, maybe a cape or tutu for dress-up clothes. What would the fabric cost? What is the fee to rent a booth? How many could I make in how much time?

And: If I made them, would anyone buy them?

Exchange

Life moves pretty quickly when you are young. And, my sewing was not very precise. I never put my plan into action. But, the

Saturday, June 7, 1997

idea stayed with me. What can I make? What will it cost me? What price will I charge? Will anyone buy it?

1974
I stuffed huge bags with cotton shirts at the church rummage sale. I cut squares, rectangles, triangles and hexagons to piece quilts. I loved the play of colours. I loved the light and dark contrasts. I loved measuring and planning. I loved making something that was both beautiful and useful. I loved pouring love into each quilt. I planned to give my first quilts to my siblings.

1977
I loved preserving old-fashioned ways of making things while I sat beside my fiancé, making a quilt for him, tiny stitches, hands expressing love, while we dreamed of our do-it-yourself homesteading future.

$ $ 1000 $ $

When we married and established our family, living on one wage, choosing the 'Self-Sufficiency' lifestyle, my crafty hands needed to make practical things. Beautiful was optional. I had to find ways to be thrifty. With the city stores 120 miles away, I had to find materials at local thrift stores.

Gift-giving seemed the only sensible way for me to make use of my crafty projects. I stuffed teddy bears. I braided rugs. I made puppets. I cut A-B-Cs with felt. I designed costumes for Christmas pageants.

My husband paid for my hobbies. Or sometimes, a neighbour cleared out her closets and gave me her bits and pieces: lace, buttons, velvet, suede, gauze curtains, a bag of colourful shoelaces.

June Chapter 5 Barter : $1000

I seldom ever gave store-bought presents. I made clever little somethings for baby showers, birthday parties, stocking stuffers.

Giving things away is fun. "Ooo - aaa" people admire my work.

Maybe I can use what I make as currency? Skip the cash exchange! Who wants a homemade quilt? Everybody. Who needs a couch, chest of drawers, shelves, a desk? Me! Would you like to trade? Sure!

$$ $ 1000 $ $$

1991

I attended a self-employment seminar. Like when I was a teenager, I made lists of possible skills, products, resources I have available. Again, calculations about costs, time, price, profit.

Could I transform my skills with children to be a tutor, birthday party entertainer, lead a dance class? Could I sew things for sale?

I listened to my classmates: bakers, painters, mechanics, cleaners, drivers. Some people already had careers but now wanted to be independent. Some people were approaching retirement and had developed valuable skills. Some hoped to make money through their hobby. Some, like me, have been stay-at-home-Moms who would like to stay at home and also earn a little cash.

"What can I do with what I have?" kept running through my mind. I don't have any money to invest. Maybe I have to be like the shoemaker and the elves. In the fairy-tale, he laid out leather for one pair of shoes. The elves came at night and made such a beautiful pair that he gained enough money to buy leather for two pairs of shoes. Soon he grew from poverty to a profitable business.

Sudden wealth comes to many in fairy-tales when a Little Man or Fairy Godmother, or another magical helper, often in

Saturday, June 7, 1997

disguise, interrupts the hero or heroine's normal life, providing a magical object. 'The Goose that Laid the Golden Egg,' 'The Tinder Box.' 'Jack and the Beanstalk.' 'The Glass Slipper,' 'Spinning Straw Into Gold.'

I don't think I will have such magic.

$$\$\$\$1000\$\$\$$

Here is my dilemma: Can I make something to sell with what I have so that I can buy more materials and increase my output? Inspired, I grab a pencil and quickly calculate. I have rhubarb! I have 2.5 acres! How many plants could I grow? How many pies could I make? How much jam? How much profit?

I divide and transplant my original rhubarb until I have 48 healthy, enormous rhubarb plants.

Slumped down, I face the facts. Both my pies and my jam are runny. Besides, people who like rhubarb already have their own rhubarb plant (and grandma's recipe). It's not really the most desirable product to take to market.

Sigh. My 'Get-Rich-Quick' scheme was a flop.

$$\$\$\$1000\$\$\$$

June 7, 1997

I am nearly 40 years old. At long last, I have earned my driver's license. As a new, inexperienced driver, I only take the steering wheel of our 4x4 truck, while Kevin is in the passenger seat. I have never gone anywhere all by myself.

I sign up for another self-employment course. My kids will be leaving home soon. I need to plan for my own future.

Same list. Same limitations. No. Wait. I can drive now!

June Chapter 5   Barter : $1000

I could keep taking the school bus as long as I am volunteering at school, which is very fun and very satisfying... but... in order to set off on my own, I will need my own transportation. "I need my own car," I mutter under my breath. "How in the world can I earn enough money to buy a car?"

$$\$\$\,\$1000\$\,\$\$$$

Thinking to myself, "I sold one quilt last year for $350. If a car costs $1000, I will need to sell three quilts. That *is* possible."

The instructor checks in with me and I explain my situation. "What kinds of quilts do you make?" she eagerly asks. "I have a car for sale."

Value

"How much do you want for your car?" I timidly ask.

"$1000."

I can probably make that a fair trade. After all, those hand-stitched Mennonite quilts I used to admire sell for $3000.

She has ideas about colour and design. I have $300 to buy new fabric.

She wants a bedspread, covering the pillows, spreading across a queen-sized bed, reaching to the floor. I have never made anything so huge! 105 inches x 105 inches.

It is heavy. It will take days and days to do the hand stitching to quilt it.

I open the fold-out couch to keep the quilt up, off the floor. The kids and I watch movies all day, all summer. They learn to make their own lunch while I sit and stitch. The garden is overgrown. My fingers are soothed with lanolin or zinc ointment, bandaged overnight to heal the needle pricks. My back aches from the head-forward posture I continue hour after hour.

Saturday, June 7, 1997

Exchange

Poof! Like wishing for a magic carpet, I turned a quilt into a car!

In early November we made the trade!

History!

Kevin took me to the lady's house, took a picture of the momentous occasion, then drove the pickup truck with the children, following behind me for the hour-long drive home. Toby was my sidekick, while I bravely entered a new chapter in my life: Independent Driver!

As we passed the place where our old one-room log cabin stood, I shook my fist, like Scarlet O'Hara shouting, promising, determined, "I'll never be hungry again!"

Weeping. Sobbing. I, too, made my pledge, standing firmly against Fate. "I will never be hungry, cold, alone, without resources, isolated, penniless, stuck at home, suffering isolation... No! Never again!"

One More Thing

Wedding quilts. Baby quilts. Gifts. Trades. For my children. For myself. I lost count after 70 quilts. Some I have donated to worthy causes. Some have sold.

$ $ 1000 $ $

2005

Then, I invented something. My three-year-old nephew was slow in learning to speak. I was going to be his Nanny for a while. I thought to myself, "He will be able to speak when I get there." I made my first 'Story Quilt' for him. I also call them 'Question Quilts.' Or 'Talking Quilts.'

I made a checker-board of picture-denim-picture-denim.

And he *did* learn to speak, naming each item: boots, bus, train, berries, apples, seashell. We laughed as he plucked the berries, pretending to munch. We 'brrruummed' for the machines. We pretended to pull on the socks and admire each other's hats. I covered a square with my hand and he had to remember what was hidden. We knew some songs for the cat, rooster and teddy bear. It was fun to learn!

$ $ 1000 $ $

Idea!

This little boy is not the only child who is having trouble with language development. Maybe I can make these 'Talking Quilts' for educators, parents, grandmothers. Learning and laughing, pretending and practising will stimulate a lot of development!

To read more about Eleanor's crafts during the shut-down...
... turn to 10 Days in July Chapter 5, page 305.

But Wait! There's More

No Fairy Godmother has arrived, showering me with wealth, but, I do have a hobby that pays for itself.

Have I spent $1000? (Probably) Have I earned $1000? (YES!) I am keeping records *and* I am abounding in satisfaction.

Now I have over 200 picture fabrics: teapots, elephants, Christmas trees, bluebirds, ballerinas, cookies, grapes, horses, bunnies. At last count, since 2005, I have made 69 of these quilts. Some as gifts. Some donated to causes. Some have sold.

Let me tell you how I make them!

BONUS: Seminar #5
Question Quilt

... since 2005

I would like to share my idea with you!
Here is the information you need to get started:

Cut: 5-inch squares.
41 picture squares. 40 denim squares.
Arrange: 9 squares across. 9 rows down.
Picture-denim-picture-denim.

Sew: The back of the quilt has a 'rag' finish. The seams show. The edges fray. Wash and dry the quilt 2 or 3 times to eliminate lint.

Your 'Question Quilt' has many uses:
- picnic blanket, baby blanket, floor blanket
- perfect for: diaper bag, Grandma's toy box
- play games in the car, wait for an appointment
- explore the world while quiet in bed

Your 'Question Quilt' can begin many conversations.
- Adult / Child asks questions

- Early Childhood Development of Language is nourished by face-to-face play, shared experiences, a sense of discovery and imagination.
- 'I spy' and 'I'm thinking of something...'
- real and pretend, bigger and smaller
- colours, shapes, patterns
- seasons, city, country
- people in your neighbourhood
- family, skills, careers
- outdoor, holiday, seasonal activities

These are some of the Themes I have made with Question Quilts:

Real & Pretend	When I Grow Up
Seasons & Holidays	A Trip Around the World
Farm & City	Eco Systems
A B C	Colours. Shapes. Patterns.
Songs.	Books.
Nursery Rhymes.	TV. Movies.
Our Family	Animals Around the World
Birds	Bears

Chapter 6
Tuesday, June 9, 1998
$100 per day for 10 days!

> In any moment of decision,
> the best thing you can do
> is the right thing.
> The worst thing you can do
> is nothing.
> —*Theodore Roosevelt*

Before we Begin
"You can always get a job if you know how to work in a kitchen." My Mom told me and I told my kids.

1971
Besides babysitting, my first paid work was washing dishes in the church kitchen. Every Friday, about 50 adults met for dinner that was prepared by volunteers. The cost was small, the companionship engaging, the pastor led a class, there was

singing, too. On Saturday morning, two teen-aged girls took turns cleaning up. $5.00 each. I thought it was fun!

1973

I found summer employment in a kitchen that prepared food for 160 residents in an 'Old People's Home.' It was like feeding a giant. I was Cinderella. Early morning start: 9 loaves of toast. Mid-morning chores: stacking the dishwasher. Noon: ladle soup. Afternoon: scrub giant mixing bowls and the biggest cookie sheets that have ever been invented. Later: dump a whole sack of potatoes into this rotating tub, lined with a rough grater to scrape away the peels. Evening: pour 160 glasses of juice: 80 orange, 20 prune, 20 grapefruit, 40 apple. Carefully carrying the heavy trays, I slide them onto the shelves in the walk-in cooler. At 2:00pm I punch my time card and wait for my Mom to come and pick me up.

1974

The next summer, it was much more fun to work in a bakery and coffee shop. Fresh bread! Golden cookies! Luscious squares! We made thick sandwiches for the lunchtime crowd. We got to wear checkered aprons and matching old-fashioned ruffled caps (and hairnets, of course). Tubs of apple pie filling, bags of raisins, cases of chocolate chips. This giant was much more fun to feed.

1978

After our wedding, while Kevin built the cabin, I was a waitress at a truck stop. Fetching and scrubbing, smiling and hurrying, always washing my hands. I worked for 4 months, earning $2.57 an hour, which was the minimum wage at that time and place.

Tuesday, June 9, 1998

Plan

I was glad for the basic skills I had learned at home and determined that our children would also become capable in the kitchen.

As soon as they could stand, I had helpers. Pouring, mixing, (tasting), shaping the bread dough into a bun for Daddy, cookies with a happy face of raisins, scooping ingredients for granola.

Standing at the sink, enjoying all of the watery and bubbly sensations, they helped to clean up too. And brought the kindling. And held the dust-pan. And fed the cat. And watered the dog.

We all worked together each day.

At about 5 years old, each child started to use the same Mark Chart method my mother used, tallying up the chores, getting paid for work well done.

Like Mary Poppins, I invented two clean-up games for youngsters who liked to pretend. At the end of the day, after homeschooling there was a lot of clutter to deal with: crafts, science projects, games, dress-up clothes, etc, (and... Kevin really didn't want to step on Legos on his way across the living room).

First: 'The Tubby Time Game.' One child is in the bathtub. Everyone else is scurrying to hang-up, tidy-up, wash-up. "Here I come!" the freshly scrubbed child announces, combed and clad in PJs. Now everyone hides. The Tubby Time child wanders about the house noticing the changes. "O, Dear, where are my toys? Has a robber taken them?" or "What happened to the dishes? Have they all been mailed away?" or "Wasn't there a pile of coats (laundry, books, blocks, stuffed toys) here? Were they sent to the Thrift Store?" Continue the rotation until all children are bathed and the whole house is ship-shape.

Second: 'The Job Jar.' We all brainstorm for tasks that need to be done. I jot down each task one-by-one on tiny slips of paper, fold them and mix them up in a big glass jar. "Reach in, grab, and pull!" I command the children one-at-a-time. Everyone holds their breath. Each person is silently hoping, waiting. "Will I get something fun, like putting the stuffed toys back in the macrame bag? Or something quick, like sweeping the stairs? Or something creative, like making a fresh bouquet for the table? Or something smelly, like taking out the compost?"

Years later, with four children in the mix, I developed a way to teach various skills, rotate responsibilities, and organize a rhythm of daily and weekly routines.

CLEAN HELPER
(wash your hands *before* you start to work)

MORNING
make juice, make toast

BEFORE SUPPER
help with food

AFTER SUPPER
wash dishes, wipe sink area

AFTER SUPPER
clear and wipe table
clear and wipe counters
put away clean dishes
put away food

Tuesday, June 9, 1998

MESSY HELPER
(Wash your hands *after* you do the work)

PORCH
tidy up, sweep
take out garbage

FIREWOOD
fill wood box

PETS
feed and water: dog, cat, chickens
gather eggs

ENTRY
tidy boots, coats, mittens, etc.
sweep

LIVING ROOM
tidy: toys, books, clothes, dishes, etc.
straighten: couch, blankets, cushions

FLOORS
sweep / vacuum

EXTRA PAY
25¢ Tupperware cupboard
10¢ fold laundry
25¢ help Mom with extra job
$1 help get a load of firewood with Dad

Exchange
1998

The summer before going away to Bonnie Hills Church School in Pennsylvania, both Elise and Michael earned the money they needed to cover their expenses by cleaning at the local motel. And, while away at school, they were both employed on campus doing janitorial work cleaning the classrooms.

When Michael came home in June, he enrolled in a 'Food Safe' course so he could work in the college kitchen the following year. Since I had to drive him to the class, I enrolled, too. $96 each. It seemed like a good idea. Exchange money for knowledge and then exchange knowledge for a job.

As they say, 'Little did I know' that the certificate would come in handy almost immediately.

1998 was a bad summer for forest fires. Significant wildfires were burning in the Kamloops region, as well as many more throughout the province. Flames took homes, reduced neighbourhoods to rubble, threatened cities. Dispatchers, pilots, ground crews, support staff were becoming exhausted. Supply trucks faced possible road closures, lengthy delays or detours. Crews came from other parts of Canada to work in the soot with shovels and hoses.

June 9, 1998

While enjoying a bicycle ride, Nicholas and Toby saw a lightning strike that started a fire across the river, about four kilometres north of our house. Kevin went to look. For the first time in my life, I phoned in to report a forest fire.

On that same day, in our area, there were 90 lightning strikes, no rain, and only one available helicopter.

My husband heard the pilot on the radio. As he made his patrol, looping past us, he called in to the Kamloops Fire

Centre, to make an initial fire report, describing the location, size, intensity, fuel types in the area, the distance of the fire from buildings at risk, wind speed and direction, slope, possible access for machinery, and availability of water.

But, no help was coming. There were no structures, no homes, no risk to human life. Let it burn.

Candling. That's when the fire rushes up to the top of the tree, brightly, fiercely. We watched that happen through the night. Orange.

Hot air goes up. Fire goes up. The steep slope was ideal for the fire to spread uphill. Hungry, devouring, always seeking fuel, everywhere finding dry wood.

A steady wind pushed the fire northward, away from our house, our neighbours, our village. It was a long way until there was anything else that was man-made that had value. Day after day, acre by acre, the fire continued to burn.

Upward, like an evil elevator to the mountaintop, northward by the wind, now the burning rubble rolled down, toward the highway. Smoky in the green leaves of the undergrowth. Smouldering where there were rotting logs. Snapping at the leading edge. Grass flares up. Trees candle. The fire is fascinating to watch.

The smell of smoke triggered an ancient reaction deep within me. I am a Mother. Save my babies! One part of my brain knew the facts. We were safe. Another part of my brain was in high alarm. Get out! Run! It was hard to focus on anything. I could only worry, and battle inside myself trying *not* to worry.

Value

Kevin's pay-day came, and I drove my car to town, hurriedly crossed off my list, and filled up at the gas station.

"How are the fires up your way?" the attendant asked. "They will need a big kitchen staff. There are a lot of firefighters coming to that fire in the next few days. Why don't you hire on?" She knew a lot about the situation and told me where to go and what to do.

I had honestly never considered working in a fire camp! Shall I stay home? Or go to work?

I signed up. And I put Michael's name down, too. It was for 12-hour days for a 10-day shift.

"We start the day after tomorrow!" I announced. First, I drove the two youngest children, Nicholas and Toby, back to town to stay with a friend. I just didn't want to think about them while I was away from home. Next, I gave Elise instructions about the garden, animals, meals, and how to do the jam, canning and freezing the 40-pound case of peaches I had just bought. Finally, I packed my car. The trunk was filled with precious cargo. What was 'irreplaceable'? Quilts, Christmas ornaments, photographs, important papers, my jewellery box.

Kevin spoke to his boss on the railroad. During the height of the emergency, he would be volunteering along the highway. His radio skills, knowledge of the area, contacts with loggers who owned equipment and first aid training all had high value.

$ $ 1000 $ $

Michael and I arrived at the fire camp. There were problems to solve. Huge cases of Styrofoam bowls, cups and paper plates had to be removed from the kitchen trailer so there would be room to work. Two young women arrived who were the head-cooks. By then we realized that we faced ever-changing circumstances. Originally planned to be a 60-man crew, by morning it was actually 150 people lined up for a meal. The camp grew. Now we had 300 people to feed! The women in charge were overwhelmed. The supplies were delayed. The refrigerator truck was inadequate. The night cook arrived one day late.

Meanwhile, Michael was Cinderella. He didn't have to solve any problems or make any decisions. Just keep peeling potatoes. Just keep scrubbing enormous pots. Just keep dragging away bags of garbage.

I was an assistant. I did as I was told: chop celery, crack eggs, slice pies, fill a tub with wedges of watermelon.

We got paid $100.00 a day! Plus room and board. It was the most money I had ever earned in such a short time. No matter how fast I had to move or how hot and tired I felt, I kept doing the math: $100 a day for 10 days! $1000!!!

One More Thing

"Maybe this is what I am supposed to be doing? Maybe this is a sign!" I thought. It was fun. It was exciting. Again, I was feeding a giant. I knew I was making the world a better place to be.

But then, I 'heard a voice from heaven.'

"No! Not this. You are a teacher. You are a writer."

And so, that was my only experience working on a fire crew. And so, here I am, still teaching, still writing.

Was Eleanor able to get more organized? Or did she just watch TV for months and months during the Covid-19 shut downs?...
... turn to 10 Days in July Chapter 6, page 311.

But Wait! There's More

After years of doing domestic work for other people, and organizing my own closets, I have developed a seminar, which I would like to share with you!

BONUS: Seminar #6
H.O.W. 2
Home Organization Workshop
(*what's the 2 for?*)

... since 1992

> Undertake difficult tasks
> by approaching
> what is easy in them.
> Do great deeds
> by focusing
> on their minute aspects.
> —*Tao*

(True) (False)
Some clutter is a bit of a problem in almost every home.

The first thing I want you to know: I am not a Neatnick! I am *good* at organization... simply because I am so *bad* at it! I have many interests, multiple projects, interruptions, supplies saved for 'someday,' plus, the normal clutter. I live in a small log cabin with my Hubby. We homeschooled our 4 children (now grown and gone), grow and store our food, and we live 70 km from a store... so I save scraps and bits and oddments 'just in case.' In the winter when I cannot get to town (nasty icy roads), I make big messes (with quilt squares and other crafts).

I developed and presented this seminar in my home after we had spent 7 months doing renovations. I needed to put everything in storage, while at the same time, I needed everything to remain accessible. Time to get really, truly, ORGANIZED.

Since then, I have made this presentation in many places, bringing a sigh of relief to many homemakers.

* * *

Eleanor Deckert's **H.O.W. 2** workshop offers practical, encouraging information. Using the **H.O.W. 2** method family members will experience a sense of freedom and balance. Participants report that they are able to see their situation differently and are able to handle everyday issues in a more calm and less frustrating manner. Whether you are downsizing, moving, or living with clutter, you will gain the skills and confidence to restore order, know where your treasures are stored, and easily find the items you are searching for.

* * *

We all have an idea of what a **Home Organization Workshop** might mean:
- My **home** will be transformed. Piles of **clutter** and unsolved **storage** problems will be clarified.

- Inefficient, frustrating **routines** will be modified by more reasonable **time management.**
- Even my **papers** will be in order! Random confusion will be replaced by **organization.**

Not by magic! Not instantly! This will require focus, time, and, yes, **work.** Let me assure you.. when you spend the **time** = you will gain more **space**... and... when you have more **space** = you will gain more **time**...

* * *

By the way, I know you are asking, *"What's the 2 for?"*
KNOW HOW + WANT TO = DO
- When you **KNOW HOW** (which I will demonstrate)
- and you **WANT TO** (you *can* increase your motivation)
- then you will be able to **DO THIS**!
- PS If one of the **2** is missing... you won't have much success.

How can I make myself **want to**? Here are a few ways to get motivated:
- challenge yourself *and* a friend
- put on some peppy favourite music
- set the timer (recommended sprint for 15 minutes... do it... it works!)
- follow your sprint with a fun activity
- reward yourself (I didn't say with a cupcake)
- PLAN TO SUCCEED: start with something you are sure you can finish successfully.

Shopping List:
- garbage bags (clear for storage, black for trash and exit to the thrift store)
- zip-lock bags (large and small)
- permanent marking pens (large and small)

- wide clear tape, paper, scissors (to make labels)
- **INDEX CARDS** and a pen
- (**most important**) Index card file box.
- 3 paper bags (ask at the grocery store)
- storage boxes (at the grocery store I ask for cardboard box egg crates, they fit inside a clear garbage bag)

* * *

Let's get to work and eliminate clutter:
1) Where in your home is clutter most likely to accumulate?
2) What times of day is clutter most likely to accumulate?
3) What cannot change? What can change?
4) To deal with the clutter, there are only 3 decisions you need to make. Label the 3 paper bags: GIVE AWAY... THROW AWAY... PUT AWAY.
5) Now schedule a time to: GIVE AWAY (deliver to a friend, donate, etc), THROW AWAY (garbage, recycling, shred), PUT AWAY (2 kinds of PUT AWAY a) deliver items to the correct place in your house, b) storage)
6) Storage: Use INDEX CARDS. Make 2 index cards with the same information. Tape one to the box. Keep the other one in your index card file box.

Example: Top left corner: 'Winter Clothes #1'... Top right corner: 'attic, top left shelf' This makes it very easy to find the box. Next: write on the bottom of the card what you put into the bottom of the box. As you add items to the box from the bottom to the top, you write the list from the bottom of the card to the top. This makes it very easy to know what is in each box.

Organize Paper:

HEART (family, photos, hobbies, artistic, music)
Use RED labels.

SPIRIT (inspirational, scripture, poetry, book titles)
Use YELLOW labels.

MIND (finances, legal, instructions, warranties)
Use BLUE labels.

BODY (health, meds, fitness, household, garden, car)
Use GREEN labels.

See the CYCLE:
Annual. Seasonal. Monthly. Weekly. Daily.

Know how often each job needs to be done. Commit to your strategy. Do not stress! You will never be 100% ALL done.

See the Cycle of each task:
   a) Get ready (gather cleaning supplies).
   b) DO the task.
   c) Clean up after the task (put supplies away).
   d) REST (yes! That is part of the cycle: being all DONE and taking a rest.)

Chapter 7
Tuesday, June 3, 2003
Learn... Teach... Dance... $1000?

> The woods would be very silent
> if no birds sang there
> except those who sang best.
> —John J. Audubon

Before We Begin

Although Mrs. Gray's creative dance class was deeply satisfying and had become nourishment and inspiration for my creative heart, curious mind, flexible body and imaginative spirit, it was not until our family attended weekly gatherings for homeschooling families in the mid-1990s that I again brought dance into my life.

Plan

1992

On a perfect, sunny day in May, our local homeschooling support group planned a Medieval Festival. Dressed in homemade historic costumes, we greeted each other as "M' Lord" and "M' Lady."

The Herald unrolled his scroll to announce the entrance of the King and Queen. The peasants provided entertainment. Midst cheering on-lookers and young maidens gasping in amazement, the audience enjoyed sword-play (armour made with hockey padding, swords made of wooden rods covered with foam used for plumbing pipe insulation), an air-band (recorded music with homemade mock instruments), a circle dance (all age groups), a May Pole, and recitations of period poetry.

At lunchtime, everyone had agreed to bring picnic blankets, but only one type of food per family, with plenty to share. In this way, we created a Market Place and bartered with each other to bring variety to the meal. "May I trade my carrots for your cheese?"

1993

The following year I met every week with the homeschooling children to prepare a theatre-in-the-round dance recital of the 'Seven Days of Creation.' Light and Dark dressed and moved to contrasting music. Water above (dancers arching a gauze curtain) and water below (dancers waving a long blue length of rippling fabric). The Earth brought forth abundant plant life. The Sun strutted boldly. The Moon was shy. Fish and birds leaped, flitted and frolicked. Animals moved as animals do. Adam and Eve regally strode, blessing and naming all of the creatures. And Rest. A day of blessed rest.

And is was very good.

1994

News travels fast by word-of-mouth in small towns.

The elementary school was considering a production of 'Joseph and the Amazing Technicolour Dreamcoat.' I volunteered to bring it to life and put about 60 children on stage.

The standing ovation made everyone giddy and me instantly famous! Who was that lady from that tiny town?

$$\$\$\$1000\$\$\$$

As soon as possible, I travelled to see Aunt Barbara in Seattle.

"The school wants me to do it again! How can I possibly? I don't know how I did it the first time? It just came to me!"

Aunt Barbara gave me her method: Form, Storm, Norm, Perform.[12]

> FORM: What are the limitations? In what way will this dance be consistent? What cannot be changed?
>
> STORM: Brainstorm: make lists of ideas without debate or editing. What can be changed, re-interpreted?
>
> NORM: Make decisions. Edit out ideas not needed this time. Simplify. Make the final plan.
>
> PERFORM: Performance is a gift to the audience. Have fun doing it!

$$\$\$\$1000\$\$\$$

Suddenly: Danger!

1994

The summer after 'Joseph,' while I was still basking in the warmth of success, there was a kidnapping attempt on one of our children!

Here's what happened.

Our family was getting ready to go on a camping trip, planning to meet at the summer church camp. The night before our trip, I told Elise and Michael to bicycle up to the Bookmobile to return our books. Since we would be away, no one needed new books.

The next afternoon the phone rang.

Michael said, "Let me answer it, Mom. Please? I never get to answer the phone."

I stood right beside him.

"Hello?... Yes... OK, Sure!... Let me ask my Mom."

Turning to me he explained, "Mom! The Bookmobile guy wants me to come and work for him. Now. He's gonna pay me fifty bucks! Can I go?"

I have worked for the library. I was paid $9.00 per hour. What in the world could the Bookmobile need a kid to do? Besides. I knew that the Bookmobile only stayed in our town for one hour. Why would they still be here overnight?

I took the phone.

"Hello?" silence... "This is Eleanor." click!

They hung up.

My entire body went cold. My worst fear!

I knew what it was: it was a kidnapping lure!

Just then a man walked past the window. I jumped in alarm! But it was my husband, coming home from work. I told him to go immediately to the three places where there were payphones in our town: the motel, the gas station and the pub. (This was before cell phones were invented.) No one was there and the owners had not noticed anything.

Tuesday, June 3, 2003

I phoned all of my neighbours who had children. Either no one was home, or an adult had answered the phone and the had person hung up. Now I was *really* scared!

I phoned the police, the library and other families I knew. I phoned the newspaper asking them to print a warning. How innocently a stranger can ask a child to "Come with me..."

The shock sent me into a state of panic that I could not control. I wanted all four of our children to stay right with me every single second.

As we drove to the campground, I was terrified every time I saw a car parked on the side of the road. Maybe someone was being brutally murdered!

I could not be sensible. I told my husband he had to make all of the decisions about the children.

"Mom, can I go swimming?"
"Mom, can I go on the boat?"
"Mom, can I go in my friend's tent?"

I could only see disaster.

I could not sleep. Or eat. Or make decisions.

$ $ 1000 $ $

I went to counselling. Through this experience, I came to see how much 'Fear' governed my life.

In ten months, through fifteen appointments with a highly skilled and very patient therapist, I unravelled the tangled, flawed, distorted views, fears and negative self-image I had been silently dragging around for so long. I pulled forward early hurts, doubts, unanswered, unanswerable questions. I made drawings, charts and maps. I recorded my dreams. I read nine psychology books. I wrote nearly 2000 pages in my Journal.

The result of this self-examination became clear: I could see myself better, make decisions, take action. Growing confidence resulted in learning to drive, earning money, making decisions like an adult.

I had, like that butterfly I was intrigued with so long ago, made a metamorphosis. Previously I was insecure, wanting to please others, anxious, indecisive. Now I could allow myself to expand, take up space, interact with more people, share my opinion without having to be so so good and so so smart.

$$\$\$\$1000\$\$\$$$

In September, 1994, I was able to allow my children to attend school, and again I could participate in community events.

For three years I volunteered at the elementary school, 70 km (45 miles) away. Every week I boarded the school bus. Three times I added dance to the school Christmas plays. Three times I added dance to their year-end production.

I was in bliss.

$$\$\$\$1000\$\$\$$$

"When are you going to give lessons?" one of the teachers asked me. "My daughter wants to be in your class."

I was stunned. People want to *pay* me to teach? Dance?

Plan

May 30, 1995

Today is my last counselling appointment.

Wearing a graceful skirt and red vest over my leotards, seated with an air of confidence, making eye contact with my counsellor, a smile flickers across my face. I have so much to tell him since my appointment a month ago.

"I earned exactly $1000 since we last met!"

Tuesday, June 3, 2003

(I wish you could see the look on his face!)

"I sold a quilt for $350. I was a substitute teacher for two days ($75 x 2) and I have 25 dance students signed up at $20 each!"

"How did all of this happen?" he sits back, watching me closely.

"I have been to the Employment Agency.

I have taken self-employment classes.

I have a sketch of a business plan.

I have filed my business name with the provincial government.

'Making Connections Making Dance'

I have a logo!

I have a purpose and determination. I need to help pay for tuition next year when Elise goes away to college."

"But, you told me you can't earn money if you ride the school bus. Only if you volunteer?" he looks puzzled. Does he think that maybe I am not seeing clearly?

"Right. In order to have a steady way to earn money, I also need a steady form of transportation and a driver's license! So, I have signed up with Young Drivers of Canada! ($$) The classes are in Kamloops, 120 miles away. I am taking the Greyhound bus ($$). I have arranged for child care ($$). I have to attend weekly in-class lessons, and in-car time with my instructor." I am beaming. "By *not* taking the children on a trip to see the grandparents this year, I have enough to pay for most of this, and Kevin is glad to pay the rest. I can really do this!"

"I notice that you are wearing contacts!" It is quite a transformation.

"Yes. And a little makeup." I feel like an adult.

Journal Entry
Today, June 3, 1995
I made history!

I opened up my own account at the credit union!

I am in business!

When I volunteer I have no expenses, no fees at the bank. I don't need to hire the lady to do my income tax, pay for transportation, or room rental, I don't even have to pay for advertising or photocopying!

Yet, there is more than cash exchanged. We all gain. We all learn. Connections are made. I am building a business.

Exchange
They came!

They learned!

They danced!

They liked it!

I'm going to do this again!

Saturday, August 19, 1995
My counsellor is moving away!

I am so sad. But also, so glad. Because I am *done*! I am so satisfied, energetic, enthusiastic. Make a list of positive attributes! That's me!

But, wait. What can I give him to say, "Thank-you"? A gift I buy? A gift I make? Write a letter? Is there time to make a quilt?

An idea flashes into my mind. Complete. No hesitation. I will make a dance.

There is a good-bye picnic planned. I have the perfect music. I can be ready on time. I can make the right thing to wear.

$ $ 1000 $ $

Tuesday, June 3, 2003

Wearing a mid-length black skirt, black leotards, bare feet, I step onto the grass. With my back to the gathering, like a mime, I show the enclosure I am trapped in, then turn, and find my way out. With larger movements, I follow the lyrics: waves, sparks, stars, mountains. I gesture receiving a precious gift, and offering one with outstretched hands.

Turning away, I cover myself with a gauze veil, secretly release the Velcro of my skirt, attaching it to my shoulders, holding the hem to spread wide like a cape, I turn back towards the audience.

Slowly rising as I turn, the veil slides down, my arms open to reveal, as if I am coming out of a cocoon: a butterfly!

Value
'Making Connections Making Dance'
Instructor: Eleanor Deckert

To me, Creative Dance means that the child is already a dancer. Whenever we move to express ourselves, we are dancing. I teach by asking questions that encourage exploration, new awareness, and attention to detail.

It is my role to develop each dancer's coordination, strength, concentration and interpretation of the music, story, character, idea or feeling so that the dancer is indeed communicating through their movement and expression.

A great deal of trust is part of my work. The children learn to trust themselves, each other, the instructor and the audience. Once this connection of trust is established, it is my experience that a great deal of creativity is opened up and wonderful things begin to be made. As children solve problems and build patterns, we make new dances.

During exercises, music awareness, and cooperation, the child makes connections and becomes more acutely aware of how their body is moving from one shape to another.

This is the purpose of my work: not so much to teach a dance routine, to imitate or perform, but to give each person this sense of connection within one's self (emotions, ideas, sensations), within the group (trust, appreciation, observation, contribution), within the world of dance.

Later
1997

By hosting annual dance recitals, children show what they have made and parents appreciate what their children have developed.

This year a bigger idea popped into my head.

"What if I invited other groups to participate? Each of them could come prepared to display their own talents and culture."

It only takes a few phone calls. Everyone wants to participate!

'Journey : A Trip Around the World'

Invitations to the event included a list of items the audience had to bring so that 'Imagine-Airlines' could take them on a trip-around-the-world through music and dance.

Upon arrival, the Cub Scouts provided the security baggage check. A table was set up with a large cardboard box, like the x-ray machine. The youngsters wore their official uniforms and their leader made sure they maintained formal behaviour.

Bleachers were set up in the school gym for the audience.

Along either side of the performance area, benches were ready for dancers to rest in between scenes. Since there was no backstage, all performers could watch the whole event.

One of the teachers set up a microphone and sound system to amplify the music. No special lighting was needed.

Four high school drama students provided airport staff. There was the pilot, a steward and stewardess, in matching uniforms. The ground control person, dressed in overalls, reflective vest and ear protection, carried a clipboard and brightly lit orange flashlight to guide the imaginary in-coming airplane.

Sit back and enjoy our performance!

A Trip Around the World
Tour departs from the School Gym
Monday, May 12, 1997
6:30pm sharp
Please allow time to be seated
All baggage will be checked
before boarding your flight
Admission by donation

Eleanor's Creative Dance Class:
Africa: Costumes: black leggings and light blue T-shirts painted with planet Earth.
Props: hoops from the gym (so young children knew their starting and returning place)
Blue tumbling mat (to represent watering hole)
Dancers move as African animals, one-by-one or in pairs going to watering hole.
AUDIENCE BRING: Binoculars (use TP tubes)

Europe: Town Criers: a women's acapaella quartet. Folk songs in original languages.
AUDIENCE BRING: Backpack

Asia: two high school students from India provided a traditional dance routine with their own music and costumes.
AUDIENCE BRING: Camera

Eleanor's Creative Dance Class:
Antarctica: Costumes: all wore black leggings and purple tops
Props: long rope held between 2 dancers, from the rope were hung threads with bits of tin foil in geometric shapes to represent the ice crystals.
Each dancer had a short stick (chopstick) and ribbons (party streamers) to represent the southern Aurora Australis.
Dancers: began as frozen, strange asymmetrical shapes to be glaciers and ice burgs.
To represent the dancing lights they moved in big, wide circles in unison, swirling their ribbons, then with variations.
AUDIENCE BRING: Winter parka

Australia: Brownies sing: 'Kookaburra' 'Waltzing Matilda.'
AUDIENCE BRING: Sunglasses

South America: Audience joined in for the 'Mexican Hat Dance.'
AUDIENCE BRING: Hat or cap

North America: Adult Country Line-Dance group provided costumes and music.
AUDIENCE BRING: Bandana (or other western gear)

GRAND MARCH: all dancers participate.

One More Thing
1996

The summer after Daddy died, my husband and children and I travelled by train to Colorado. So many childhood experiences flashed into my memory as we went from one familiar place to another.

Aunt Esther made me a gift of her time. "I'll take you anywhere you would like to go. Stay as long as you like. I have a book to read in the car."

"Is Mrs. Gray still alive?" I was anxious as I made arrangements to meet my dance teacher. 1966 was 30 years ago! "I wonder if she will remember me?"

Yes, she did! She was thrilled that it was my time of life to pass dance along to the children of the next generation. She gave me four of her most helpful books, sharing her philosophy and method. Treasure!

Later, Mrs. Gray wrote me a letter!

December 15, 1998

Dear Eleanor,

Thanks for your greetings and your newsy letter. You are a remarkable woman blessed with too many talents. I hope one day you will find the time and inspiration to write the story of your life and family.

I am happy to hear you are still teaching and planning for the future. Your energy and creativity are amazing.

Isn't it amazing to think of changing from 1900 to 2000? I often ponder about it.

One piece of advice – never lose your enthusiasm – this is what makes all the difference. You are talented and dedicated – that's more than money can ever buy, believe me.

You are rich beyond words – with a fine husband and children. Life has been good to you.

Have a peaceful holiday season with your loved ones,

Love,

Ursula

Tuesday, June 3, 2003

Today is my Graduation! Yes!

Cap. Gown. Diploma. I have earned the Provincial Instructor's Diploma.

I figured that since I have been volunteering, tutoring, teaching dance class, developing seminars... since people like what I am doing... I might as well make sure I am doing the best I can.

This program was developed because there are so many people who know their trade or art, and so many others who would like to learn from skilled people. In my class there were beauticians, electricians, potters, massage therapists, carpenters, butchers. And then there was me, with my ideas about parenting, homeschooling, Sunday School and dance.

Now, I can 'begin with the end in mind,' and use a variety of techniques to convey instruction. I can evaluate myself and the students and the curriculum. I can feel confident about the content I prepare, the manner with which I deliver information, and the value of the experience to the participant. And, for the first time in my life, I feel confident with the fees I charge.

How did the lock-downs impact the performing arts?...
... turn to 10 Days in July Chapter 7, page 315.

But Wait! There's More

After years of volunteering with children, I wondered if I could develop a worthwhile Professional Development Day seminar for adults?

BONUS: Seminar #7 Teach Dance

... since 1998

> The only limit to our realization of tomorrow
> will be our doubts of today.
> Let us move forward with strong and active faith.
> —*Franklin D. Roosevelt*

Drawing on a lifetime interest and involvement with children, theatre, dance and music, I wish to fully utilize my skills and experience by encouraging teachers to include dance in their classrooms.

I teach by asking questions that encourages exploration, new awareness, and attention to detail. As children solve problems and build patterns they make new dances. Kinesthetic awareness is developed and vocabulary is expanded as children choose words to describe movement.

I enjoy working with the teachers in the classroom. I enjoy seeking ways to include creative movement while learning science, art, literature, math and social studies.

I enjoy working with directors planning a production. I must be aware of the interpretation of the script, limitations and possibilities of the set, costumes, and props. I draw ideas from the children as we become familiar with the music, story, and characters. Because my ideas blend with theirs as we build the dance together, we can prepare for the audience fairly rapidly (3-5 hours of class time).

This is the purpose of my work: not so much to teach a dance routine, to imitate or perform - but to give each person a sense of connection: with one's self (feelings, ideas, body), within the group (trust, appreciation, observation, contribution), within the world of dance.

Teach Dance
3 Hour Professional Development Day Workshop

Is your school developing an elementary school
dance curriculum?
Do you need training, ideas, encouragement?
Eleanor Deckert can help you begin.

Eleanor's experience as a choreographer for elementary school productions:
1998: Teach Dance: Professional Development Day Workshop
1997: Journey : 'A Trip Around the World'
1996: 'The Swingin' Piper'
'Dandelion'
Girl Guides weekend: Fine Arts Camp
'Surfin' Santa'
Holiday Dance and Piano Recital
1995: 'Alice in Wonderland'
'Christmas Mischief'
'Plant a Seed and Watch it Grow'
1994: 'Joseph and the Amazing Technicolour Dream Coat'

'Santa's Holiday Hoe-Down'
1993: 'Seven Days of Creation'
1992: 'Medieval Festival'

Related Experience:
1986-1992: develop reading programs while employed by the public library
1985-1998: develop curriculum while homeschooling
1978-present: volunteer in schools (reading, guitar, singing)
1973-present: directing Christmas plays, both religious and secular

Teach Dance

1st hour: What does a dance class look like? Participate in one.
2nd hour: Lecture. Video. Discussion.
3rd hour: SMALL GROUP A) Now it is your turn to create a dance. SMALL GROUP B) Go on a treasure hunt. What are the resources available to you? music / poetry / props / costumes

Teach Dance

1-hour dance class:
HELLO (greetings, news, info)
WARM-UP (stretch, isolations, strengthen, body awareness)
CROSS THE FLOOR (walk, skip, slide, gallop, jump, turn)
LISTEN (FORM)
EXPLORE (BRAINSTORM)
BUILD (see EXAMPLE below) (NORM)
SHARE (PERFORM)
THEATRE (classical music, simple props ie: scarf, flower, shawl. Teacher introduce information about a piece of music, individual or groups interpret)
CLOSING (cool down, rest, talk about the care of the body, review what was learned, relaxation skills)

CURTSY, BOW, THANK-YOU, DISMISSED

EXAMPLES: BUILD:

> Can you tell a story with: facial expressions? hands? gestures? body language?
> 4 counts x walk. 4 counts x hold body still in a shape.
> Expression: add emotion: 4 x walk, 4 x shape.
> Teach: Specific moves
> Folk dance steps
> Rhythm instruments

1-Hour Lecture
Video examples: When does ordinary movement become dance?
'Pete's Dragon': washing the windows 'It's a brazzle dazzle day'
'Snow White': sweeping 'Just whistle while you work'
Many examples: walking becomes marching becomes dancing.

Definitions:
This is the pattern you will use over and over again.
FORM = listen to the music, give instructions, set limitations, set a task or problem or challenge.
STORM = brainstorm with the whole group to generate ideas to solve the problem or meet the challenge.
NORM = break into groups, build a short piece from all the possibilities. Choose, order, edit, practise.
PERFORM = each group shows the class what they've made.

1-Hour Small Groups
A) Create a dance.
B) Search for resources within the school.

Teach Dance

A – 1 Create a Dance : 'The Wind and the Sun' Aesop's Fables

The sun and the wind challenged each other.
"I am stronger than you!" each one claimed.
"Let's see. We'll have a test," they agreed.
"See that boy walking along? He's wearing a coat. Whoever gets him to take off his coat: that is who is stronger."
First, the wind tried. He blew and blew, harder and harder.
The boy clutched his coat more and more tightly.
Then, the sun tried. He shone and shone.
Soon the boy took off his coat. "I am stronger!" said the sun.
And so it was finally decided.

A – 2 Create a Dance : 'The Sower' Matthew 13: 1–9

The sower went out to sow his seed. As he worked, some seeds fell on the pathway and the birds came to eat them.
Some seeds fell on stony ground. First, they sprouted and then, since they had no root, they withered away.
Some seeds fell in thorns and thistles. They were choked and could not live.
But, some seeds fell on the good soil and they produced fruit, some thirty, some sixty and some one hundredfold!

A – 3 Create a Dance : Peer Gynt Suite

4 counts = hands open, 4 = hands closed
4 = spine open, 4 = spine closed
4 = hands and spine open, 4= hands and spine closed
8 = stand arms open
4 = to centre, 2= arms up, 2= arms down
8 = left to right arch
4 = stand arms in front, 4 = arms open 8 = turn

Small Group B
Search for resources and create a file for your school.
Library: books, photo file, biographies, music, video, cultural.
Music room: rhythm instruments, recordings.
Drama: dress-up, scarves, ribbons, flowers, other props.
Literature: poetry, folk tales, culture, holidays.

* * *

Techniques to Prepare for School Play
- Explain the whole story of the play.
- Listen to the music. Explain the songs.
- Who, what, where, when, how, why, feelings.
- What leads into __? What comes after __?
- Talk about the story. Ask questions. Content, characters, conflict, order of the story, notice surprises or changes.
- Notice construction of songs: verse, chorus, verse, chorus.
- Ask students to move to music. Make a note of their ideas.
- Watch, gather and add to what they present. *It is easier to build with what students invent than to copy what teacher designs.*
- Extend natural movement into dance (rhythm, count to 4, repeat sequences).
- Teach an easy part of the dance that repeats (like the chorus). This will make sure they are successful with their first attempt. Next time they will come to class satisfied, eager.
- Teach the hard part that will need lots of practice. Break this down into tiny pieces.
- Teach the ending early. Rehearse so the ending is strong.

Chapter 8
Thursday, June 2, 2006
Parent Educator : $1000

What need we teach a child
with our books and rules.
Let him walk among the hills and flowers.
Let him gaze upon the waters.
Let him look up at the stars
and he will have his wisdom.
—*author unknown*

Before we Begin

I watched my Mother. I listened. I asked. I remembered.

There are so many facets. So many unseen, immeasurable, sacred, intuitive, interconnected parts.

I know this: I want to be a Mother.

Plan

Having kids was always part of the Plan. Taking care of kids is something I have always been good at. Big sister. Babysitter. Volunteer. Live-in Nanny. I had so much experience before I got married, I thought that being a Mother would be a piece of cake. As easy as pie. The way the cookie crumbled.

I watched my Mother. I listened to my aunts and grandmothers. I paid attention when I was employed by other families. I noticed how Ma and Pa did things in the 'Little House' books by Laura Ingalls Wilder.

My ancestors had children. I want to have children.

My descendants will also have children.

I loved being pregnant. (I read so many books and asked so many women about their experiences.) I loved giving birth. (Almost impossible to find words to describe.) I loved caring for infants. (Kevin worked at night during those years, so I had the babies sleeping close to me.) And I loved all of the learning, discoveries, pretending, storytelling, singing and customs.

Besides reproducing and raising healthy bodies, I knew I would need much skill to manage the home and finances, plan ahead for seasons, holidays, the unexpected.

Like the song in 'Fiddler on the Roof,' I'm singing, 'Tradition!'

Ah! But there is more to being a Mother than just filling their empty little heads with the wisdom of the ages!

Deep down inside there is a real person, an individual. I do not want to trample my muddy boots on their field of pure white snow! There must be ways to preserve individuality while providing an enriching education, appreciation of the arts, adventurous travel, exploration of religion, all the while watching for ways to nurture their interests and talents.

Like Sammy David Jr., I'm singing "I've gotta be me!"

I knew from observing two-pay-cheque families that I wanted to stay home full-time. I wanted to dry every tear, see

Thursday, June 2, 2006

every 'first time,' encourage invention and tuck each child into bed myself.

Like Jim Nabors, I am singing,

'To Dream the Impossible Dream.'

$$\$\$\,\$1000\$\,\$\,\$$

They say, "A woman's work is never done."

I say, "A woman's work is also entirely unpaid."

Which is fine. I did the math. Between the things I would not have to buy (second car and all related expenses, business wardrobe, childcare) and the things I could do myself (haircuts, mending, gifts, firewood, garden and preservation of food) or make-do (Thrift Store, here I come!) I knew I would not really have less by earning less.

Exchange
1984-2004

1984

After six years of living in the bush and two babies, we moved into town. Now we had bills. Electricity. Phone. Propane. Water. Land taxes. Sometimes I had to 'Rob Peter to Pay Paul.' Even while running a tight budget, there were times I could only pay $10 here or $20 there, and wait until later to finish paying the total.

The children learned that there was more than one way to get what was needed. They watched Kevin make our furniture, repair the truck, install a window, clean the chimney, hang a door, build a porch. They saw me baking bread, making clothes, braiding rugs, laying out quilts, barter. They knew we did favours for people, who later did favours for us.

June Chapter 8   Parent Educator : $1000

2000

Once we came back from a trip back east. Upon returning home, Nicholas asked me, "Mom, are we poor?" He had seen bigger houses with multiple bathrooms, big televisions, wall-to-wall carpet, beautiful drapery, matching bedroom suites, more than one vehicle in the garage, trampolines, backyard swimming pools, horses.

"Grab a pen," I said. "Add this up." I started to tally up "What we need right now" and the price it would take to buy everything brand new. What would it cost if everyone had new sheets and a store-bought bedspread, lamp, furniture, winter coat and boots, haircut and swimming lessons, towels and dishes, silverware and kitchen appliances? I was dizzy! $80,000? $100,000? More?

Unthinkable to mention including a new pickup truck for Kevin and a new car for me as well as the full price of college tuition for four young adults. Yipes!

And yet, we already had all of those needs provided for, mismatched as they were. Tuition grants, DIY, second hand, they all kept us supplied and content.

$ $ 1000 $ $

Still, as our children grew and no longer needed me to tie shoes and zip coats, I realized that my role as all-day-every-day 'Mom' was fading fast.

Is there anything I know, or can make, or can do that others need? Is there any realistic way that I can earn a significant amount of money?

Having quit university (twice) I now lived the rural lifestyle without the advantage of registering with adult education or job training courses. I was pretty limited. I did earn the Provincial Instructor's Diploma by taking most of the courses online.

Volunteering was fun. Having a hobby that pays for itself was fun. Earning my own 'pocket money' was fun. But seriously, by 2004, all four of our children were going away to private school or college, and I was home alone. Not only that. Kevin could not afford tuition, texts, room and board, travel, and eventually, four weddings on his one wage.

Value
2005

The phone rang. It was my brother in New York.

"I'll be travelling overseas quite a bit for the foreseeable future. Would it be at all possible for you to come and live here, to be the Nanny for our two children?"

So I did. For a whole year.

In fact, one-by-one, I have been a Nanny for each of my siblings' children while they travel, or go back to school, or start a business, or advance their career.

Airfare paid. Room and board covered. Enough cash to cover our sons' monthly tuition payments. I'm in!

One More Thing
June 1, 2006

"Eleanor. Call me. I was just at a meeting. They want to hire someone and the job description suits you perfectly." It was an email from Cheryl. She was my neighbour at home. I was still in New York City.

I phoned her to find out more. "The community organization is expanding. They want to hire people to support parents in their homes, observe how the family members interact,

model parenting skills, keep the children in their families and out of Foster Care. You'd be perfect. Here's who to contact."
 I phoned the agency and set up an interview. Pretty soon I was on an airplane, going home, starting a career! My skills are essential. I can provide in-home coaching for parents!

$$\$\$\$1000\$\$\$$$

Babies need stimulation. I knew face-to-face nursery rhymes, bathtub play, showed the parents how to tell if their child could hear, see, be safe, get enough nutrition and sleep, recognize developmental milestones.

Toddlers need stimulation, too, not life in a restrictive playpen, highchair, or in a bedroom with the door closed, not with endless TV droning on and on. I showed the parents how to pretend, ask questions instead of reading the words in books, how beneficial it is to repeat words, songs, games, routines of the day.

School-aged children need stability. Rules. "Yes" means 'Yes,' and "No" means 'No.' I made charts, taught children self-care skills, encouraged everyone to do chores, helped with homework, strengthened readers, pointed out the benefits of bedtime routines, hygiene, I even bought the children books from the Thrift Store as rewards for jobs well done.

Pre-teens need to develop self-governance. "Tell me three times when..." became an often repeated phrase I used to make them stop and think about their words, actions, reactions and decisions. "Tell me three times when it is OK to throw something? Tell me three times when it is dangerous, even criminal to throw something?" Spit. Hit. Kick. Be loud. Push. Slam the door. You can decide what to do to express yourself, without hurting yourself, hurting others or damaging property.

Thursday, June 2, 2006

Parents need encouragement. These teen mothers were stuck at home, unprepared, single. There was a need for education and coaching. I was good at it.

Parent education can also be delivered through meetings and classes. I did that, too.

$$\$\$\,\$1000\$\,\$\,\$$

Then, I developed my own! I took my seminars on the road. I made them laugh. I made them cry. The room was silent. Everyone was talking at once. The day after the seminar, participants told me solutions to problems that I never gave them answers for. I simply showed them seven patterns found recurring in nature, and how they might apply them to their situation. I simply told them how the pattern of a fairy-tale holds information about child development. I simply gave them a few pointers to be able to address normal, predictable, daily moments when children might be grumpy, or resist, might need a reminder, maybe need the adult to hold strong to one thing, or maybe shift a little and be flexible.

$$\$\$\,\$1000\$\,\$\,\$$

Being a Mother, I have to keep myself in balance, too. Now, that is a hard thing to do! I have given up my own sleep, my nourishment, my air and blood and experienced those ever-changing hormones. I have struggled with doubts and renewed my courage, reached for my hopes and battled my fears. All of this is so that I can focus on my children. I am exhausted. It will take more than 'a bubble bath and a candle' for me to be refreshed and face tomorrow anew. I will need other women. I will need to Journal or draw or sing or punch a pillow. I will need privacy and a social life. I will need information about so many things and not enough time to learn it all. I need to trust my gut and realize I know nothing for sure.

Being a Mother is an impossible puzzle. Every mother I know doubts herself. Yet, every mother I know is pouring her 'Self' out 24/7. No box of chocolates or Mother's Day poem can ever express enough appreciation for the unpaid work done in the home.

I know you do it. And I respect and admire you. It is the most valuable work on the Planet. Find a web of Mothers. Feel the support. Draw in what you need. You can do this!

How were parents impacted by the "Stay Home" orders?...
... turn to 10 Days in July Chapter 8, page 319.

But Wait! There's More

After years of volunteering, working as a Nanny, raising our own four children, I have developed a parenting seminar. I would like to share with you! . Meaningful . Practical . Realistic .

Mealtime
Storytime
Bedtime
Chores
Charts
Money
Holidays
Customs
Ethics
Discipline
Development
"No"

BONUS: Seminar #8 Mommy Matters

... since 1998

Children learn what they live.
When they grow up, they live what they've learned.
If a child lives with criticism,
> He learns to condemn.

If a child lives with hostility,
> He learns to fight.

If a child lives with ridicule,
> He learns to be shy.

If a child lives with shame,
> He learns to feel guilty.

If a child lives with tolerance,
> He learns to be patient.

If a child lives with encouragement,
> He learns confidence.

If a child lives with praise,
> He learns appreciation.

If a child lives with fairness,
> He learns justice.

If a child lives with security,
    He learns to have faith.
If a child lives with approval,
    He learns to like himself.
If a child lives with acceptance
and friendship,
    He learns to find love.
—Dorothy Nolte

The **Mommy Matters** workshop is not about tips and bits of advice. It is about developing a wholesome philosophy, moving from 'discipline' (parent telling child what to do) to 'self-discipline' (child can make decisions for himself-herself).

During my work as a Nanny and Parent Educator, I have observed a frequent struggle that many Mothers seem to have: not feeling 'Good Enough.'

Here are some ways to replace self-doubt with more wholesome messages to yourself.

Wholesome things for Mommy to be thinking

"I am not the best. I am not the worst.
I am in the middle somewhere."

Think of a Circle – a Cycle.

Spring – Summer – Fall – Winter
Morning – Noon – Evening – Night
Childhood – Teen – Adult – Old Age
Prepare – Do the task – Clean up – Rest
Think: "Where am I in the CIRCLE?"

I cannot make the cycle go faster or skip any steps. It helps to realize where I am and not feel frustrated.

The misbehaviour of the child is not a measure of my worth. Keep some distance. Keep cool. I can think of a way to solve this problem.

Think: "What can I do with what I have?"

Whisper: Children have excellent, sensitive hearing. So, instead of raising my voice, I can sing or chant or whisper instructions.

Fill-up Prevents Flare-up

HEART: Give lots of love often: eyes, voice, smile, touch, words.

SPIRIT: Show you value each other. Manners, waiting, everyone will get some, you are special.

MIND: Tell child the plan. Share information.
Give an explanation.

BODY: Provide for physical needs. Warm - Cold.
Need to be active - Need to rest. Hungry – Thirsty. Need toilet.

An empty child is ready to flare up.
Look after my own needs, too.

Making choices:

There are many times in a day when I can allow my child to make choices: clothing, snack, toys. There can be many options and possibilities.

"I want!"
Be aware of how often I say, "Do you want...?"
Be aware of the hazards of child saying "I want."
"I want! I want!"

Teach my child by my example to say:
"Do you need__?" or "Would you like___?" not always "Do you want___?"

Teach my child to ask:
"May I please have ___?"

Ask myself "Who is in charge?"
"I want" puts the child in charge.
Then the child is ruling the adults.
When the child does not get his/her way, this is usually the start of a meltdown.
"I want ___!"
"I don't want ___!"

Making decisions

Usually "Yes" means 'Yes' and "No" means 'No.'
Often there is room for a middle answer.
"Not yet."
"When it's your turn."
"Pretty soon."
"After ___"
"Good idea... but not today."
"It's not your turn yet."
"Let me think about it."

Time to obey

There are many times in a day that I expect my child to obey. There are no options or choices. Seat belt. Toothbrush. Safety. Getting ready on time.

Here are some ways I can indicate to my child that this is not a time for choices. It is a time to obey.

"N - O spells No."

"Shall I stop you? or can you stop yourself?"

"When I tell you to (do something) I want you to go forward in a forwardly motion!"

"When I tell you to (do something) I want you to go as straight as an arrow!"

"When I tell you to (do something) I want you to get a nice fresh 'Yes, Mother' ready!"

"You may ___ or you may ___, but you may not say, 'No' to me."

Practice obedience games:
Mother May I
Simon Says

Transitions
Practice stop and start in fun ways:

Red Light - Green Light

"In ___ minutes we are going to ___."

Predictable ways to begin or say "Hello."
Predictable ways to end or say "Good-bye."

Plus, Zero and Minus Ethics
There is a lot to learn about getting along with other people. These ideas and words can help.
"You may join in or you may stay out,
but
you may not wreck what (I am, s/he is, they are, we are) doing."

"Tell me 3 times when..." is a helpful idea.
  a) "Tell me three times when throwing is helpful?" (kicking, hitting, pushing). People will say, "Good for you!" (sports, strength to help others, succeed at a difficult task)
  b) "Tell me three times when throwing is harmful?" (kicking, hitting, pushing) People will say, "Stop! Danger!" (hurting a person's body, breaking something, knocking something over)

Serenity Prayer
What are the things that cannot change?
What are the things that can change?

Selfish / Sorry
Sometimes children grab, or want to be first.
"Wait until I give it to you."

Sometimes children accidentally do harm.
It is important to admit "I did it" and not walk away, make an excuse or blame someone else.
Set an example by saying:
"Oops!"
"Tut-tut!"
"I'm sorry!"

Helping
Children like to join in, feel needed. It feels good to have a sense of belonging and accomplishment: food prep, clean-up, carry, message, care of siblings.

'Tubby-Time'

While one child is in the bathtub, the other family members hurry to put away toys and tidy up. Then all of the helpers hide. When the child comes out of the bathroom, they act surprised and say, "O, wow, where did the toys go?"

'Job Jar'

On small slips of paper write down each job one-by-one: sweep the stairs, empty the trash, clean off coffee table, etc. Put in large jar. Each family member must pick one. Fun surprise if I have something easy. Exaggerated moaning if I get something hard.

"What can I do to help?"

Give many opportunities for child to ask, "What can I do to help?" Loading/ unloading the car, washing machine, dryer. Pet care. Kitchen tasks. After a meal. Weekly chores.

Charts

Making a chart helps me see "what can change and what cannot change." It's like putting the Serenity Prayer to good use.

A chart shows the child things that cannot change.
Examples: What to pack in your lunch. What to do before bed.

Use a clock, timer, chart, calendar, or list.

This will reduce the struggle between the parent and child. Coaxing. Whining. Uncooperative. Repetition.
Now the child will see what is expected on the chart. The chart is not negotiable.

"Are you done with your chores? Go look at the chart."

"We will do this ___ after you finish ___ that is on the chart."

"First ___ then ___."
"Go look at the chart."

Bedtime

A regular bedtime routine ends the day smoothly, most of the time.

It can begin with a simple announcement:
"Toilet…Teeth…Book…and Bed!"

Here are fun ways to tuck my child in.
"Big hug…Small hug…"
"I love you so much" (say a ridiculous form of measurement like "My love would fill a barrel to the brim")
'Story Back Rub' (plant garden, bake cookies)
Tell a story of my own life, or grandparent's life, or my child's life, remember when___.

Chapter 9
Tuesday, June 28, 1988
Tuesday, June 17, 2008
"You will pay me $1000 to read?"

> I am only one,
> and yet, I am one.
> I cannot do everything,
> yet, I can so something.
> —Helen Keller

Before we Begin

While I grew up, reading was my favourite activity. I read the cereal box at breakfast time. I read my library book on the school bus. I read my lessons at school. I read books from our family bookshelves before bedtime.

In school, I loved the SRA cards that encouraged independent reading and strengthened each student's reading skills. When assignments were done, students were free to select a new card at the reading level exactly right for them. Not too easy. Not too hard. The cards were colour coded. Red. Brown. Turquoise. Green. You knew what section you could choose to experience reading with success. Each card had a story and multiple-choice questions. Each student had an answer sheet to fill in. The answer code was on another card at the back of the SRA box so each person could check their own work. By recording the score, students knew when they were competent at that level, and could move on to more difficult reading.

Plan
1987

I am at an interview for a real job! There is an opening at the Avola Library!

"Yes, you can bring your baby with you. It's only for three hours a week. You will have a partner to take the other three hours per week. Your duties include: checking out and re-shelving the books that were borrowed. Keeping records and mailing your statistics into headquarters every month. Looking after the petty cash for buying stamps, craft supplies, or other incidentals. If you're not sure about anything, phone us first, before you take action. Twice a year we exchange about 300 books, so you have to withdraw those you think are of less interest to your patrons, and then put the new books into the right place. You have an additional hour each month for mopping the floor, cleaning the washrooms and dusting. Of course, you have to keep the room tidy every week. You can't loan out the key and you have to make sure everyone who comes in obeys the rules: no smoking, quiet voices, care of the books. The pay is $9.00 per hour."

Tuesday, June 28, 1988 Tuesday, June 17, 2008

It doesn't take me very long to decide. The library is in the Avola Schoolhouse right across the street from my house! I already go to the library every week with my children.

"Yes!" I can hardly contain myself. "Yes, I would like to do this job."

When I get home I scribble on a piece of paper: $9.00 per hour x 3 hours per week x 4 weeks x 12 months = I'll be making over $1000 in a year! Practically a fortune!

$$$ 1000 $ $

The one-room log Avola Schoolhouse was built in 1939. Many other one-room schoolhouses in British Columbia have been taken down. This one was still in use as the school gym while the three modern portable units were used. When the portable units were removed after the school closed in 1984, the old log building became the new library.

Set in a beautiful landscape, seasonal changes frame the building: spring's flowers, summer's lawns, autumn's foliage, winter's soft snow.

The Avola Schoolhouse is the only major, visual, historic, attraction in Avola. It is a significant source of community pride and identity. There are residents, relatives and visitors who remember attending the school. Questions lead to conversations and relationships are strengthened. Younger generations begin to understand their ancestors. A Geocache site welcomes visitors to pause and learn something of the construction and history. Guests and tourists are curious about the Avola Schoolhouse and enjoy strolling through the area. Local artists have captured the Avola Schoolhouse in a variety of mediums including pen and ink, paint, quilting, charcoal sketches and of course, the schoolhouse has been photographed by international guests as they gain an appreciation of the mountain lifestyle of Canadians and one-room rural schools.

The regional government provides for libraries in small towns. Recently, a system was designed to link all of the libraries together, exchanging books, making the entire collection available on request. This means there is an expanded collection available to even the smallest population. The Avola Library opened only a few years ago. It has become a very popular place to be for three hours, twice a week.

$$ $$1000$ $ $

"Let's have a Spelling Bee!" Ideas pop into my head. We need two teams, a leader, and a prize. Maybe refreshments. Wait. There are three-year-old tots, eager students, university-educated teachers and senior citizens all coming to the library. How can it be 'fair' to have a competition with people who have such different skill levels?

"We'll collect words here on the chalkboard. There will be three categories," I explain. "You can study your list until the day of the Spelling Bee. Then the board will be erased, teams chosen, and the competition will begin."

"The leader will tell you a word and use it in a sentence. When you are ready you 'Say it. Spell it. Say it.' That way the leader knows you are finished. You have to say out loud 'hyphen, capital, new word, apostrophe,' or anything else that is part of spelling the word. If you are correct, you stay. If you make even one mistake, you have to go sit down."

The kids collect words all month. There are over 50 words for each level of difficulty.

December Spelling Bee
Easy: elf, toy, fun, star, ball, tree, sled, wish
Medium: Noel, snowman, feast, secret, egg nog
Hard: mistletoe, decorations, tangerine, North Pole

$ $ 1000 $ $

Most fun of all, I was given the freedom to design Reading Programs for the children. I worked there for five years and I enjoyed every minute of it!

$ $ 1000 $ $

Jack and the Beanstalk: Beanstalk wall mural with castle and giant at the top. Each child has a 'Jack' (a paper doll shaped like a gingerbread man). They can decorate their 'Jack' and write their name and the titles of the books they read.

Hickory Dickory Dock: Each child has a mouse that climbs higher on the clock as they do 12 tasks.

Pirate Map: Each child has a map. Each symbol on the map indicates library skills.

Snowflake: Six points indicate six kinds of books to read.

Christmas Paper Chain: Write the title and author of your book on a strip, add the strip to your chain.

Reading Tasks: Read different kinds of books: Biography, History, Canadian, How-to, Sports, Animals, Poems, Romance, Adventure, Novel, Western, Science, Bible Story, Pamphlet, Magazine, Fairy-Tale, Fantasy, Mystery, Legend, Fable, Myth, Folk Tale.

Library Skills: Table of Contents, Index, National Geographic, locate a book by author's name, locate a book by Dewy Decimal System, locate a book by title, use the dictionary, encyclopedia, atlas, globe, sign out your own books correctly, put your returned books away properly, read about something you saw on TV, read aloud to another person, find a book about your favourite animal, find a book about a place you have been, find a book about a job you would like to do.

$$\$\$\$1000\$\$\$$

Theme: **Princess and the Pea**
Start Date: June 28, 1988
Party Date: August 30, 1988
Poster / Wall mural / Chart: all illustrate the Princess sleeping on top of ten mattresses.
Chart: colour one mattress for each book
Entertainment: Skit
Prize: Pillow
Refreshments: Layers: cookies, sandwiches
10 Tasks: Read 10 books in 10 weeks
Who – read a book about a person
What – what is your favourite animal
Where – read a book about where you live
When – read a book about the old days
How – read to learn how to do something
Why – read a mystery
That's Silly – read a funny book
Poem – read a collection of poems
Order – order a book that especially interests you
Read aloud – to someone who can't read

$$\$\$\$1000\$\$\$$

When the school closed in 1984, everyone who could leave, left. The logging was also slowing down.

Even the railroad needed fewer employees as more machinery took over the work of man and muscle. The population of our tiny town was shrinking.

Exchange
1992

A letter from headquarters announced the upcoming closure of the Avola Library. In exchange, we were offered a Bookmobile, scheduled to visit Avola for one hour every three weeks.

In an attempt to communicate with the decision-makers, the children launched a letter-writing campaign. I encouraged them to take on the experience of attempting to influence this level of local government.

> I would like the Bookmobile to be bigger, until it fills up the whole playground and we can use it for a gym. I wouldn't like the library to be closed for ever and ever and ever.
> Danny

> I would really like the library to be open and not locked up always. Because, maybe, if you guys would like to, you could keep it for a big place for people to play in. And, if you close the library and use the bookmobile, can you please move something in so people can sit? Can people bring their own toys and play?
> From, Nicholas

> We think that the Avola Library should be left open. We can't go to the bookmobile because we will be at school. So we will keep printing letters till the library is left open.
> From, Will Tooker

June Chapter 9   "You will pay me $1000 to read?"

To whom it may concern,
My name is Elise Dellmar. I am twelve years old. I received my first library card when I turned five and have been taking books out of the Avola Library ever since. I remember helping move our previous library into the present building.

I enjoy reading. It has been my hobby since I was three. I want to be a Lawyer or Grade Seven Creative Writing teacher. To do this, I must be able to read.

I helped protest the coming of the bookmobile the first time even though I was in bed with the chickenpox. The bookmobile will not be able to provide me with adequate material often enough.

I usually take out from four to eight books a week. The selection at our library sometimes doesn't satisfy me. I go to Blue River for school Monday to Friday. I leave the house at quarter past seven and return home at three-thirty. If we receive the bookmobile's services it will have to come after three thirty to benefit me.

Although I don't welcome the bookmobile with open arms, I am willing to accept it providing it suits my needs.

In closing, I wish to say that losing this library is like losing my lifelong best friend.
Yours Truly, Elise Dellmar

If the Library is closed and the Book Mobile comes, I will not be able to go because I will be at school. We kids take out most of the books. So soon you will take the Book Mobile too. We get 15 minutes in the library at school and it doesn't have any good books. If the Book Mobile must come, make it after 4:00.
From, Michael Dellmar

Tuesday, June 28, 1988 Tuesday, June 17, 2008

> Hello.
> I hope this will save the Library in Avola.
> The Library is my best place.
> I would like the Library to stay open for weeks and weeks and weeks.
> No bookmobiles allowed!
> If we don't have a library anymore, I won't have my Garfield books that I like.
> Toby
> PS Now <u>that</u> will save the Library! They'll read that and they'll get out'a here!

$ $ 1000 $ $

June 7, 1992

Representatives from Library Headquarters met with Avola residents. I read my letter aloud.

> I know that on your pages of statistics, our library is an enormous cost for very few books and people.
> Yet, in some ways, your money could not be better spent.
> Do we have a public swimming pool? Skating rink? Sports centre? Youth club? Adult club? Service organizations? Church? School? Public meeting place? No.
> Yet, if we had any of these, it would only fill one need for one group.
> The library fills a little bit of several of these needs.
> Without it, we'll have almost nothing.
> *Something* is so much more than *nothing*.
> Sometimes a small service can make a big difference.
> Eleanor Deckert, Avola Librarian.

Protests and phone calls, letters and newspaper articles, even radio interviews did nothing to change the decision. The proposed Bookmobile would do little to re-create the experiences

June Chapter 9   "You will pay me $1000 to read?"

the community has been enjoying with their neighbours. But, since the school closure, the population of the village had become so small, that the statistics simply could not support the project.

$ $ 1000 $ $

November 10, 1992

After the library closure, while the children were still so loyal, we decided the Avola Community Reading Room would stay open, now run by volunteers.

So, I designed another Reading Program, this time to build team spirit and encourage the children to continue coming to the library. Each child was given a paper chart that looked like a big, round, black soup pot. I read aloud the traditional story of 'Stone Soup.' During a time of poverty and lack, the people in the village each shared the little bit of food that they had. Together, they made enough food for everyone.

Each time a child performed a task in support of the Reading Room, they added an ingredient to their soup pot.

black pot = read story of 'Stone Soup'
white barley = come to Reading Room for first time
salt and pepper = invite someone to the Reading Room
orange carrot = write a thank you note
brown potato = bring an empty box
green pea pod = tell about when people work together
red tomato = donate a book
tan bone = say "We can do this together" or "Yay team"
purple turnip = donate a magazine
yellow beans = make a poster for the Reading Room
white onion = bring an adult to help

Tuesday, June 28, 1988 Tuesday, June 17, 2008

$\$\$\$1000\$\$\$$

Meanwhile, we sold chocolate bars to raise money to buy books. Headquarters offered us books they were going to discard for $5.00 per case! A desk and chair, a table for puzzles and crafts were donated, but, no one had extra shelving.

We used some of the chocolate bar money to buy lumber. A retired carpenter, Len, offered to design and construct a clever set of two-sided shelves on casters that could roll over to the side of the room so that the space could also be used for larger events.

The Avola Schoolhouse has continued to be a meeting place, activity centre, library, and multi-purpose community room for many more years.

Value

2001

"So, basically, you are going to pay me to read?"

Again, I was applying for a real job. $15.75 seemed a lot of money to me. What, exactly, would be my responsibilities?

"It is the Self-Employment Program you took a few summers ago. Now it is delivered on a one-to-one basis instead of as a group seminar. People can choose which components they want to cover. You set up appointments to meet with individuals."

"But, I am not an employment counsellor!" I couldn't imagine giving expert guidance to people.

"Here are the workbooks, you just read them aloud with your client!"

Sounds easy. And valuable. I took the job. In four months I earned a whopping $3000... enough to re-outfit my kitchen!

One More Thing
June 17, 2008
Mother Goose

Another opportunity seemed perfect for me. The 'Mother Goose' program coaches parents to stimulate language development through face-to-face play with their babies and toddlers. Nursery rhymes, finger games, rhythmic actions and peek-a-boo are just what I like to do.

A paying job? Bliss!

Reading... you can do this during the pandemic...
... what is Eleanor reading? See 10 Days in July Chapter 9, page 325.

But Wait! There's More

After years of volunteering with children, employment in over 80 families, taking courses in Early Child Development, completing training as a Parent Educator, I went back to college.

One of my assignments was to take two disciplines and blend them together into a presentation. I have my own ideas about Child Development... *and* I love Fairy-Tales. Could I fit them together?

Here is my seminar.

BONUS: Seminar #9
What do Fairy-Tales tell us about Child Development?

... since 2001

> The universe is made of stories not atoms.
> —Muriel Rukeyser

Families within our society are so diverse.

What resources do parents and educators have that, like a bridge, can relay important information about child development in language, images and sequences that participants will remember and use in the fast pace of everyday family life?

Fairy-Tales are one such resource, a shared experience across generations that holds age-old wisdom and contains a reliable 'map' to guide caregivers and parents as they provide for children's ever-changing developmental needs.

Some say folk and fairy-tales are pure entertainment, told in the firelight to nodding children. Some say that as humans evolved they invented stories to explain the forces of Nature.

Scholars catalogue the archetypes, theorizing about how languages and cultures mingle. Historians claim that biographies, tragedies and battles expand to heroic proportions in the telling and are passed on as fictionalized accounts of actual events. The religious point to the deterioration of sacred texts after many oral repetitions and may shun the crudely twisted folkways.

But, just suppose for a moment that there is something deeper, timeless and very powerful within the fairy-tale.

What if the stories we know and love, passed on through centuries, over mountains and deserts and across oceans are actually 'true' stories? Could simple oral traditions hold rich symbolic meaning? Perhaps we can find here, carefully preserved, a true map for the invisible Journey of our innermost being.

How else could these tales circumscribe the globe, reaching into huts and mansions, connecting the wise and the very young of so many nations and cultures? Why would unwritten stories be revered and preserved over such an expanse of time? And how is it that similar stories can be found in unrelated cultures?

Infancy, Toddlerhood, Childhood, Youth and Young Adulthood, each with their own fascinating characteristics are described in well-known fairy-tales. As the Hero or Heroine meets loss, endless tasks and faces death, so, too, we each pass through these inner wanderings, battles and reach for the happy ending.

And if this theory is worth considering, then the valuable information hidden within fairy-tales is available to parents and others who work with children to better understand, protect and provide for them as they begin their journey through life.

Many patterns are repeated in well-known fairy-tales. Think of Snow White, Cinderella and Sleeping Beauty.

What do Fairy-Tales tell us about Child Development?

Once upon a time.....

King and Queen have waited so long...
now... their special baby is born.
Rejoice! Gifts! People gather! All is well!
(How does this tell us what an **Infant** needs?)
(Abundance. Precious. Cared for 24/7. Bliss.)

Sadly, the Mother dies...
King remarries, then travels (or dies).
Toddler is an orphan.
Stepmother raises Tot.
(How does this tell us what a **Tot** needs?)
(Parents say "No." Tot no longer has pure bliss.)

Stepmother makes strict rules and much work.
Rules. Rules. Rules.
Every day is much the same until...
(How does this tell us what a **Child** needs?)
(School. Coach. Parents. All insist on Rules.)

Teen runs away to forest...wilderness...
Teen feels alone.
Magical helpers come.
(How does this tell us what a **Teen** needs?)
(Teen is away from home more and more.)
(Teen finds peers, team, group to belong to.)
(Mentor helps Teen with problems.)

Great battle. Good vs. Evil.
Threat of death...
Prince conquers threat.
(How does this tell us what an **Adult** needs?)

(Adult must make moral decisions.)
(What is 'good? What is 'evil'? What will I do?)
(Adult can provide for and protect his/herself.)

Wedding. Rule together.
(Both Prince [mind/logic] and Princess [heart/emotions] are within each person)
("Happily Ever After" = sustainable balance.)

Participants are:
Parents, educators and other child-care professionals who observe changes and guide children through transitions.

Participants learn from:
instructor
brainstorming
noticing patterns within well-known fairy-tales
noticing patterns typical of development
small group discussion
self-observation and personal experiences

Participants benefit:
Ability to recall and apply concepts in parenting/child care decisions.
Notice signals of child's developmental changes and therefore the need to adapt parenting strategies.
Feel a sense of encouragement and satisfaction about their work with children of different ages. Share experiences.

Participants continue to:
With a sense of exploration, discover ways to apply this new knowledge to situations and problems in the workplace, at home and in their own personal growth.

Chapter 10
Thursday, June 25, 2015
$1000 : Ink

> Insist on yourself; never imitate.
> Your own gift you can offer
> with the cumulative force of a whole life's cultivation,
> but of the adopted talent of another,
> you have only half possession.
> —*Ralph Waldo Emerson*

Before we Begin

All of these attempts at earning money and self-employment over all of these years have been fun, but nothing has really been sustainable. If I make some kind of product myself, I have to repeat and repeat, one-by-one, and hope there is someone out there who wants to buy them. My pies, jam, baking, etc. are not consistently good enough. Neither is my sewing or other handwork. If I am paid by the hour, there is no room to explore or develop or be creative. The creative things, like dance, teaching or coaching parents involve hours and hours of preparation and driving, both of these expenses I cannot factor into the one-hour meeting time. I live in a region of low-income, small population, great distance, harsh winter weather. How can I overcome these obstacles?

What could I possibly do for both creative satisfaction and significant pay and magically continue to sell this 'something' without me reproducing it myself? or arriving in my car? or lugging equipment around all over the place?

Plan

Writing!

For many years Mrs. Mary Gibson wrote a weekly column for the local newspaper sharing tid-bits of Avola news. Then Mrs. Fran McRae took a turn. Baby showers, visitors, children's activities and school functions, seasons and holidays. Maybe Mrs. Eleanor Deckert could give it a try?

I think the first time I wrote for the newspaper was 1987, describing the Library Opening in Avola! There was a need for a weekly column from our village, so I accepted the responsibility. There isn't much news. Also, I found it difficult to write as a Journalist, reporting without also sharing my opinion.

I asked if I could write a column about whatever popped into my pretty-little-head? I sent in a few samples.

Poetic seasonal descriptions. Concern over safety in a rusty playground. Report on Ladies' Auxiliary Club activities. School kids hosting a fundraiser. I could turn everyday events and common knowledge into sparkling prose.

$$$1000$ $ $

I was offered $1 per column-inch. Write about 350 words per week. Averaging about $15 for each column. It takes about one-and-a-half hours to hunt-and-peck-peck-peck on my keyboard. (I type with two fingers) OK. I'll do it. At this rate, I will have to write 67 columns to reach $1000. But, I can do it.

Exchange
1998

Before I completely accepted the responsibility to write a weekly column, I wanted to meet with the editor. He had said some pretty encouraging things about my style of writing, and he really wanted me to continue. But I had one invisible obstacle to overcome.

The editor was a very quiet fellow, a little older than me. I hardly knew him, except as the guy with the camera whenever there was a community event. I needed to tell him something pretty emotional, so I drove to town. We agreed to meet outside at the library.

"I want to tell you a very personal thing: The religion I was raised in held as sacred some books written in the 1700s. They said, as Holy and unalterable text, that women who write, speak in public or preach will go insane and go to Hell. I learned this *after* I went to the Pastor and declared that I wanted to enter the clergy. I was 13. I was devastated. I left home, lived a spartan lifestyle, endured frigid cold, poverty and isolation."

I felt awkward and agitated. But I gathered my courage to continue. "When I started to write for the newspaper and you asked if I would like a column, I wanted to meet with you to talk about this barricade. I feel such danger to be crossing into this forbidden territory. Breaking this Taboo. Looking directly into God's face and saying, 'Tough!' and 'I'm going to do it anyway!' However, I don't actually feel rebellious! I feel like a colt running, a bird flying, a child singing, a flower opening. How could the 'Gift' the Creator gave me somehow be filthy?

Wouldn't neglecting my Gift actually be more disrespectful? I am telling you this because, yes, I want to write, but I feel more than 'stage fright.' You say I have talent, great, but I am also dealing with a *lot* of anxiety!"

He quietly listened, observing my stress, perhaps a little confused about my 'I can't - I have to' struggle. Obviously, he is unaccustomed to a woman pouring out her heart. He stepped back and simply said, "Think about it. Let me know what you decide. You are good at what you do."[13]

Value

Let me think. I've been writing columns for one newspaper for about 25 years! They pay $1 per column inch.

I just got off the phone with the Editor of another newspaper. She'll pay me 10¢ per word. She wants 700 – 1000 words!

$15 per weekly column? Or $70-$100 per weekly column? It's not hard to do that Math!

One More Thing

One year, I volunteered to start a newsletter for homeschoolers.

Later, I wrote my own 'Seven Predictable Patterns® Newsletter' and had 150 subscribers. The subscription covered photocopying and postage. I broke even.

More recently, I asked local businesses for advertising, and produced the 'Mountain Wellness' coffee-shop style newsletter for a little over two years. I never made much of a profit, but I made a lot of amazing trades. I swapped an interview on the front page with a business owner in exchange for their product or service.

Now I write a column transforming ink on paper. I have earned $3000 to buy my own car!

Thursday, June 25, 2015

$ $ 1000 $ $

On January 1st, 2014, I suddenly realized, my Mom is turning 80 this year. If I want her to read the book I am going to write someday, I'd jolly well better get it written!

Steadily, weekly, wrapped in my blanket during the dark winter days, I eventually had my whole story written down. Ink on paper. I printed one chapter every week and mailed it to her, rough, but done. '10 Days in December... where dreams meet reality' was taking shape! A city girl's Journal. A coming-of-age story. A newly-wed romance. A memoir.

Cleaning and polishing took time. Two-finger typing is not the best method! Kevin did the research and recommended FriesenPress, which offered a form of self-publishing that included skilled coaches, editors and training in marketing strategies. I visited the office and found everyone welcoming, information clear, and the project manager was straightforward. Owned in Canada, the Friesen's printing press has been in business since 1907. I toured the huge printing facility. Bliss!

June 25, 2015

From: Project Manager: FriesenPress: Publisher

Hi Eleanor,
I received your final manuscript. Very exciting!
I have news for you too—your cover designs are complete.
As you know, with self-publishing you have full creative control over all content. Please look closely at these proofs of the book text and cover.
Check the following: font type, font size, line spacing, text spacing, spelling/grammar/punctuation, image resolution/ alignment/colour/ positioning, etc.

$ $ 1000 $ $

While I meticulously went through the process of checking every decision and detail, I wondered, "Do I dare put 'Book 1' on the front cover? Can I write more?"
Since I was eight years old, I knew I wanted to write a book. Everyone else in my family seemed to be authors. I have written one. How hard would it be to write more?
I grabbed a pen and paper, drew lines to make a chart, filled in the months and numbers one to ten.
It didn't take long to realize: I could write an entire series! Really? Yes! There are anniversaries and seasons, holidays and achievements, turning points and personal goals, grief and celebrations.
My husband has retired. Our children are grown and gone. I have lived a varied and deliberate life. I am not embarrassed to talk about what I think, feel, observe, discover, how I puzzle through decisions, and when, where and why I changed direction, who has influenced me and what I believe, where I came from, where I am now and where I think I am going.
There won't be any thrilling chase scenes, no 'sowing wild oats', no dangerous criminal activity or frightening violence. 'Read Wholesome' is my slogan. With so many people making lifestyle habits surrounding their physical health, surely there are Readers who would enjoy following the inner workings of an individual who was trying to also be healthy on the inside. Seeking goodness, light, kindness. Aware of the impact that attitudes and intentions have on the people we interact with. Aware of our footprint on the earth. Aware of our own Path.

$ $ 1000 $ $

Is there a Plan?
I ask. I listen. I watch. I try to remember.

Thursday, June 25, 2015

I cannot see up ahead. But, I can look back, follow my own trail, notice the stepping stones, see the patterns. And yes, I think there is a Guide. I think there is a Plan. Not a predetermined script, but rather, a welcoming Potential.

I am like a butterfly, leaving behind the limitations of my Caterpillar-Self. Ready to be released from the restriction of the Cocoon I made for myself from misunderstandings, silent lies, constricting taboos, outdated roles. Stretching and unfolding, pushing towards light and air and life itself. I believe there is Someone with my best interests in mind, Who, with little nudges, prompts, and whispers is leading me towards fulfilling my Purpose.

Not just me.

You, too.

To learn how Eleanor's writing developed during the lengthy isolation of the Covid-19 shut-downs...
...turn to 10 Days in July, Chapter 10, page 329.

But wait! There's More

After three years of speaking at libraries, schools and book stores, I have developed this seminar for authors. I would like to share it with you!

BONUS: Seminar #10 "Eleanor Deckert's Memoir Writing Method" . Title . Theme . Topics . Tips .

... since 2018

Look to this day, for it is Life...
... For yesterday is but a dream
and tomorrow is but a vision,
but today, well lived
makes every yesterday a dream of happiness
and every tomorrow a vision of hope.
—*Sanskrit Proverb*

My husband is a Tracker:
    He follows clues others leave on the trail.
    I am a Writer:
    I leave a trail for the Reader to follow.

I was eight years old when I read the last page of Laura Ingalls Wilder's *Little House in the Big Woods*. Laura wrote, "This is now... it can never be a long time ago..."

Wikipedia: A **memoir** is a collection of memories that an individual writes about moments or events, both public and private, that took place in the subject's life.

Biography. Autobiography. Memoir. Creative non-fiction. Which will you write?

A *very helpful book:*
"The Book You Were Born To Write"
by Kelly Notaras ©2018 Hay House
"Everything you need to know to (finally) get your wisdom onto the page and into the world"

There are **3 kinds of memoir.**

    1: **Narrative: The reader enjoys good storytelling**
    2: **Teaching: The reader learns**
    3: **Transformational: The reader is inspired**

I used all 3 kinds of memoir writing styles in Book 1 *10 Days in December... where dreams meet reality...* by Eleanor Deckert, ©2016 FriesenPress

Teaching Memoir: Inform

I described: where my husband and I came from, our trip west, how we found land, built the cabin and use the woodstove.

Narrative Memoir: Entertain

I described: our wedding, how a city girl felt confused and embarrassed when facing problems. Humour: "Who ate the fruitcake?"

Transformational Memoir: Inspire

I described: emotions brought on by each Christmas carol, the agony of isolation, and the gradual realization of one part of Christmas I had never before experienced.

Writing Exercise:
    a) Write one sentence, the same way you would say it in a conversation.
    b) Now write one word at a time in a column.
    c) Add a little info explaining each word. Do this again and again to build a paragraph.
    d) Now add a back-story, what led up to this? How is this the same or in contrast to other events?
    e) What happened next? What did you learn? How did this shape you? Why is this significant in your life? How will this benefit the Reader? (remember: Inform. Entertain. Inspire.)

Example:
I forgot my lunch... then... I felt... what happened?

I (How old? Describe location? Destination?)
forgot (Morning routine? Interruption? Realization?)
my lunch (Who made it? What was it? Lunch box?)
Then (When you realized? Who reacted? Who helped?)
I felt (Emotions? Resources?)

Title
Title: Sub-title - Chapters - Structure

I will tell you my story.
    I knew since I was a child that I would someday write my memoir... the same way that Laura Ingalls Wilder did. Normal, everyday experiences. 1965 would someday be 'long ago.'

"Eleanor Deckert's Memoir Writing Method"

I paid attention to my parents and their decisions. I noticed my own turning points. I remembered sequences. I was aware of my own Faith Journey.

I had a pretty 'normal' upbringing. As newly-weds, my husband and I joined the 'Back-to-the-Land' movement. (Now people say 'Off-Grid.') I realized that our first winter was 'the story' I would write. There was so much to learn as a 'homesteader,' many years of 'hair-straight-back' parenting our four children... homeschooling... volunteering... writing a newspaper column. Eventually, I got the quiet time to write.

But I didn't want to make a list: "and then we moved to Canada, and then I met Kevin, and then we got married, and then we found land, and then we built our cabin..." Boring!

One day, out of the blue, walking along: BINGO! I suddenly got the title of my book. I realized: I could write my entire life within those first 10 days when we lived in our log cabin during that bitterly cold winter of 1978.

I could make flashbacks to my childhood, where I lived, first jobs, how we met, how we built the cabin, etc... "10 Days in December..." with a subtitle... "where dreams meet reality."

Now the Reader knows: this is a Journal. This is an idealistic person who has a rude awakening to an unexpected challenge.

Could I write a book for each month?

Yes!

The subtitle indicates the theme for each book.

Now, I don't know exactly how to coach anyone else how to find a title, but I DO know that it does a lot of work for you as you find Readers.

Theme
https://literarydevices.net/a-huge-list-of-common-themes/

DO take a moment to open this link. Save it. Treasure.

Keep the Theme for your book clearly in mind. Inspiration. Avoid detours and sidetracks. Focus. Emphasis. Details.

Theme: Isolation
Title: 10 Days in December... where dreams meet reality
(a city girl's homesteading journal)

Theme: Identity
Title: 10 Days in January...
... 1 Husband, 2 Brothers, 3 Sons, 4 Dads
(family dynamics, bright and dark portraits)

Theme: Enough / Not Enough
Title: 10 Days in February... Limitations
(winter blues, SAD, depression)

Theme: Connection / Community
Title: 10 Days in March... Possibilities
(creativity, volunteering)

Theme: Doubt / Trust
Title: 10 Days in April... a detour through breast cancer
(confusion, decisions, trust)

Theme: Early Childhood
Title: 10 Days in May, 1966... freely receive... freely give
('a day in the life' of an eight-year-old)

Theme: Can I earn money with my talents?
Title: 10 Days in June, $1000
(how volunteering became paid work)

Theme: Does one person make a difference?
Title: BONUS: 10 Seminars
(If I can teach children, maybe I can teach adults?)

Theme: Creativity during hardship
Title: 10 Days in July, 2020... shut down... open up
(How did the pandemic impact creativity?)

I honestly didn't think about **'Theme'** until I was well along writing my first book. I shared my manuscript with a relative who works in marketing. She kept saying *"What is the benefit to the Reader? What is your book about?"* I was kind of stunned. The Reader? I just wanted to TALK! I didn't think about anyone LISTENING? Benefit? It was a benefit to *me* to get my life-long dream accomplished.

I had to go back and observe each phrase as an outsider, listen to my own story, writing, emphasis. I needed to focus on what was meaningful about each experience. After I realized the **Theme**: "Isolation," then I realized this truth: "In the Universal is the Particular. In the very private is the Universal."

Topics

I am using the word **Topics** to cover such things as: food, clothing and details that are specific to the time you are writing about, such as available technology, or location, or limitations, or music, or the weather. How are these details part of the story?

Maybe family traditions or holiday customs are side **Topics** you want to include to add colour to your writing, or to compare 'then and now.' Another side **Topic** is pets. If you bring pets into your writing, then you can't leave them out, you have to continue to include them in the story.

Topics are little details that are not really part of the overall story (plot) but bring realism of your experience to the Reader.

To decide what **Topics** to include or leave out: How much is your experience the same or in contrast to people today? Inform. Entertain. Inspire. Keep checking for these.

Make a list of Topics you might include.

Tips
Sequence of steps (check off what you have done)

[   ] **Title.** Even if you are unsure, it helps to have a 'working title.'

[   ] Outline. Hold your ideas still long enough to identify, collect, cluster, compose.

[   ] Write 4 pages per chapter. This is enough to hold the basic construction. You can move pieces around and expand later.

[   ] Expand: Action - Description - Dialogue.

[   ] Find the time of day or night when you won't be interrupted.

[   ] **Time Line** I have a large roll of adding machine paper. I cut off about 2 meters/yards. I folded it in half - half- half to make 8 sections. Each section is 10 years. I wrote the year and my age at intervals within the 10 years. Then I added significant events: births, deaths, moving, school, my own achievements. This is a way to collect facts in very few words.

[   ] Now go back to the one-sentence exercise and build a paragraph for the events you recall clearly.

[   ] **How to write 'Back Story'**

[   ] Start in the middle. Then go back to the back-story. They use this technique in movies all the time. On the printed page, you have to leave a gap, or a symbol ~ ~ ~ to show the reader you have switched from the present to the past, or from outside yourself to your own inner thoughts. Whenever I need the Reader to know the back-story, that's when I use this method. Where do I use this technique in my writing? As I fall asleep, when I first wake up, riding

along staring out the window, telling my story to someone, in conversation with my husband.

[   ] Keep pen and paper beside your bed. Jot down ideas.
[   ] Write down the details you decide. Be consistent.
ie: *italics* or " or ' for titles, music, names.
[   ] Make Lists - Brainstorm - Use Thesaurus.
- emotions - people - music - places - 5 senses
- food - weather - dates – resources - research
[   ] 'Make a Frame... Then the Picture.'
ie: Describe the wider setting... Then zoom in to the detail.

Glossary: difficult words, spelling, abbreviations, other languages, technical terms.
[   ] Dedication: Write for one specific person.
[   ] Cut anything that does not link to the **Theme.**
[   ] Answer this question: How will this writing benefit the Reader?
[   ] After all of the revisions and corrections, when you think you have something that might be good...
Ask Readers for feedback.

[   ] Are you ready to see your name in print? Have you decided? Submit your manuscript to a publisher? Self-publish for sale? Self-publish for your family? Each pathway has its own challenges and benefits.

As a 'homesteader' (we make our own bread, pickles, jam, grow a garden, sometimes raise chickens, rabbits, ducks, pig, hunt, gather firewood and have gravity feed water, build our own house and furnishings, etc. etc.) I was trying to decide. Will I actually make the books myself? Buy a printer, binder, produce and mail out every copy one-by-one?

Then my husband took the time to research. He found FriesenPress. In 2015, I toured their office in Victoria, British Columbia, and in the summer of 2019 I toured Friesen's printing press in Altona, Manitoba (south of Winnipeg). Every staff member is cheerful, encouraging and informative. I am completely satisfied! Take a look at their web page. There is a lot to learn.

https://www.friesenpress.com/

Why I chose FriesenPress:

- The FriesenPress web page, representative and contract all match.
- Variety of editorial and business services. Fair prices.
- Over 15 years experience. More coaching than 'self-publishing.'
- Global distribution. Royalties and Marketing options.
- Hard cover, soft cover, e-books, ISBN, copyright registration.
- Printing presses in Canada, USA, UK, Australia.
- The books themselves are well constructed and beautiful.

How to claim the available Discount: When you sign the contract with FriesenPress, Mention that you were recommended by: **Eleanor Deckert** *You get a discount... and so do I!*

[   ] Research publishers / self-publishing.
[   ] Submit. Follow their guidelines. Stay on-time.
[   ] Design cover.
[   ] Write foreword, dedication, acknowledgements, epilogue, author bio.
[   ] Research Marketing.
[   ] Schedule dates for Book Launch Events.

EPILOGUE

"Kevin?"

"Hmmm?"

"I'm all packed up: car, food, overnight, seminars, phone numbers, water bottle. It seems like I'm always leaving. I never like to say 'Good-bye' to you! I feel like you are the steady, reliable one. I am flitting here and there. Together we are like a boat. I am the flapping sail. You are the sturdy keel. Twogether we make new things happen."

"Be safe. Come home."

> If one advances confidently
> in the direction of his dreams,
> and endeavors to live the life which he has imagined
> he will meet with a success unexpected in common hours.
> —Henry David Thoreau

10 Days in July, 2020
... lock down... open up

There is in every woman's heart
a spark of heavenly fire,
which lies dormant
in the broad daylight of prosperity;
but which kindles up
and beams and blazes
in the dark hour of adversity.
—*Washington Irving*

a memoir by
Eleanor Deckert
BOOK 8

Table of Contents
10 Days in July
... lock down... open up

Introduction   286

Chapter 1
Wednesday, July 1, 2020
Is there a Plan?
Canada Day   287

Chapter 2
Saturday, July 4, 2020
Border Closed   291

Chapter 3
July, 2020
A Month of Sundays   295

Chapter 4
Wednesday, July 8, 2020
School? Homeschool?   301

Chapter 5
Tuesday, July 14, 2020
Vision Board   305

Chapter 6
Saturday, July 18, 2020
Stuck at Home   311

Chapter 7
Monday, July 20, 2020
Sing? Dance? Alone?   315

Chapter 8
Friday, July 24, 2020
Stay-at-Home-Mom   319

Chapter 9
Thursday, July 30, 2020
Win-Win Win-Win   325

Chapter 10
Friday, July 31, 2020
Writing for Clarity Through the Fog   329

Epilogue   335

INTRODUCTION

For forty-four years I have lived beside the river.
 Where does it come from?
 Where does it go?
 How can 1+1+1 snowflakes make the river rise 9 feet?
 How can 1+1+1 raindrops flow over 400 miles to the sea?
 How can the salmon return to find the place where their parents came to spawn, so they can continue the life cycle?
 How do the geese fly away and return at the right time?
 When the sun rises, I stand on the river bank. I stretch my arms tall and circle wide. Air. Earth. Fire. Water.
 When the sun is high, my children wade, exploring, sensing. Here. Now.
 When the sun is low, I imagine myself as a leaf drifting peacefully, trusting, slow and steady.
 When the sun is gone, I hear a coyote howl, an owl call.
 Mist rises.
 Rain falls.
 What have I learned?
 Where did I come from? Where will I go?
 What will I do? Here? Now?

> The purpose of life is not to be happy.
> it is to be useful, to be honorable,
> to be compassionate,
> to have it make some difference
> that you have lived and lived well.
> —*Ralph Waldo Emerson*

Chapter 1
Wednesday, July 1, 2020
Is there a Plan?
Canada Day

More than ever was I convinced
that the old way of seeing
was inadequate to express this big country of ours,
her depth, her height, her unbounded wildness,
silence too strong to be broken
– nor could ten million cameras,
through their mechanical boxes,
ever show real Canada.
It had to be sensed, passed through live minds,
sensed and loved.
　　—Emily Carr

National Holiday

Ottawa, Ontario, is pretty far away from the mountains of British Columbia, so it is our family custom to watch the Canada Day Celebrations at the capital city on TV. A huge stage is set up in front of the Parliament Buildings. Politicians speak. Entertainers sing. Famous fiddlers, children's choirs, French and Acadian, Native and Meti, tried-and-true and up-and-coming talent are showcased. The crowd is dressed in red and white, silly hats, faces are painted with red maple leaves, mini-flags wave while commentators interview folks in the crowd. New immigrants from the four corners of the world share the happy feelings of belonging to the wild and wonderful country of Canada. Meanwhile, news cameras around the country have been collecting portraits of families, cities, vast landscapes, wildlife and natural geographic formations to remind us all of how special it is to live here. 'A Mari Usque Ad Mare' which being translated is the nation's motto: 'From sea to sea!' As evening cools and the sky darkens, there is one more treat: the finale festival of fireworks.

Our family lives in such a small town, I want our kids to know that they belong to this vast land. But, not only through the television screen. Small towns are well-known for hosting small-town events!

Sometimes, we go north, 40 kilometres (25 miles) to Blue River, to participate in the Canada Day parade and family fun. The Fire Truck leads the way and the Ambulance brings up the rear, crawling slowly through the streets. Kids decorate their bicycles. There are a few horses. Once we decorated our pick-up truck and threw candy. Once we made our little red wagon into a covered wagon and I pulled the baby along. Michael dressed as a cowboy and rode his little hobby-horse. Elise dressed as a pageant princess with white gloves, sparkly sash, tiara and bouquet.

Wednesday, July 1, 2020

❊ Pandemic + Holiday? ❊
This year?

Covid-19 necessitates a very different experience. No parades. No gatherings. No small-town picnics. No festivities at the capital.

How will we be able to participate when abundant outpouring of national loyalty and community spirit is limited to each socially distant front yard?

From the start, restrictions have been put in place, dictating how many people can be 'in your bubble.'

Weddings have been postponed or very private. I saw on YouTube where a Bride and Groom danced down the street. Their guests were parked along both sides, all tuned to the same radio station. Music, balloons, friends waving, confetti, all sharing congratulations and cheer.

Birthday parties for children have become parades, too. The guest of honour is seated on the lawn. The friends pass slowly by with posters instead of cards, throwing candy instead of sharing birthday cake, blinking lights instead of candles, honking horns instead of singing.

A funeral that hosted 65 guests made the news, when 45 people who attended became infected with Covid-19.

❊ ❊ ❊

July 1? I was almost going to skip the whole thing. The disappointment might feel less if I simply forget what day it is. Who cares? But, my curiosity got the best of me. I found the Canada Day celebration on TV.

An oval stage. Two hosts. No audience.

Where the sunny crowds would usually be filling the lawn in Ottawa, this time there was a darkened studio. Where the enormous stage would usually be, new acts every few minutes, offering such a variety of song, dance, displays of traditional clothing, this time there was a huge screen, sharing 2-dimensional samples of talent from across the nation. Where cheering fans would usually be, this time there were tiers of empty seats, each row had a TV screen showing the faces of individuals and families, looking into the studio, somehow watching from their own home.

* ❋ *

Covid-19. Together. Apart.
 "Stay home," they said.
 "Two weeks," they said.
 "Wear a mask," they said.
 "Tiny droplets," they said
 "Flatten the curve," they said.
 "Social Distancing," they said.
 "Only 10 people in your Bubble," they said.
 "You can have it without knowing it," they said.
 "Your symptoms might not show up for a few days," they said.
 "Be kind. Be calm. Be safe," Dr. Bonnie Henry said. Sometimes I see tears in her eyes. She is our Provincial Health Authority. She grieves each and every death.
 Every day there are new statistics. Every day there are more and more deaths. Every day there is this sense of gloom and anxiety and fear.
 And, like the Canada Day celebrations, it all pours into my eyes through the TV screen.

Chapter 2
Saturday, July 4, 2020
Border Closed

> For yesterday is but a dream
> and tomorrow is but a vision,
> but today, well lived
> makes every yesterday a dream of happiness
> and every tomorrow a vision of hope.
> —*Kalidasa*

Travel

I was born in the USA. I live in Canada.

I have four siblings. Only I live in Canada.

I have four children. Only one lives in Canada.

I have a zillion classmates, cousins, former neighbours and Facebook friends, who all live in the USA. My Canadian neighbours and friends do not seem to feel the weight and confusion and alarm that I feel.

I deliberately live in a small log cabin, in the mountains, far from a stoplight or mall, far from the hurry and pollution and pressures of city life.

✹ Pandemic + Travel? ✹

The borders are closed. I cannot see my Mother. Papa. My newborn granddaughter. They are all in the USA. So? I watch the USA news on TV. Alarming news. Scary news. Shocking news. Relentless news.

* ✹ *

My son, Michael, sent me a graph showing the various radio and print and TV news stations. 'Left' and 'Right' leaning as well as the ratio of 'Facts' and 'Opinions.' That helps me choose what I want to hear and see, and helps me realize why there are such significantly differing points of view. I compare the same story reported by USA and Canadian news. I find UK and German news, too, which gives a wider point of view. China. Italy. Brazil. Poverty. Science. History. World Health Organization. International communication. Graphs. Interviews. Daily announcements from authorities. Who are the authorities? Scientists? Politicians? Researchers? Pharmaceuticals? Statisticians? Religious leaders? Medical specialists?

Who do you trust?

* ✹ *

There is a new appreciation for 'Essential Workers.' Who tends to the care of the elderly? Who mops the floor in the hospital? Who removes garbage? Who buries the dead?

Saturday, July 4, 2020

Essential? Are the gym instructor, hairdresser, chef, waitress, bartender, bus driver 'essential'?

Appreciation? I see people who live near hospitals stepping out on their balconies to bang pots and pans and wave flags at 7:00pm to encourage the hospital staff as they change shifts.

Balconies? I see people in Italy playing music from their balconies, flying their country's colours, the airplane fly-by trailing smoke the colour of their flag. The whole country is in Lock-Down.

Lock-Down? Lock-Down is expected to last until there is a vaccine.

Vaccine? Up-dates regarding research for new vaccines pepper the news. Hope. Pressure. 'Why is it taking so long?' And 'Why is it ready so fast!" Lies. Confusion. Misinformation. Science. Everybody has an opinion. Trust. Or. Doubt.

Everybody? I see tin-roofed shacks, the people tightly pressed together. There will be nothing like two meters distance if the virus ever comes to these poverty-stricken places in the world. There will not be hospital beds or ventilators for these people. If/when vaccines are developed, will they ever receive them here? And: Who is going to pay for all of this?

* ✻ *

Like peering through a crystal ball, through my TV screen I can see the whole world. I see wealth. Privilege. Poverty. Patriotism.

Patriotism? I see that in the USA the 4th of July celebrations have been cancelled. I see the presidential election gearing up. Crowds wearing red. No masks. They are making a statement. They are following their leader. I see other candidates, much more cautious, speaking to people in parked cars, all tuned to the same radio station.

July Chapter 2 Border Closed

I see protests. Protests joining protests. Marchers joining marchers. The television is filled with surging crowds joining each other to grieve and shout and point to the injustice of one man smothering another man, right in broad daylight. A single cell phone captured the entire 9 minutes, 22 seconds.

I see government officials kneeling, silent, for 9 minutes and 22 seconds... the same amount of time that this individual suffered, called for his mother, begged for a breath, and then went limp. By kneeling, many people want to indicate that they, too, join the surge of overwhelming realization of the history of being shut out, silenced, rejected. Privileged people become aware and take a pledge to use their voices to make a difference, make a change, open up what has for so long been locked down.

Fires. Broken glass. Tear gas. Police with shields. Police behind barricades. Police on the run. Police opening the pathway for a man with a Bible. The crowd, the reporters, the church officials, the visual impact of this one act rocking the nation.

I see flags. The stars and stripes. The Confederate flag.

The Confederate flag?

I see guns. Lots and lots of guns.

* * *

I try to stop. No TV today. But, I am so anxious. I know people who live in these cities. It all has nothing whatever to do with me. Or not? The roar of the crowd so far away in miles, yet echos in whispers inside very private places within me as I search my own mind and heart and conscience.

The words and actions, captured on film, broadcast through satellites, fuels the ideology of millions... This era will take decades to unravel.

Chapter 3
July, 2020
A Month of Sundays

> Do what you can
> with what you have
> where you are.
> —*Theodore Roosevelt*

Group Participation
What day is this?

From the very beginning, I have cancelled all of my volunteer work. I do not want to enter any group. Masks? Social distancing? Some believe and comply. Some say it's all fake shouting, "Conspiracy!" and "The government can't tell me what to do!"

Everybody doubts everything!

✸ Pandemic + Groups? ✸
I just don't want to participate in any risky behaviour. I'll wait. I'm staying home.

Stay home?

I realize that my husband and I are in a very small category of people: retired, steady income, safe home, cozy companionship, our children are grown and gone. We have stability, security.

Others stand in food lines. Others live in a place where violence is possible. Others have no income. Others face risks and threats and pressures I know nothing about.

I have the luxury of not knowing what day it is, not watching the clock, or the bank account, or fearing for my own or my family's safety.

I'm feeling pretty emotional these days, though. Especially on Sundays.

One Sunday this month it is our daughter's 40th birthday. I wrote a letter. I sent a card. I tried to make contact. I know her address and that's about all. In this world of distance and isolation, this is the hardest part for me. Being away from family.

One Sunday this month it is our youngest son's birthday. The one who was so naughty as a little boy. I never knew how to handle his energetic pretend, his inventions, his curiosity, his risk-taking and apparent lack of respect for rules and norms. I can't send a letter or card or gift. He lives on a sailboat! In this world of lock downs and restrictions, this is the happiest part for me. He has found his lifestyle. His cleverness is put to good use.

One Sunday this month is the due date for our 4th grandchild and only granddaughter. I anxiously await the news. Too far for me to go. The Canada/USA border is like a barricade that I cannot cross. Digital photos will keep us up-to-date and connected. Still: my arms are aching for the soft warmth, my eyes are aching for the darling face, my heart wants to connect with my son, his wife, this child. When will we ever be together?

July, 2020

• ✹ •

Some restrictions are lifted, or rather, better understood. New recommendations are posted. An announcement from the Provincial Minister of Health allows gatherings with specific protocols. The Bishop sends out an email letter confirming compliance with these instructions.
    I go to church! So glad! So upsetting!
    Sign in. Hand sanitizer. No hugs. Every face covered. The pews have green tape indicating where to sit and where to leave space. No singing. No songbooks. No lingering to talk.
    The Mass unfolds in predictable ways. I feel so comfortable. Everything is so familiar. It is good to be back. I might forget that there is a global emergency. Then comes the prayers... My heart stretches far and wide. I saw the Pope on TV, standing in St. Peter's Square on Easter Sunday... *alone*! I know that church gatherings are not possible in many countries where the rate of infection and death statistics are so high. I know there are 'Christians' who oppose any government at any time for any reason if they restrict church attendance. They believe that God will somehow protect them. My heart screams in agony knowing there are children in cages, held at the USA southern border without their parents.
    My heart is broken. Tears flow. How can I enjoy this comfort and security and believe that God is close to me, helping, loving, providing... when other people suffer so much, hopeless, hungry, powerless.

• ✹ •

My mind travels to the people I know in places where Covid-19 cases are spiking. Florida. Arizona. New York City. Mass graves in New York City? I know people in 19 states, 7 countries, each with their own set of difficulties, each with a death count growing daily. There is a moaning, a wailing, inside my heart.

To try to relieve my stress I have been making phone calls. My aunts. My uncles. My cousins. I have learned to Zoom with my family: my Mother, my siblings, my children.

After church, it is time for the weekly family Zoom call. I drive 3 blocks to the library. It's Sunday. It's locked. I can stand outside and pick up the WiFi on my cell phone. Tiny faces. Familiar voices. Up-dates. Confidence. Safety. No alarm.

I glimpse my mother, my estranged daughter, my son who is now a new father with his little baby. I can hardly speak. I just want to listen. Memorize each message. Store up each face. Feel the bonds that connect us. Hold on tightly to the memory of each voice.

• ✺ •

Tomorrow is not promised to anyone.

• ✺ •

It seems so impossible that I am not making birthday cakes as these Sunday celebrations come and go. I open a photo album, looking for pictures of my own newborn babies.

A-ha! Here is a letter I wrote while awaiting a birth. Now my emotions rise, fill and expand my heart. Sometimes we must wait. The unknown is really all there ever is. We plan and make arrangements and think we know what is coming... but really? Do we have any control over the future? Maybe all that we can do is monitor our own attitude. Choosing hope, although despair is so very near. Choosing commitment, although uncertainty is ever-present. Choosing trust while fear taps at

July, 2020

the door. Choosing kindness which trumps power. Choosing life, even when death is waiting, so nearby.

❋ ❋ ❋

Dear Little Un-Born Someone!

There are so many questions I want to ask you!
What colour are your eyes, hair?
How soon will you arrive? sit? stand? walk? speak? ride a bike?
But all I can do is...
...WAIT...

There are so many things I wonder!
Will you like sports? music? books? math? animals? science? machinery? travel?
Will you explore? perform? earn awards? join a club?
But all I can do is...
...HOPE...

There are so many gifts I want to make for you!
Books, music, toys, quilts, powder mitt, bean bags,
family heirlooms to share, memories to recall, stories to tell.
But all these do is express my...
...JOY...

There are so many ways I want to welcome you!
To touch and hold and hug you,
to feast my eyes on your features and expressions,
to listen and laugh and sing and dance and play with you.
But all of these things express one thing...
...LOVE...

There are so many things I impatiently want *right now*!
Where did you come from? Where are you going?

What can I do to help you achieve your goals?
But all I can do is...
... sigh a sigh that reaches across the miles...
... smile a smile that wisely knows that things will unfold as they will...
... stand and join the line stretching unbroken back, back to the beginning of time, a line of all your grandmothers and great grandmothers and great great great...
...hum a lullaby and remember how much my grandmothers loved me...
and so...become grounded, settled, safe, still, become calm, and quietly send you...
...PEACE...

Chapter 4
Wednesday, July 8, 2020
School? Homeschool?

> Education sows not seeds in you
> but makes your seeds grow.
> —Gibran

School

All of the schools were shut down, all of a sudden, in the middle of the spring term. The radio hosted interviews with parents, teachers, administrators and education experts. Teachers had to scramble to adapt their curriculum to provide instruction on Zoom. Parents had to stay home from work to look after their kids. Students in the graduating class had to give up all of those end-of-the-year parties, outings, once-in-a-lifetime trips, The Prom, even the graduation ceremony itself.

Everyone wondered: Will school re-open in September? And, if it does, what will it look like? Will everyone wear masks?

July Chapter 4   School? Homeschool?

Sit behind Plexiglas cubicles? Stay 2 meters apart all through the day?

✸ Pandemic + School? ✸

Many families chose homeschooling. The internet became a flurry of questions, ideas, sales, coaching. I wanted to do something to help. I contacted local homeschoolers to meet outside at the lake. I started an Instagram account to post the underlying concept I developed while homeschooling for 15 years. I hope it will be helpful to someone, anyone.

People worry about the students 'getting behind.' Some students get more food at school than they do at home. Some children live with domestic violence. How can worried, unemployed, stressed out, ill-equipped parents focus on such an important task? There are Facebook jokes posted about day drinkers as homeschoolers. Will children become germ-a-phoebes? I see news footage from Europe where lockdowns are so strict that the children are only allowed outdoors for one hour per day, the parents hovering close, hand sanitizer at the ready. And what about younger children who learn to talk and interact by viewing the human face? Will small children be afraid whenever the day comes that they see unmasked faces?

I have friends on Facebook demanding that the schools open. Parents having meltdowns. Children who do and do not have supplies. Parents who need the computer to stay employed. Children who do not have access to the internet for their lessons. I have friends who are teachers, fearing for their lives if schools reopen. I have volunteered in schools enough to wonder: what if a child drops their mask on the floor, on the bus, on the ground? What if the mask gets lost, or never washed? How does a child eat lunch? I remember the humiliation and embarrassment of having an inferior picture on my lunch box. What status symbols will be on masks? Will there be that age-old 'Mine is better than yours,' teasing, bullying? Don't children need to see each other's faces to be able to interact in a social environment? Doesn't the teacher need to see the child's face?

• ✹ •

I just wish there was something I could do to participate, to share what I know, to encourage the parents, to comfort the children, to soothe the anxiety, to give confidence to everyone.

Children love to learn. They will come through this. It won't last forever.

We are living through history. Parents in the past held their little ones in bomb shelters, singing nursery rhymes. Parents on ships waited for the new land. Parents in hiding shushed their children to avoid capture. Parents in quarantine bathed feverish foreheads. Parents in covered wagons left civilization behind. Parents screamed as their children were ripped out of their arms, sold to slavery, sent to residential schools. Parents grieve for vanished children kidnapped into the sex trade, dead of an overdose.

How can we possibly whine about this minor inconvenience? This pause? Is it an opportunity? Will some families find creativity and thrive? Seek adventure? Make their 'Bubble' a fine place to be?

When the confusion clears, will we go 'back'? Or 'forward'? How can we even imagine 'The New Normal'?

Chapter 5
Tuesday, July 14, 2020
Vision Board

> Champion the right to be yourself.
> Dare to be different.
> Set your own pattern.
> Live your own life
> and follow your own star.
> —*Wilferd Peterson*

Normal

Since I can't go anywhere, I'll have to make do with what I have.

I'm pretty used to that. For the whole 40+ years we've lived here, I've been saving (not hoarding) fabric and yarn, instructions and patterns, felt and paper, embroidery floss and paint. I need to have a stash of colourful things for the long months of winter when the roads are icy, the sky is gray, the days short and the distance to the city might as well be the distance to the moon.

Before Christmas I make cards and gifts, wrapping paper and decorations. I am like the elves at the North Pole.

After Christmas, I am like people in the cultures of the North who turn to storytelling and embroidery, elaborate carvings and tatting lace for layers of petticoats, preparing a trousseau for the bride or a layette for a new-born. I make quilts, read books and dabble in other crafts. On-going creativity and the warmth of the woodstove bring a sense of satisfaction.

Wintertime quiet. Happily moving hands. Colours. Textures. Imagination. Progress.

✹ Pandemic + Normal? ✹

But something is different now. First I was shut in for five months of winter. So far I have had four months of Covid. There is no end in sight. I stay home, not because the highway is potentially unsafe, but because the air I breathe while indoors with other people is potentially unsafe.

I am not alone in being alone. The strain is felt all around the world. Curfews. Lockdowns. Quarantine. These are serious matters. I am hardly in the mood to stimulate crafty creativity.

• ✹ •

With nothing on my to-do list, no place to go and an empty calendar, I scroll through Facebook endlessly. I get a lot of ads.

"Be a coach!"
"Make 6-figures!"
"Learn technology!"
"Write a book in 90 days!"
"I can edit your book!"
"I can market your book!"
"Get clients on Instagram!"
"Here's how I made my first million!"

Tuesday, July 14, 2020

"Here are templates to design your online course!"

* ✸ *

I click the remote control exploring YouTube. I can find a lot of info for free. I start taking notes. Tips for writing. Tips for editing. Tips for speaking. Tips for marketing.

I am working on my next book. I might as well learn as I go.

What exactly is a 'webinar'? How exactly do I sign up for an online course? Can I really pay with the push of a button? How do I keep track of all of these passwords? What is a Vlog? a PodCast? Who wants to video chat?

What can I do with the equipment I already have?

I pay money for a writing coach. Dissatisfied, I find one for free! I sign up for a free training, only to find it is bait for a costly long-term plan with a hefty enrolment fee.

* ✸ *

I was so eager for this year, intending to expand my own business. I bought two daybooks. One for home and one for my business.

With a fancy pen, I printed a motivational quotation on the title page:

> By failing to prepare you are preparing to fail.
> —Benjamin Franklin

The depth of disappointment right now will become even bleaker if I dwell on what is missing. How can I use this year, these resources, my own eagerness, to focus on what I *can* do? How can I learn? What do I need? How can I benefit from this vast stretch of time that has now become available?

I begin using one of the daybooks to take notes while I check out multiple resources. Name. Contact. Date. Notes. Here is a woman encouraging others to begin online businesses. Here is a Christian self-publishing company. Here is a woman who wrote 1000 pages, trimmed it to 300, then developed a monologue and went on the road with a speaking tour. Here is a writer's workshop in France! Here is a theatre school looking for books to interpret into plays and eventually film.

What would I say on a PodCast?

How can I improve my website?

In what ways can the different social media platforms help me expand my contacts?

Do I really want to earn 6-figures?

Since it takes me a year to write, edit, polish, proofread, design the cover and publish a book, how can I keep Fans connected, curious and entertained?

I listen to a fantastic webinar. This author is so informative, so energetic, so descriptive, so inviting. I join her Facebook writing group. Yipes! The other authors seem to be mostly sci-fi, fantasy, thrillers. Most authors in this group write with various levels of sexually descriptive material. Time for me to exit.

I try to find my way into Goodreads. What exactly will be the benefit to my book sales by spending time making comments here?

I feel very confused and overwhelmed. The people who read my books like them enough to pass them along to family and friends, up and down generations, even purchasing multiple copies for book clubs. But, how do I attract attention? Collect more Readers?

It seems strange to be spending so much time looking at my computer screen.

Tuesday, July 14, 2020

Email. Facebook. YouTube. TV. Solitaire. Looking for a funny movie. Watching oldies. Shirley Temple. Favourite singers. 1960s black and white after school TV. (Guilty Pleasure: I'm finding all the TV shows my Mom said I couldn't watch! 'I Dream of Jennie,' 'Get Smart,' 'Gilligan's Island') O my goodness! I am spending almost the entire day sitting. Screen time. There must be something else I could be doing?

Where has my creativity gone? Where are these extra pounds coming from?

OK. Now I look for exercise coaches. Yes. There are all kinds of ways I could look at a screen and follow the moves. I try. I give up.

What can I do with what I have?

* ❋ *

"Debbie?" My go-to method for inspiration: phone a friend. "It's Tuesday! Do you want to get together today? 10:30? I have more magazines to cut up. Do you want to make a collage?"

Lately, there have only been the three of us, Debbie, Paulette and myself, but we continue to get together, safely, signing in, sanitizing our hands, wearing masks, staying at a distance from each other, no hugs.

Debbie has collected pictures of birds, butterflies and greenery. It looks like she will fashion an oasis of tranquility. Paulette seems to be puzzle-piecing her cutouts together to make a unified scene. Sky, pathway, hiker, dog. It makes me curious to see what is beyond the hill.

Me? I cut out words. You know. The kinds of words that abound in enthusiastic advertisements. However, at the moment, I am finding it hard to conjure up a positive worldview or even care about improving my self-image. 'Happy' and 'Bright' seem far away at the moment, but, then again, maybe a Vision Board is what I need to jump-start my mind. Wake me up. Return to 'good energy.'

Here is what I have so far, scrambled fonts, phrases, single words, searching for a question mark. It is hard to find letters in the same size and colour to make my name! If I line the words up just right, I might actually have something. OK. Here goes. I'm going to glue this down now. (This is mildly embarrassing to publish in a memoir for all the world to see... a Vision Board is, after all, private, like a Journal entry.)

What's good for Eleanor?

How can you have a wholesome balance?
Traditional. Dramatic. Whimsical.
Exercise. Rest. Time out. Health.
Smarts. Focus.

A little light reading, a quote.
Favourites: pamper, needs a hug, and big smiles!
Use this new winning attitude for well-being
It's not easy. It's new.
START NOW!
I'm ready.
Today.

I can't go anyplace. I can't go back in time to 'Normal.' But, I can do THIS. I can make a Vision Board. Today!

Chapter 6
Saturday, July 18, 2020
Stuck at Home

> The grand essentials in life are:
> Something to do,
> Something to love,
> And something to hope for.
> —*Joseph Addison*

Home
Stay home.
   Maybe I will think less about the 'Stay' and more about the 'Home.'

✱ Pandemic + Home? ✱
I know that many of my Facebook friends started to super clean their homes right at the beginning of the Covid-19 restrictions. Some did renovations they had been putting off. Some had to

make office space to work from home. Or make changes to better adapt to homeschooling.

• ✺ •

Me? I scrolled for jokes on the internet.

It was annoying, then alarming, then ridiculous, how the toilet paper shortage became newsworthy. Cell phone cameras captured fights in stores, long rows of empty shelves, and hoarding. I laughed out loud to see the Easter Bunny all dressed in bright springtime colours delivering rolls of toilet paper. Then there was this photo of a Great Dane in the living room with shredded toilet paper all around and that guilty puppy face. The caption was "You've destroyed the family fortune! My lifetime savings!"

Existing factories cannot be changed overnight. Existing factories cannot increase their output overnight. Covid-19 safety procedures for employees impact the process.

One news host explained how there were sure to be other shortages, and mostly for the same reason.

Usually, people spend only part of the day at home. The rest of the time people are at their workplace, or school, or recreational facilities such as the gym, restaurant or other public places. Food, toilet paper and other supplies are needed at these places. Factories make products differently for these places than the ones produced for use at home. Tiny, individual servings of jam, ketchup, soy sauce. Large industrial-sized toilet paper rolls for public washrooms. Milk for school lunchrooms and restaurants. The list goes on and on.

When I realized how the dominoes were falling throughout the world, I could see more clearly and feel less alarm.

Then there are products that have a 'best before date.' My heart drops when the TV shows Ontario dairy farms pouring out surplus milk. What a waste! What else is possible?

I understand a little better when I see a photo on Facebook from California showing a heap of flowers as high as a house. This caption (used with permission) pretty much sums up the entire scramble going on.

* ✱ *

Farm Girl Flowers, March 25, 2020

We had to throw out $150K in flowers this past week which just about killed me. The farms we work with have had to throw out millions of dollars in flowers collectively. Here's a picture I took today at one of those farms.

Post update: OK a lot of you are asking why these aren't donated. This is not a normal situation.

First, we were given 12 hours notice to shut down our operation, so we gave away as many flowers as we could in those hours, however then there was a 'stay at home' mandate which means everybody needed to be in their homes so, therefore, we couldn't leave them out on the sidewalk (which also comes with a very large fine in San Francisco).

Second, we contacted hospitals nearby and they asked us NOT to bring them because they didn't want anybody subjected unnecessarily to potential contagions within the hospital and also they don't currently have the bandwidth to deal with taking free flowers around when they're trying to save peoples lives right now.

So, I know you're trying to be helpful by giving all of the suggestions, however now is an unprecedented time where we need to do what's right for society even though that means a lot of wasted resources and money, which we understand completely is very, very sad.

* ✺ *

"If there are going to be shortages, let's take action now," I conferred with my husband.
We usually have a lot of food stored up. Right away we collected more. Kevin made an inventory list. Non-perishable foods are in storage tubs: milk powder, rice, pasta, sugar, oats, flour, barley. In the pantry are canned goods: cases of soup, tomatoes, tuna, canned milk. Also: peanut butter, syrup, cooking oil, dish soap, laundry soap, other toiletries. In the freezer is the food we grow in our garden: spinach, beans, peas, fruits, meat. And dog food, stored in a brand new sealed garbage can.

* ✺ *

Right now I am feeling domestic. And very, very privileged. And grateful. A flood of appreciation flows through me as I organize, clean, cook, even do laundry. All of my domestic tasks feel unusually exceptionally marvellous, not drudgery and repetition and 'poor me.'
I have a home. I am safe. I have food. I have water. I have a husband. He is retired and has a steady pension. There are many without these basic necessities. I ache for them.

* ✺ *

Renovations?
I won't tackle anything grand, but I can re-organize, reduce, re-purpose.
Staying home does have some advantages.

Chapter 7
Monday, July 20, 2020
Sing? Dance? Alone?

> When we step to the edge
> of all the light we have,
> and step off into the darkness of the unknown,
> we need to believe one of two things:
> either we will have something solid to step onto,
> or we will be taught to fly.
> —Patrick Overton

Sing and Dance

My childhood friend, Laurel, re-posts lovely things. Fairies and flowers, gentle paintings of landscapes and moonlight, close-up photos of birds and encouraging quotations. And choirs. Just now she shared a YouTube video unlike anything I have ever seen before.

It is like a mosaic of many faces, each adding their part to a choir. I have been in several choirs in my life. I have even been in a choir with Laurel. Her Dad and my Dad were in the same choir for a while. My grandparents were in choirs. Being in a choir is one of the best experiences I have ever had. Cooperation, harmony, confidence, my small part is of benefit to this magnificent whole. Sacred and humorous, cultural and historical, different languages and meaningful messages are preserved and passed forward through choirs. All of this draws me back into joining a choir at every opportunity I get.

✸ Pandemic + Sing?... Dance? ✸

Fact: singing is a risky thing with this Covid situation. Small droplets are carried further when the voice is casting itself with boldness. We aren't even allowed to sing at church. I already know that the Community Christmas Choir will be cancelled if this pestilence is not eradicated before rehearsals start in the fall.

Why then did this mosaic of singers, this 'cyber choir' bring me to tears?

Because each singer is alone. Can they hear each other? Or maybe just the accompaniment? Can they see each other? Or maybe just the conductor? The harmony was gorgeous. My heart was lifted. Quickly I looked for and found more. Children's choirs, church choirs, acapella choirs, and soloists who recorded themselves at home, singing multiple times, layering in the harmonies.

Basking in the loveliness, I also felt deep sorrow. Part of the experience of being in a choir is the camaraderie. Part of being in a choir is giving what you have practised and polished to the audience. Both of these elements were missing.

• ✸ •

Suddenly another thought flashed into my mind. If there cannot be any audiences now, then what about theatre? what about dance?

Monday, July 20, 2020

A singer or actor might not lose momentum if left out of rehearsal, off stage, away from applause. But a dancer? Daily, rigorous, discipline is required to maintain their strength, stamina and flexibility. Wherever they are and whatever other strains and stresses are around them, a dancer must continue to dance. Daily. For hours.
So. I looked.
Yes. There they were.
Alone.
My eyes could not leave them. In the kitchen. On a balcony. In the playground. On a small practice mat. In the snow. Leaping around the cull-d-sac. The human spirit cannot be denied. The determination shines through. The beauty, elegance and world-class skills are evident. Even with a broom as a partner. Even with a vacuum cleaner. In Russia, New York City, Italy, England, France.
Dancers dance.

* ✻ *

Sports are cancelled. Live theatre is cancelled. Musicians are writing new songs, recording in their homes. Performers and audiences alike remember the lights, glitter, sounds.
Audiences are hungry. Watching TV is just not the same.
Covid-19. You are robbing us of so much while you wander, seeking new victims, instilling fear, evading the scientists, dividing the politicians, shutting us in, as we cry out, "When will this be over?"
And the unspoken silent question: "Will it be over?"
And yet: Dancers must dance.

Chapter 8
Friday, July 24, 2020
Stay-at-Home-Mom

You have survived 100% of your bad days.
—*author unknown*

Mom

It's hard enough to tend to little ones. Guessing what they want. Providing what they need. Saying, "Yes." Saying "No."

✹ Pandemic + Mom? ✹

Covid is having such a huge impact on Mothers!

I so much want to reach out to the parents of preschoolers. Many families are two pay-cheque families with their children in daycare. They don't have the stamina, experience or mindset to be able to cope with toddlers and preschoolers all day every day with no end in sight. No Mommy-and-Me groups. No play-dates. No babysitters. No let-up. And then, if parents do take their kids outside, there are all of the fears about contamination, even at a playground.

24 / 7!

Yipes!

* * *

Here are the things I wish I could convey:

Think of the **Serenity Prayer.** "What can change? What cannot change?"

Preventing Melt Downs

Your consistent examples of loving, firm, values, principles, ethics, social skills, healthy lifestyle, long-range plans, goals, fitness, etc. are GOLDEN!

All of my suggestions are NOT to negate the exceptionally delicious parenting you are doing and meanwhile managing your own stresses, and life situation, and career, and family matters, and grief, and travel, and finances, and infant care.

May I remind you: Your preschooler is only 3! Although s/he has an amazing vocabulary and knowledge and is so smart - s/he is only 3. So self-regulation and self-control and logic all day is not entirely realistic.

"I want"

If s/he says "I want" all day, and bumps up against "YOU HAVE TO__" at bedtime (brush teeth, bath, wash hair, etc.) you can expect a meltdown. In real life: not everything is going to be "I want."

Friday, July 24, 2020

Language:

You might try to change from the child saying, "I want" and the parent always asking the child "What do you want?" or "Do you want____?"

Instead say, "Today there are 3 choices____" or "You may choose____" You could even model "I have decided" instead of "I want."

When there is a Melt Down:

All the talking parents do can make this whole thing last too long. S/he can't recover from the crying after it starts. This small child is not capable of logic.

If you find yourself too many times in a day saying, "I'm counting to 3" or facing a Melt Down or putting the child in 'Time Out,' you might try saying, "Oops, I think it's time for the Peace Place."

Peace Place

This is not a 'Time Out' place where the child does not want to be, this is a nest, comfortable, relaxing, a place of nourishment. 'Peace Place' is NOT a 'Time Out' that happens *after* the 'Melt Down' or misbehaviour. 'Peace Place' is a special nest for *preventing* a 'Melt Down' and for making a transition such as waking up after a nap, coming home a bit grumpy or tired. The 'Peace Place' is a quiet place to pause and think about options before making a decision and taking action.

You can demonstrate that you need the 'Peace Place,' too, if you feel frustrated or need time to think about a decision.

In a small space, build a nest-like pleasant place with a favourite blanket, yoga mat or other soft material. Add stuffed toys, music, or other cozy items so the child can have a rest, a haven, a safe place to calm emotions instead of a 'Melt Down.'

Learn to Take Turns:
Mommy, Daddy, Oldest, Youngest. Everyone in the family gets to take turns.
    Not always what the oldest child says.
    Not always, "I want."
    Often there is so much attention on the 1st child, who can speak, the baby is set aside, however, the 2nd child needs to make choices, too.
    There are so many times when it is important to learn to take turns: talking, singing, toys, bath, food, after dinner play. Find ways to let each family member be first, or lead the way, or get the praise, or be the centre of attention.
    "Wait for your turn."
    "You will have a turn soon."

Transitions:
A potentially difficult time in the day, and often the place a Melt Down might occur is during transitions from one activity to another. Children really focus on what they are doing. Now. It is quite a jolt to stop something interesting. It is important for the parent to let the child know in advance that a transition is coming.
    "In ___ we are going to ___."
    Can you make a song or chant or repeated message for the beginning and ending an activity?
    Say out loud what you are planning: "The next 3 things___" or "When we get home___" Children are so quick and may already have a plan in mind. When your idea is stated, it is a sudden interruption of their own plans and causes disappointment. S/he bumps up against an unexpected plan you have in place already.
    "When we get home: shoes off, wash hands, then we are going to___."

Friday, July 24, 2020

"I need to ___ so we can ___."
"After ___ we will___."

After dinner play:

Children get excited when the parent comes home from work. Suppertime might be the most important part of the day for the family to be together. Adults want to share their news. Children have to be still and eat what's on their plate. After supper, there is just a little time to play with both parents. A good romp before bed can be fun, but it might get too rowdy. This could set the child up for another potential Melt Down as the transition from well-behaved at the table, to energetic play, to the non-negotiable bedtime routine is too much to handle smoothly.

Especially if the play is scary, chasing and hiding, loud roaring, big surprises or tossing, wrestling etc. It is important for the child to transition to calm down, otherwise, bedtime might find the child upset, too tired, stubbornly refusing, or waking with bad dreams.

Choose quiet or cooperative or peaceful activities or take turns choosing an activity.

"Today Daddy gets to choose and he decided ___" (after supper play, front yard, back yard, etc)

Charts:

Use a clock, timer, chart, calendar or list.

This takes away the coaxing and counting, demanding and resisting. Now the necessary task is not between parent and child. It is between child and chart. Not negotiable.

Ding! Ding! Ding! "I hear the timer!"

Bedtime:

"What are you thankful for today?" is a moment for each family member to share, just before tucking children into bed.

Once you establish this valuable custom, be sure to expand your child's vocabulary and skill in self-regulation by talking about other emotions. "Did you feel___ today?" (sad, lonely, waiting, hungry, frustrated, disappointed, stubborn, brave, creative, curious, excited, happy, friendly)

Acknowledge that everyone has feelings and that it is OK to have many feelings, no one is happy and positive all of the time.

Celebrate Progress:

Notice the GOOD things! Tell them. Touch them. Make eye contact. Smile.

> Our children are watching us live
> and what we are
> shouts louder than anything we can say.
> —*Wilferd Peterson*

Chapter 9
Thursday, July 30, 2020
Win-Win Win-Win

> To have made
> even one person's life a little better,
> that is to succeed.
> —Henry David Thoreau

New Friend

Very soon after the initial Covid-19 pandemic shut downs, the library found ways to be able to serve the public.

The Bookmobile is coming today!

I am not allowed to go in. What if I am sick and don't even know it yet? What if he is sick and he doesn't know it yet? The librarian greets me through a clear curtain.

Since I cannot browse, I make requests by email. What if there is live virus is on the surface of the books? The librarian brought my books in a paper bag. Since there is scientific evidence that the virus can live on surfaces for 72 hours, the books were packaged 72 hours ago. The books I am returning are collected in a box on a table outside of the Bookmobile. He will not touch them to put them away for 72 hours.

❋ Pandemic + New Friend? ❋

Three weeks ago I asked for a copy of 'Charlotte's Web,' by E. B. White. Why? Because I am reading aloud over the phone. Every day at 9:00am the phone rings. Not long ago, while on one of my book tours, I met a cheerful lady who came to Canada from China about 8 years ago. Rosie wants to improve her English and I love to teach, so this is our strategy!

Up until now, during Covid, we have stayed friends over the phone, talking about where she used to live (in the city near the ocean) and where I live (in our tiny town in the mountains). She told me about where she goes with her friends. I told her about how I get together with my neighbours once a week in the old log one-room schoolhouse. My friends and I read (a little), talk (a lot). We make puzzles (in the winter), go for walks (in the springtime), gather and scatter seeds to spread the splendid purple lupins along the highway (in the summertime), and share produce from our gardens (in the autumn).

Rosie is amazing. In China, she was studying English at school and with her father for years. She knows there is always more to learn. She has a notebook for new words, and asks me questions to be sure she understands the meaning before she writes down the equivalent Chinese word. I also write down the words she wants to learn. I send her emails with simple sentences using the new word and ask her to write back to me. Of course, her cell phone has a translation feature, so she can always check.

I tried to learn a few Chinese words. Really? I think she showed me the word for 20. Then with a twist and a dot, the meaning changed entirely. No. I am too chicken to try something so hard. I am glad she wants to learn my language because I am not strong enough or patient enough to learn hers.

Besides the words, I pause to check with her about the cultural meanings as we read through the story. Just about everyone in North America knows the story of 'Charlotte's Web.' Do children in China behave like this? Do they change into play clothes when they get home? Play outdoors without supervision? Ride the school bus? Pretend that animals can talk? Do they have harvest fairs? rides? cotton candy?

First 69, then 124, later 472 words are in her notebook. Imagine!

Reading with Rosie is the best part of my day! I feel like I won the Jackpot to have someone so eager so that I can have the fun of teaching, reading, learning from her, building our friendship.

She told me that she feels very lucky, too. When she told her friends in China about our reading together they were so jealous! A private tutor for a whole hour every day... for free? Big Win!

* ✸ *

One day her English-speaking husband answered the phone when I called her. He was so happy. He was happy that he can understand her more clearly. He was happy that they have so much more to talk about. He was happy that her day was more interesting and she was more independent. He was happy that she was happy.

Not to mention how happy my husband is because I am so happy, too.

Win-Win Win-Win!

Chapter 10
Friday, July 31, 2020
Writing for Clarity Through the Fog

> Turn your face to the sunshine
> and you cannot see the shadow.
> —*Helen Keller*

Event

Planning events is one of my favourite things to do. Committee. Place. Date. Time. Budget. Theme. Posters. Creativity and teamwork. Community Spirit. Smiles. Fundraising. Holidays.

Part of the small-town-living and the do-it-yourself lifestyle is creating your own entertainment.

Need ideas? Set-up? Clean-up? I'll be there.

❈ Pandemic + Event? ❈
I am so disappointed.

I had the most perfect Book Tour planned. 30 days! 16 events!

Yes, I knew the Covid-19 virus was making trouble in China, spread to Europe, was serious in Italy, impacted my brother in England, was a big controversy in the USA... but somehow I convinced myself that it wouldn't happen here, in Canada.

• ✺ •

I was wrong.

That day in March, 2020, when Mrs. Trudeau came home from the conference in England and tested positive for the virus, when her husband, the Prime Minister of Canada, Justin Trudeau, was also quarantined and could not go to work, and he had to hold daily press conferences outdoors on his front porch, that's when I realized: I had to contact each of my event and overnight hosts.

Postpone? Cancel? At first, everyone was talking about "flatten the curve" and "2 weeks." But, no. This is going to last so much longer. Libraries, books stores, churches and schools. Poof! All gone. I cannot enter any of these to share my books. My seminars!

Social isolation. We are all in this.

OK, I admit, I spent a few days of pouting, then sharing jokes, eventually realized how serious this is and understood that we might be in 'Stay Home' mode for a while.

How dare I pout!

• ✺ •

Thousands and thousands of people are dead and dying. Thousands and thousands more are suffering the long-term consequences of this invisible threat. Thousands and

Friday, July 31, 2020

thousands don't believe this is real, talk of conspiracies, pray for protection, refuse to participate in protocols, gather on beaches, parties, churches, political events.

There are so many dead bodies, the funeral services can't keep up. The coffins are stored in chilled transport trucks. Coffins? Cremation becomes the norm, even required. No funerals. No gatherings. Mass graves? in NYC? What is the world coming to?

• ✺ •

I am immobilized. My brain cannot handle all of these facts, process all of this grief, comprehend the lineups for food, sympathize with this sea of anxiety, imagine how this will come to an end.

Wait. I don't need to concern myself with international data. I don't need to panic about the turmoil south of the border. I can get relevant updates closer to home.

Every day the British Columbia Provincial Health Officer, Dr. Bonnie Henry, speaks on TV, sharing condolences, stating the information, asking for cooperation, closing her remarks every single day, "Be kind. Be calm. Be safe."

• ✺ •

"Free time." That is the only direct impact on me. I have cancelled all responsibilities outside of my own home. And yet, I cannot seem to find any brainpower to use my time for anything productive at all.

I unpack and re-pack my collection of beautiful fabric. Nothing stimulates my creativity. I open and close books. The words seem too hard to understand. I sit at the desk. Solitaire.

Really? That is how I am going to spend my day? That is my legacy for surviving this historical era?

"What can I do with what I have?"

Well, I did prepare a marvellous seminar. Maybe I can deliver it through my Facebook page? That idea kept me busy during the month of April.

I re-write my nifty new improved workbook into 12 lessons and post them daily on my Facebook page. Does anyone read them? I doubt it.

Hmmmm... how to find an audience? Ugh! I'll have to learn new computer skills? Too complicated.

May.

Of course, I have to plant the garden.

I go outside.

It really is summer. I really do have a choice about how to spend my time. I open up my senses. The river doesn't know there is a crisis. The birds are still doing what they have always done. My dog is eager to sniff, dig, splash and explore. The flowers are not anxious. The trees are alive. My garden is growing.

Let me learn here. Let me trust. Let me belong to this reality. There is satisfaction here, in the garden. Real reality. Not upheaval, media hype, opinions. No talk - talk - talk.

June.

I began noticing: I am still my Self. The things I like, I have always liked. The contributions I have made, I might still be able to make. What brings me satisfaction could still be enjoyable.

July.

I put up my Vision Board where I can see it. I seem to awaken.

Friday, July 31, 2020

* ✹ *

I participate in a weekly coaching session on Zoom. Tessa Smith McGovern is an author and a professor of writing and a coach, encouraging beginners. "Loving kindness" she says. "You don't get extra points for being harsh with yourself." She greets each participant with "a wave of the magic wand" a big smile and congratulations for any progress, or reassurance that "filling the well" with rest is also part of the writing process.

I am not alone!

The fog lifts. Clarity. Creativity. Concentration. Confidence.

I return to my writing. First: the outline. I have decided to print three books in one volume. May & June & July. 10 chapters each. Maybe I'll add a BONUS: the seminars I have developed which I can no longer deliver? It's a lot to organize. Charts. Scribbles. Flitting ideas. Jotted notes. Midnight is my time to remember. The wee hours is my time to type. It begins to take shape.

* ✹ *

But, I *so* much want to speak!

My writing seminar is *so* good!

I go back to my earliest log cabin days of poverty and remember my motivation: "What can I do with what I have?"

People are using Zoom. I have learned to use Zoom. Maybe one or more of the libraries I was scheduled to visit are hosting courses?

I start to make contacts. Yes!

I can do this!

* ✹ *

Eleanor's April 2020 Book Tour has been cancelled, due to library, school and bookstore closures.
   However, there just may be:

Readers who want to write!
Writers who need a nudge.
People in isolation who may be writing Journals.
Relatives connecting (while maintaining physical distance) who are wanting to collect family history.
Treasured elders who could be interviewed and their stories preserved.
Students looking for an interesting project while schooling at home.

Expect: Ideas you might use, other writers that will stimulate your imagination in various ways, encouragement, and coaching through the process.

• ✸ •

Meanwhile, while I organize content, details, anticipate questions and answers for this new way to deliver a seminar, I could take my own advice. I could start to write *my* next memoir.
   A memoir can be defined as: "preserving history through the eyes of those who lived it." I guess that could be me? We are all living through a very big historic event. What else has happened in my life? What stories would I like to preserve?
   What will I write for my one-and-only newborn granddaughter, believing that someday we will be together, intertwined by our stories of 2020.
   Type type type

Friday, July 31, 2020

EPILOGUE

We are both staying home.

I thought I might feel upset. I love to travel! We have a new granddaughter! When will be able to see her?

I have re-set my wish-list, expectations, goals.

Here. Now.

Kevin and I walk on the sand bar together. The river is ever-new, summer scents, weather sounds, animal tracks, there is much to observe. Kevin and I do seasonal work together. The deep beds are producing well. The lawn mower bag fills with mulch for me to use in-between the rows of carrots. Kevin is building me a tiny log cabin. I bring him iced tea and admire his progress.

"Kevin?"

"Hmmmm?"

"I'm glad to be home."

"Me, too."

"Me, Two."

Alone Twogether. It actually feels wonder-full.

> Take good care of the future
> because
> it is where you are
> going to spend
> the rest of your life.
> —*Charles Franklin Kettering*

Titles currently available through the Author's web page

www.eleanordeckert.com

or order on-line from the publisher
books.friesenpress.com/store
then search for 'Eleanor Deckert'

Book 1 ~ 10 Days in December... where dreams meet reality

Book 2 ~ 10 Days in January...
... 1 Husband... 2 Brothers... 3 Sons... 4 Dads

Book 3 & Book 4 in one volume

Book 3 ~ 10 Days in February... Limitations
Book 4 ~ 10 Days in March... Possibilities

Book 5 ~ 10 Days in April... a detour through breast cancer

Book 6, 7 & 8 in one volume

Book 6 ~ 10 Days in May, 1966... freely receive... freely give
Book 7 ~ 10 Days in June, $1000... BONUS: 10 Seminars
Book 8 ~ 10 Days in July, 2020... lock down... open up

Watch for future titles Eleanor Deckert is working on:

10 Days in August... so many good-byes

10 Days in September... learning... teaching

10 Days in October... glad, sad, mad, afraid, thankful

10 Days in November... maiden, mother, crone

Endnotes

[1] Read full story in *10 Days in December... where dream meet reality.* A memoir, by Eleanor Deckert © 2016 FriesenPress

[2] How we built the stackwall house is described in *10 Days in February... Limitations.* A memoir, by Eleanor Deckert © 2018 FriesenPress

[3] Phonics Skilltext Copyright 1945, Charles E. Merrill Books, Inc.

[4] https://soundcloud.com/gilslote/school-is-a-useful-tool.

[5] Photo on cover of of *10 Days in February... Limitations* & *10 Days in March... Possibilities.* A memoir, by Eleanor Deckert © 2018 FriesenPress

[6] More family stories in *10 Days in January... 1 Husband... 2 Brothers... 3 Sons... 4 Dads.* A memoir, by Eleanor Deckert © 2016 FriesenPress

[7] *The Shining East,* by Cornelia Hinkley Hotson, 1964, Vantage Press

[8] Hymn lyrics were written in 1841, by Jemima Thompson Luke, the wife of Rev. Samuel Luke. This song is in the Public Domain

[9] More school stories in *10 Days in September... Learn... Teach.* A memoir by, Eleanor Deckert. Coming soon!

[10] *Home School Burnout, What it is, What causes it, How to overcome it,* by Raymond and Dorothy Moore, 1989, Wolgemuth & Hyatt, Publishers, Incorporated

[11] Seven Predictable Patterns® is the Registered Trademark protecting the Intellectual Property of the owner, Eleanor Deckert, in business since 1995.

[12] Tuckman, Bruce W (1965). "Developmental sequence in small groups". Psychological Bulletin

[13] To read some of Eleanor's newspaper columns, search for: Clearwater Times, or Valley Voices, or Valley Sentinel, or Eleanor Deckert https://www.clearwatertimes.com/our-town/valley-voices-the-in-between-season/

What Readers Are Saying

Your words are vivid. It's is like looking through a window and seeing everything you see. I love it!

— **Carol, educator**

When we leave our childhood home, there is sorting to be done, possessions and values – what to affirm – what to leave behind – what to integrate into new understanding of Self. For Eleanor Deckert this process was extreme. She left behind much of what had provided her with a sense of identity. Her telling of the process she undertook to emerge with a deep sense of integrity is truly inspiring. In addition, she generously shares the workshops she has developed so that others, seeking wholeness, for themselves and those they love, may do the same.

— **Rev. Jeanne M Randels, B.A., M.Div, Michigan**

Eleanor took the courageous path, not only less travelled, but of more risk. And, she succeeded. She left the safety of the world created by her parents. With her husband, Kevin, she 'chopped wood, hauled water and cleaned her rice bowl,' not just for 6 years like the Buddha or 2 years like Thoreau, but for the rest of her life. Both the Buddha and Thoreau were driven to talk publicly about what they learned. Eleanor belongs in their realm.

— **Glenn Olien, Unified Transition Theory, British Columbia**

Memoir: What were my dreams? What did I long for? Could I get it then? Can I get it now?

—**Tessa Smith McGovern, writing coach**

Seminar Testimonial

Animated presentation. Really opened my eyes. She demonstrated rapport with the entire group as well as each person as an individual.

— **Susan Frindt, educator, Colorado Springs**

Review

Changes, like a kaleidoscope. Stability, like a foundation. Eleanor's experiences and observations are thoughtful, heartfelt, authentic.

10 Days in May, 1966... freely receive... freely give

Life as an eight-year-old big sister brings Eleanor responsibility, anxiety, joy and contentment.

Sharp details bring a sense of nostalgia to the Reader while Eleanor recalls memories of childhood, family, school, seasons and community life in the 1960s.

10 Days in June, $1000

Will practical Kevin and idealistic Eleanor be able to make their newly-wed dream of the 'Back-to-Basics' lifestyle possible? What will she give up? What will she gain?

Anyone seeking the 'Off-Grid' lifestyle, or even making tiny 'Green' decisions will gain insight and helpful ideas from Eleanor's Journey.

BONUS: 10 Seminars

Eleanor's desire to be of service is evident on every page.

10 Days in July, 2020... lock down... open up

How will Eleanor's creativity be impacted by the Covid-19 restrictions? As always, she will find a way!

About the Author

"When does a person become 'who' they are?"

Heredity? Culture? Education?
Is a child born 'empty'
and needs to be 'filled up'?
Is a child born 'flawed'
and needs to be 'fixed'?
Is a child predestined
to 'turn out' a certain way?
Is a child already a 'person' and simply needs to develop naturally?

I cannot answer this question.

So, I observe. Myself. My children.

Through Memoir: I share my own Path. Ten talents seem to be significant throughout my life. My earliest creativity brought a delicious sense of 'Me.' All too soon, I was bombarded by conflicting messages, smothering fears, taboos, religious shame. Self-doubt clouded my creativity.

Like a caterpillar, I shuffled along. I chose a Spartan lifestyle, believing that these talents were unnecessary, irrelevant, could be discarded. That time of isolation and poverty was like a cocoon. Silent. Alone. Inner struggles. Inner changes. With great effort, even pain, I wrestle, emerging, uncertain. Look! It's 'Me.' Like a butterfly! Expanding. Light. Beautiful!

Potential. I believe that is how each child is born. Overflowing, swimming in, bursting with, dancing to express: Potential.

O how precious each child is. O how fragile. O how sturdy. O what a privilege it is to be a companion to a darling child as they make their own self-discovery and reach for their Potential.

Contact Eleanor Deckert

email: 10daysindecember@gmail.com
to request seminars currently available in person or on-line:

7 Healthy Habits
Seven Predictable Patterns®
Home Organization Workshop H.O.W.2
Mommy Matters
Eleanor Deckert's Memoir Writing Method

Printed in Canada